Worst-Case Scenario?

ABOUT THE AUTHOR

STUART PRICE is Reader in Media Discourse and Principal Lecturer in Media, Film and Journalism at De Montfort University, UK. He is the author of *Brute Reality* (2010), *Discourse Power Address* (2007), and a number of other books on media and communication theory. His research encompasses studies of politics, rhetoric, cultural formations in antiquity, film and adaptation, and configurations of state power.

Worst-Case Scenario?

Governance, Mediation & the Security Regime

STUART PRICE

Zed Books

LONDON | NEW YORK

Worst-Case Scenario? Governance, Mediation and the Security Regime was first published in 2011 by Zed Books Ltd, 7 Cynthia Street, London N1 9JF, UK and Room 400, 175 Fifth Avenue, New York, NY 10010, USA

www.zedbooks.co.uk

Designed and typeset in 10½ on 13 Monotype Bembo Book by illuminati, Grosmont
Cover: www.thisistransmission.com
Printed and bound in Britain by the MPG Books Group, Bodmin and King's Lynn

Distributed in the USA exclusively by Palgrave Macmillan, a division of St Martin's Press, LLC, 175 Fifth Avenue, New York, NY 10010, USA

A catalogue record for this book is available from the British Library
Library of Congress Cataloging in Publication Data available

ISBN 978 1 84813 529 1 hb
ISBN 978 1 84813 530 7 pb

Contents

Acknowledgements

The genesis of *Worst-Case Scenario?* was a public lecture delivered in 2010 for De Montfort University's Cultural Exchanges programme. Later in the same year, the material was reworked for a seminar given at Loughborough University, before it was turned into a proposal for Zed Books. My editor, Ken Barlow, deserves thanks both for his early enthusiasm and for his patience during the gestation of the project. Members of the Media Discourse Group in the Faculty of Humanities – including Rivers Barry, Hazel Collie, Steph Collins, Scott Davidson, Alastair Gordon, Kaitlynn Mendes, Simon Mills, Margaret Montgomerie, Rona Murray, Ruth Sanz Sabido, Paul Smith, Diane Taylor, Andrew Tolson, Cassian Vian, Jo Whitehouse-Hart and Helen Wood – helped to create a positive academic environment. In addition, the presence of colleagues from other departments and centres – especially Deborah Cartmell, Tony Graves and Heidi Macpherson – helped to keep the whole enterprise in perspective.

Some of the material in this book was presented within academic networks and institutions, including the Media, Communication and Cultural Studies Association, the Media Group of the Political Studies Association and the British Film Institute. Permission to reprint illustrations and text has been obtained from the *Independent* for 'Techie Challenge to Save the Lives of Soldiers' and 'Shoot to Kill', and from the *Sunday Telegraph* for 'Spy in the Sky'. The two photographs that illustrate the *Sunday Telegraph* piece are reproduced with the permission of Associated Press photos. Steph Collins made the screenshots that accompany the analysis of 9/11 in Chapter 6. Part of Chapter 5 is based on my article 'Missiles in Athens, Tanks at Heathrow', which appeared in *Social Semiotics* 18(1), March 2008, while Chapter 7 contains material first published as 'The Mediation of "Terror": Authority, Journalism and the Stockwell Shooting', in Boehmer and Morton's *Terror and the Postcolonial* (Blackwell-Wiley, 2010).

Stuart Price
January 2011

NOTE ON THE TEXT Where attributions appear as (Author, 2010: 4) this represents the standard reference to a monograph, book chapter or article (full details are available in the References), while (Author, 30 September 2010: 4) indicates the use of a newspaper or periodical. In this case, page numbers (where known) appear at the end of the reference. The transcript in Chapter 6 obeys the following conventions:

[word] Authorial comment on source
(1) Length of pause in seconds
(.) Pause of less than a second
utterance Emphasis placed on word by speaker
uttera::ance Lengthening of vowel sound

In memory of my father, Gerald Price, 1931–1978

Preparing for the worst?

Fires, floods, pandemics: preparing for the worst. Universities'
business continuity staff are developing strategies for crisis response.

C. Stothart (*Times Higher Education Supplement*, 17 April 2008)

Forms of authority

References to hypothetical dangers are a standard feature of the discourses produced by influential organisations, appearing within a
variety of formats, including political speeches, newspaper articles,
policy launches, web pages, official dossiers and corporate reports.[1]
These allusions are so numerous that they sometimes appear to take
precedence over the release of timely information about substantial
events, yet their proliferation is in one sense entirely understandable.
In turning their attention to the unknown, institutions – in both public
and private sectors – follow the general human propensity to try to
anticipate the uncertainties of life.

At the same time, the tendency of some groups to imagine a particularly severe challenge or threat – based on the pretext that dealing
with anything short of disaster will be easier if an acute emergency
has already been rehearsed – can be used to augment an inflexible and
essentially dystopian world-view. This form of institutional activity
does not consist solely of preparations designed to mitigate the effects

of public trauma. The argument advanced in this book is that planning for contingent events, even where it does not predict the appearance of the worst possible case, is actually a technique of governance (see Chapter 2).

Although the general administration of the social order is rationalised through reference to concepts like community, democracy and accountability, it is actually dependent upon a less exalted and more practical technique – the seizure of political initiative. Operating within a spatially distinct environment, the various bodies involved in regulation and oversight issue directives and requests to a dependent clientele: it is this process that is exemplified by the right to manipulate (from a safe distance) the procedural and temporal conditions within which subordinate groups must frame their responses.

The reproduction of security

In preparing for generic events, the hierarchical configuration of powerful groups is duplicated in those ancillary organisations, such as the 'resilience forum', that are devoted to the reproduction of security as a practice. In reality, therefore, it is the bureaucratic disposition of government departments, private industries and internal police agencies that helps to standardise the conception and performance of contemporary crisis management.

Although the modelling of alternative futures is a long-established practice, associated with the growth of economic forecasting and the management of urban populations, its incorporation into the protocols of contemporary governance has been (i) driven by an interest in the mechanisms of pre-emptive administration and (ii) substantiated and enlarged by the development of digital technology. The spread of predictive analysis has been assisted by a form of electronic calculation that began, according to one source, with the first 'probability-based model for measuring the threat of natural disasters', produced in 1987 by a US company based in Boston (Ripley, 29 March 2004: 40).

The procedure used by this group, the AIR Worldwide Corporation, was to record a series of measurements, from 'the wind speed of hurricanes to the lengths of fault lines', to provide data for insurance firms. The insurers would in turn use this information to estimate how often a disaster might strike and the amount of damage it could produce (Ripley, 29 March 2004: 40). Now known in some quarters as 'probabilistic modeling technology', this kind of service became more popular after 11 September 2001, when various firms decided that they needed 'a new model that would capture the risks of terrorism' (40).

In order to establish a comprehensive picture, the AIR Corporation entered a list of 300,000 potential targets into a database, and then estimated what kind of damage could be expected in each location, from a number of different terrorist acts. These encompassed 'airplane crashes to chemical weapons to nuclear bombs' (Ripley, 29 March 2004: 42). Once this had been done, the company called in former FBI and CIA operatives, so that they could give an opinion on how likely it would be that any one of the hypothetical outcomes would actually occur. The model eventually produced was supposed to be able to run 'tens of thousands of attack scenarios and estimate the potential loss' (42). Yet, despite the existence of a model that was supposed to identify the real locus of the terror threat, federal funding (the distribution of money from the Homeland Security budget) actually ended up in places that came very low on the list of probability.

Various state officials had been engaged in 'a perverse competition for antiterrorism dollars', which were disbursed on the basis of a funding formula that divided some 40 per cent of funding to all states, irrespective of the actual risk to which they were thought to be subjected (Ripley, 29 March 2004: 42). According to the journalist who studied this process, a 'strange thing happened': rural officials became convinced that their states were 'just as threatened as Washington, New York and Chicago' (44). One man 'rattled off his doomsday scenarios', which amounted to a list of infrastructure and industrial sites, any one of which was supposed to become vulnerable to terrorist attack.

In the end, the terror mentality was spread far and wide, because 'in order to get homeland security money' various states had to 'frame their needs in terms of terrorism' (Ripley, 29 March 2004: 44). A similar situation prevails under any funding regime, including that related to academic provision, where the identification of particular necessities produces a form of conformity: if that is where the funding lies, then the bid must be framed in the terms set by the authority concerned.

The extension of the 'crisis paradigm' into civic and private life does not mean that the depiction of an apocalyptic threat will necessarily appear within every recorded example of risk assessment, because the nature and severity of the hazard imagined depends on the institutional function of individual organisations. Many centres of authority are devoted to organising the 'capacities of individuals and collectivities' (Miller and Rose, 2008: 2), but not all are directly concerned with the overt reproduction of the national security agenda. Public and private bodies will, nonetheless, take advantage of any hypothesis that reinforces their ability to regulate the lives of their clients and subordinates, and in this sense are unlikely to be actively hostile to the managerial advice issued by government agencies.

The scenario and established practices

If the communiqués issued by bureaucrats and managers are oriented towards an uncertain future, the depiction of threats to national infrastructure furnishes an opportunity to invoke rather more dramatic hazards. Insurgency, financial meltdown, natural catastrophe, cyber attacks and terrorist assault are nominated, not only as challenges to the exercise of executive power but, in order to draw the wider social order into the project of security, as existential threats. In the case of military, police, surveillance and security functions, the vast array of stories devoted to the representation of risk should be recognised as an attempt to address one proposition – that the precautionary practices organised by the state are both necessary and legitimate. While the habitual practice of the serious analyst is to test the credibility of this perspective, the public relations mechanisms employed by the political executive are devoted to its promotion.

One of the most common and effective methods of disseminating the dominant conception of insecurity and risk is the creation of the 'scenario', a postulated condition that functions both as a parable (offering a warning about a convergence of undesirable circumstances) and as a regime of activity. As a tool of governance, scenario planning produces two benefits for the authorities: first, it provides a credible rationale for the pre-emptive posture adopted by powerful institutions such as the armed forces, the police and the security services; second, it helps to reinforce the type of *security regime* described in this book as a clandestine form of internal administration (see Chapter 3 and below), rather than a type of transnational relationship established between states.

'Scenario planning' consists of various international, national and local schemes designed to facilitate a series of practical exercises, all of which are predicated on the rehearsal of contingencies that encompass various simulations of crisis and disaster. Although modelled on the command structures of military organisations, these exercises are played out by a cast of participants that includes civilian operatives.

Based on existing workplace hierarchies, this practical approach to 'emergency' rule can be used to align employees and functionaries with the political conceptions of the dominant class. It represents a method of social incorporation that, though openly propagandistic in a narrative and propositional sense, is founded on the ability of a workforce to repeat key terms and follow established procedures. The emergency training exercise, for example, demands the use of the same set of skills already reinforced through the emotional, cognitive and physical labour expended in the service industry. The need to conform to managerial precepts about the importance of teamwork, customer service, record-keeping, auditing and review provides a more reliable method of ideological orientation than the unadorned repetition of any particular 'party line'.

When, for example, an individual is made to occupy a specific role in the emergency scenario, such as the 'first responder' in a crisis, belief in the virtues of the wider political system is not required. Quite besides the perspectives absorbed during the subject's early socialisation, basic assumptions about the character of the social order are enacted simply by fulfilling assigned duties in a systematic manner. Attitudes, like the notion that the general public needs firm direction in an emergency, are enshrined in the protocols that are practised during the security exercise.

Evacuation, for example, serves a dual purpose. It removes individuals from a potential source of danger, but also represents the seizure and control of public space, a procedure that can be employed in a variety of situations that in no way resemble the one used in training. The scenario exercise can be seen, therefore, as a way of reinforcing the structures of hierarchical governance, without requiring even the most perfunctory form of democratic oversight. In effect, political decisions are built into material practices and are therefore removed from the arena of debate and controversy. A similar argument, founded on the relative invisibility of harmful authoritarian practices, has been made about the despoliation of the environment, and with regard to the needless deaths (of women and children in particular) that occur throughout the world as a consequence of 'human decision-making' (Roberts, 2008: 4).

If widespread belief in a dominant concept is not required for the successful administration of the social order, the fact that – despite the scepticism that attends their reproduction – media forms circulate a series of propositions about risk and security demonstrates the continuing importance of this form of publicity (see Chapters 6 and 7). Equally, though outright ideological conviction may be unnecessary, familiarisation with a limited number of arguments about an issue, particularly those predicated on the maintenance of the status quo, is sufficient to maintain the basic assumptions that underpin patriarchal capitalism as a coherent set of social practices. The appearance of such material in the public domain also means that those who exercise local executive power do not have to invent a unique rationale for their actions. This takes place at a higher level and is passed down, releasing CEOs and their functionaries from the chore of having to understand and present particular arguments.

Risk and the security regime

In order to illustrate how the practice of scenario planning extends the culture of an essentially authoritarian form of governance into public and commercial structures, the examples in this book are taken from the security practices of the US government and from the British state, with the latter providing the bulk of the material. The UK is a particularly useful case study, since it illustrates the problems that ensue when a political entity proclaims its independence, but acts as the obedient factotum of another government. Since the British reconfiguration of the terror threat, in both narrative and practical forms, relies in large part on the foreign policy positions adopted by the United States, comparisons are made throughout the text with the North American superpower. There is also some analysis of Greece's subordination to the US foreign policy agenda (see Chapter 5).

The particular focus of this study is not, however, an abstract conception of the British state, nor the larger generic category of risk (Beck, 1992; Lash et al., 1996; Adam et al., 2000). Academic perspectives which share Beck's assertion that 'the discourse of risk begins where trust in our security and belief in progress end' (Beck, in Adam et al., 2000: 213) cannot inform the kind of critical analysis undertaken in this book. The idea that a useful enquiry might start at the point at which faith in 'our security' has been exhausted not only depends on the selection of a particular community of interest, expressed by the possessive adjective 'our', but suggests an unhealthy dependence on the agendas set by conservative scholars, government personnel and security professionals.

The present work does not lament the (exaggerated) loss of bourgeois confidence, exemplified by the more paranoid scenarios circulated in the media, but concentrates on the communicative behaviour of those agencies, both public and corporate, that make up the operation of an undeclared *security regime*. The security regime is defined here as a permanent but flexible organisational resource that exists beyond the realm of formal democratic control, and that is primarily concerned with the dramatised pursuit of that chimera known as the 'national interest'. The use of the term 'regime' is therefore quite distinct from its use in standard 'regime theory' where the reference is designed to draw attention to 'those principles, rules and norms that permit nations to be restrained in their behaviour in the belief that others will reciprocate' (Jervis, 1982: 357). While the study of transnational governance is entirely legitimate, my use of *regime* is designed to emphasise more than its basis in diplomatic protocol and rule-based management. It is meant to draw attention to a practice that is not subjected to the restraints – both legal and moral – which are supposed to apply to the social order as a whole. It is, therefore, not just the organisational character of the security regime that is of interest, but the fact that its highly influential activities take place in a realm that allows a high degree of operational autonomy. This perspective is close in spirit to the work of those theorists who seek to understand how dominant modes of political rule are reproduced in 'open' societies (Young, 2003; Wood, 2003; Neocleous,

2008; Nitzan and Bichler, 2009, among others). Young, in particular, shares an interest in analysing the ways in which authoritarian principles are disguised as a form of paternalism: she identifies the existence of 'an apparently benign form' of male domination ('masculinist protection') that has been used to justify the emergence of an *internal* security regime in the United States (Young, 2003: 223).

Structure of the book

The first chapter deals with the various myths of security propagated by state agencies. Project ARGUS, a training exercise initiated by the UK's National Counter Terrorism Security Office, is used as an initial example. The chapter includes critical analysis of the fictional productions aimed at ARGUS's target audiences, and refers in addition to the historical context of the emergency exercise, with particular reference to activities undertaken during the Cold War. This section of the book extends the thesis presented in the Introduction, to the effect that emergency planning represents the creation of an auxiliary system of semi-privatised hierarchical authority, one that is not monitored or subjected to democratic oversight. The second chapter presents a detailed critique of the concept of governance, covering managerialism, regulation and the 'reform' agenda associated with the political culture that flourished under the aegis of New Labour. The role of technology in the maintenance of order is explored, before a response is made to those perspectives that attack neoliberalism but not the capitalist system itself. Chapter 3 offers a definition of the *security regime*, beginning with an unusual description of this condition contained in an official report into the conduct of the Iraq War. The differences between the various forms of secret state apparatus are also subjected to analysis, before a distinction is made between the concepts of 'regime' and 'regimen'. The question of hierarchical structure provides another focus for study, and is supported by various empirical examples. The later parts of this section deal with the relationship between normative habituation and ideology. Chapter 4 presents a thorough overview of the 'event' as both a practical and philosophical category, and compares its qualities to the production of the scenario as an instrument of power. The fifth chapter is primarily concerned with the *security event* and how this can be distinguished from the exercise or rehearsal by the fact that it represents a 'real world' mobilisation of resources. The primary case study used in this instance is the appearance in 2003 of armoured vehicles at Heathrow airport, but the relationship between Greece and the USA during the 2004 Olympics is also drawn upon, for the purposes of comparative analysis. Chapter 6 concentrates on the *mediated event*, and sets out a critique of the ways in which the events of 9/11 were analysed by academic authors. An extensive transcript of BBC News 24's broadcast of 11 September is provided, together with a series of screenshots that illustrate that coverage. The seventh chapter examines two events: the human disaster that followed the landfall of Hurricane Katrina, and the material generated by the British press in the immediate aftermath of the Stockwell shooting, in which Jean Charles de Menezes was killed by police officers. Both incidents provide a stark contrast to the imaginary occurrences that are generated through the use of the 'worst-case' scenario. The last chapter covers the practices of perception management and presents a study of Prince Harry's highly theatrical appearance in Helmand province, Afghanistan. The Conclusion presents an overview of the book's theoretical perspective, and argues that the role of the academic analyst is not to help the various branches of the state manage the perceptions and feelings of the citizen (a role advocated by Richards, 2007), nor to provide advice about how best to construct a more realistic model of the terror scenario, but rather to draw attention to those authoritarian practices that appear to underpin the practices and rituals of 'democratic' governance.

ONE

Myths of security

Officials outlined two 'catastrophic' scenarios, the overcoming
of 'electro-mechanical arming devices' by terrorists to produce a
'nuclear yield' or explosion, and the use of conventional explosives to
blow up the plutonium core of a bomb.

> C. Milmo, 'Shoot to Kill, Britain's Answer to Massacre
> at Munich Olympics' (*Independent*, 9 June 2009: 17)

In the worst-case scenario, staff and students could be killed or
injured, and the premises destroyed or damaged in a 'no warning',
multiple and coordinated terrorist attack.

> Association of Chief Police Officers, Counter
> Terrorism Protective Security Advice for Higher
> and Further Education (NaCTSO, 2009b)

Project ARGUS: spreading the word

Project ARGUS – which stands for Area Reinforcement Gained Using
Scenarios – is a training exercise initiated by the UK's National Counter
Terrorism Security Office (NaCTSO). Established in 2002 to provide
'expert security advice' to government agencies and the corporate sector,
NaCTSO went on to create a network of more than 250 Counter-
Terrorism Security Advisers (CTSAs) around the UK, including seventy
staff who were recruited between 2008 and 2009 to 'support the delivery
of the Government's crowded places programme' (NaCTSO, 2009a:

107). Within a period of just over two years, beginning in January 2007, these CTSAs had 'run over 700 scenario-based training events' for city and town centre businesses, to help them identify measures they could take to 'protect themselves and their customers' from 'a terrorist attack' (107). As the central component of these events, ARGUS, which encompasses Retail, Professional, Hotels and 'Night-Time Economy' subdivisions (Pindoria, 10 June 2010), is predicated on the assumption that the response of the managerial class to a *simulated* incident will help it acquire skills that can be used in a real situation.

The proliferation of organisations, networks and professional roles dedicated to the promotion of security is not simply the consequence of an increased awareness of public hazards. It also represents the creation of a parallel structure of authority, one that has not been sanctioned by any form of popular mandate. So, for example, the formation in the UK of the Media Emergency Forum, an '*ad hoc* grouping of senior media editors, government representatives, emergency planners, emergency services and other interested bodies' (Cabinet Office, 2004: 107), allows the composition of an authoritative narrative about security, before this same perspective is disseminated throughout the mainstream media. The question of power and agency, therefore, is analysed throughout this book, but the immediate concern must be to examine the concept of the *scenario* itself.

The scenario

The original and still principal meaning of the term 'scenario' is an outline or textual framework for a play or operatic libretto. This definition has been supplemented in recent years to include the kind of synopsis used to set out the projected content of a film or other creative project. Accordingly, the concept is meant to indicate a postulated development, not an actual sequence of events that can be described after they have taken place. Nonetheless, 'scenario' is often employed as a substitute for 'situation', which would suggest that it is sometimes thought to refer to a verifiable set of circumstances, and therefore a physical condition that can be experienced and then related to an audience.

This semantic mutation has meant that *scenario* is sometimes associated with the notion of having to face a dilemma, a meaning

THE INDEPENDENT SATURDAY 9 MAY 2009

NEWS 17

Shoot to kill, Britain's answer to massacre at Munich Olympics

➤ Secret document reveals MoD advice after 1972 slaughter of Israeli athletes

West German policemen take positions in the Olympic Village in Munich in 1972 in a bid to release Israeli hostages being held by Arab terrorists, below. The incident prompted a swift review of British counter-terrorism measures
AP/GETTY

By Cahal Milmo
CHIEF REPORTER

IN THE WAKE of the 1972 Munich Olympics massacre, military commanders gave soldiers carte blanche to shoot hostages should nuclear weapons be the target of terrorists. The murder of Israeli athletes at the Games sent a wave of panic through Western governments at the bloody arrival of a new breed of terrorism. In Britain, the atrocity struck such fear into the hearts of military chiefs that they believed their nuclear weapons could be the next target.

A top-secret document obtained by *The Independent* under the Freedom of Information Act details how the Ministry of Defence made preparations for an attempt by terrorist groups including the IRA and Black September, the Palestinian extremists behind the Munich killings, to ambush military convoys carrying nuclear bombs and set off a "dirty-bomb" explosion.

The file shows that after the attack at the Olympics, which ended in the murder of 11 Israelis by their Palestinian captors after a bungled rescue attempt by German police, the MoD drew up new guidelines based on the knowledge that a well-trained terrorist group would be capable of arming a stolen nuclear weapon "within a small number of hours", and cleared a "recapture force", led by the SAS, to open fire on hijackers and any hostages to regain or destroy the bomb.

The rules of engagement, which were later extended to American forces based in Britain, stated that the potential devastation caused by the detonation of a stolen nuclear weapon meant that hostages were "lower-value pawns" whose safety should not "deter the taking of decisive, prompt and effective

action" against terrorists. A memo from a senior MoD official, written in March 1973, marked "*Secret UK Eyes A*", said: "When something as sensitive as a nuclear device is involved, time is of the essence, and hostages do assume a lower value as pawns in the game where the stakes are so high."

The heavily weeded document makes it clear that defence officials took seriously the threat of a terrorist incursion on a British or American airbase, or an attack on one of the convoys used to shuttle missile components and warheads between storage bases and active units.

An internal MoD report, entitled *Security of Nuclear Weapons* and dated 24 November 1972, less than three months after Munich, said: "There [is] a potential risk of hijackers from such terrorist organisations as the Black September Movement, PFLP or the IRA manning a determined and well-planned attack using a group of the equivalent strength of the Munich Olympic attack and employing automatic weapons, grenades and possibly other devices.

"Because of the political consequences and potential danger of a successful hijacking, it would be imprudent and irresponsible not to have adequate counter measures."

The file refers to the formation of a special SAS unit, codenamed Pagoda, which was set up in the aftermath of Munich to deal with terrorist hijackings and hostage situations, as a response team to crises such as the 1980 Members of Pagoda were used to end the Iranian embassy siege in 1980.

Officials outlined two "catastrophic" scenarios, the overcoming of "electro-mechanical arming devices" by terrorists to produce a "nuclear yield" or explosion and the use of conventional explosives to blow up the plutonium core of a bomb.

The document warned: "If a stolen weapon were blown up by terrorists in the UK, there would be widespread radioactive contamination leading to death and serious illness among many people exposed to the contaminant and also entailing the evacuation and cleansing of many acres, with costs running into hundreds of millions of pounds. It would be a disaster on a unique scale and completely unlike that of the most serious terrorist incident to date."

In the face of such consequences, officials declared that a shoot-to-kill policy was permitted against a retreating terrorist "even though this may endanger the lives of hostages or others". The rules of engagement stated: "Although the safety of hostages and other innocent persons which such action may place directly at risk will be given due consideration, it will not, given the potentially very grave consequences of a successful theft, deter the taking of prompt and effective action."

> "Hostages do assume a lower value as pawns in the game where the stakes are so high"
> MEMO ON THEFT OF A NUCLEAR DEVICE SCENARIO

A shoot-to-kill policy devised over thirty years before Operation Kratos (see Chapter 7)

reproduced in a Microsoft news article entitled 'RAF pilots given "suicide scenario"' (Microsoft News UK, 3 April 2007). In this piece, Air Vice-Marshal David Walker is cited as having asked pilots if they would 'think it reasonable if I ordered you to fly your aircraft into the ground in order to destroy a vehicle carrying a Taliban or al-Qaeda commander?' (Microsoft News UK, 3 April 2007). From this example, it is possible to discern the existence of an underlying rationale, one that is often obscured by the standard model of emergency. Whereas Project ARGUS is used to imagine a security dilemma that is created by the malicious actions of an enemy, and is therefore seen as a defensive response, the 'suicide scenario' presented to the RAF pilots is actually an assessment of their willingness to carry out an aggressive strike against a target, the designation of which they must take on trust. Although disguised as a test of character and the readiness of the individual to carry out an act of self-sacrifice, this particular version of the 'worst-case' scenario is meant to discover just how far a subordinate is prepared to go in order to attain a specific goal. The underlying purpose is therefore to find out who will accept unpalatable orders in general, including instructions that might involve the use of extreme or illicit force.

Depending on the circumstance posited by the authority concerned, this could include actions that are clearly immoral: once the principle of obedience has been established, then the action itself can be produced in a situation that is *quite different to the original scenario*. When it was revealed that, after the Munich Olympics massacre of 1972, British military commanders 'gave soldiers *carte blanche* to shoot hostages should nuclear weapons be the target of terrorists' (Milmo, 9 June 2009: 17), it is the creation of a new practice, together with its concomitant training regime, that is significant, not the general proposition about the inherent severity of particular *kinds* of risk. The seizure of nuclear weapons is one of those 'worst-cases' that is used to establish principles that can be applied in any situation that pits the authorities against a determined opponent. In the example given here, civilians became 'lower-value pawns', the presence of which should not 'deter the taking of decisive, prompt and effective action' (17).

'Worst-case scenario': communication and training

Another drawback associated with trying to describe the worst possible outcome is that it can of course always be supplanted by an even more uncomfortable account of contemporary hazards, so that there comes a point at which an extreme projection might begin to appear ridiculous. The circulation of the worst-case depends on exaggerating some quite reasonable assumptions about the uncertainty of everyday life, making the idea that caution should be exercised in unfamiliar situations into a more grandiose edifice of pre-emptive behaviour. When applied to conduct in the everyday world, such an attitude – the anticipation of possible developments – seems no more than common sense. The transition from this point of view, to the more extreme proposition that it is essential to prepare for the *worst* eventuality, is one of the features of contemporary institutional existence, and can be explained as an attempt to protect the material and immaterial assets that constitute either the market value of the capitalist enterprise, or the structural integrity of the modern state.

In other words, while references to the human scale of any disaster may feature in propaganda designed to persuade the general populace that here is 'a serious and sustained threat from international terrorism to the UK and UK interests overseas' (www.nactso.gov.uk/threat, n.d.), the main concern appears to be the resilience of the security infrastructure, the reputation of the state, and the financial losses that might be incurred by an attack. The secret Ministry of Defence memo written after Munich may have described the lives that could be lost if a stolen nuclear weapon were to be detonated by terrorists, but it also mentioned the costs of a clean-up operation that could amount to 'hundreds of millions of pounds' (Milmo, 9 June 2009: 17).

Since the amorphous mass known as 'the public' is perceived to be the immediate target of the terrorist assault, through which the malefactor strikes at the authorities, any such disruption to 'normal life' (where the disturbance is conceived as the production of social and not just physical chaos), can be interpreted as a threat to the hierarchical order and thus to the state itself. The population in general is therefore regarded by the security professional as no more than a significant variable in the equation of risk.

The public is also seen as essentially passive and more than a little fearful: in advice issued to 'first responders' under the Civil Contingencies Act of 2004, section 7.31 of 'Communicating with the public' noted that 'research suggests that people look to the authorities to 'do something', and that they will be relieved and reassured to see that plans are in place' (Cabinet Office, 2004: 97). The promotion of 'scenario training' is, meanwhile, a means of assimilating existing civic and corporate structures into the lower and more informal levels of the security state. In a period when the ruling political elite seems to find it difficult to motivate citizens through the provision of a clear 'ideological' rationale for their behaviour, practical training provides a reliable and less controversial method of aligning individuals with their goals, which extend much further than the reproduction of public safety.

The narrative composition of Project ARGUS

Project ARGUS, introduced as a *scenario-based* and thus an essentially 'live' procedure, also encompassed the production of video material, which focused – as mentioned above – on the security challenges encountered in crowded places, such as shopping centres and university campuses. What is remarkable about these narratives is the far from sober approach they choose to adopt. It is as though the progenitors of the Project were caught between two conflicting impulses: the need to present a realistic and credible assessment of projected risks, and the desire to dramatise the notion that – in the words of the main character who appears in these video dramas – 'the threat posed by terrorism in the UK is *real*' (NaCTSO, Department for Innovation, Business and Skills, www.communityforum.org, 2009; original emphasis).

When, however, an audience feels that a danger has been exaggerated, or that the authorities have not been entirely candid about their own shortcomings, it is possible that the whole premise of an emergency exercise will meet resistance. A major problem of this type occurred when the PR company Ogilvy, running a 'Topoff' anti-terrorism exercise for the US Department of Homeland Security, found it difficult to overcome the belief held by many of its intended audience – senior administrators and managers – that their own government had been complicit in the events of '9/11' (see Price, 2010: 129–30).

The production of any public address is therefore founded on the belief that either there will be some resistance to the message promoted by the security apparatus, or that it will in certain cases be greeted with a measure of indifference. This is why the obligations of the target group, described in one document as 'Shopping Centre managers, Store managers, Loss Prevention managers, Security managers, Building-Facilities managers, Health and Safety managers' and 'anyone *in a supervisory role* of both staff and public' (www.liverpoolchamberblog. org, 28 August 2009; my emphasis), are often emphasised as a legal 'duty of care'. In most cases, attempts are made to tailor the content of any communicative act to the perceived requirements of particular constituencies or 'stakeholders'.

The intention behind Project ARGUS was first, in common with all official schemes, to identify and assemble a captive audience, and then to subject this collective to a series of propositions about the nature of the real. The challenge, in the case of terrorism, is to materialise a condition that is not always immediately apparent. The impression that 'terror' constitutes a substantial threat has, therefore, constantly to be renewed. For most people it is an experience that is only known through its mediated form, a circumstance that is exploited in one of the three Project ARGUS videos currently available. Knowing that the practices of news media attest to the existence of a social reality beyond the realm of immediate experience, the ARGUS storyline incorporates a television 'report' into its imaginary account of an attack on a city centre. A fictional newsreader declares that

> It has been confirmed that the three explosions in the central entertainment district were bomb blasts. Police have said that it is still too early to say whether these were the work of any particular terrorist group, or indeed if they were, as has been speculated, suicide bombings. While it is impossible to ascertain the precise number of casualties at present, it has been estimated that no less than forty and as many as ninety people have died. (NaCTSO *Crowded Places* video, www.mefeedia.com, 11 February 2009)

In another of its productions, aimed at managers in higher education, exactly this kind of concept – the substantiation of a specific threat – is dramatised in a section that warns of the risks posed by terrorist attacks on (once again) crowded places. The action is set in what appears to be a university precinct, surrounded by a number of faculty buildings that seem to belong to the architectural tendency sometimes known as 'brutalist'. In the midst of this grey, deserted concrete environment, the protagonist, a middle-aged man in a suit – who appears as the paternalistic authority figure in all three productions – is seen describing the malicious intentions of the would-be terrorist bomber:

> We know that crowded places are attractive to those who want to make an impact – if they can find a place that is contained, and busy, a place where they can expect a pattern, or predict a routine – that is a place where they can pass *undetected*. (NaCTSO *Higher Education* video, www.continuityforum.org, 2009)

If the routine reproduction of the inclusive, first-person-plural 'we' is the hallmark of the rhetorical address (Atkinson, 1984), then the next noticeable device is the use of an assertion that it is 'crowded places' that are 'attractive to those who want to make an impact'. The problem with the ARGUS video is that the large space seems to be occupied only by the speaker. No one else is in sight. This empty and depressing vista is supposed, nonetheless, to represent the epicentre of an imminent threat. Of course, it may have been the case that, from a practical point of view, the film's producers thought it easier to control the message if the viewer had only one figure upon which to fix his or her attention (or else the film-makers were not allowed access to the institutional space when it was in regular use). Whatever the explanation, there is a clear contradiction between what is claimed in the script and what is shown on the screen. The next sequence presents an even greater contrast between the actual scene and the 'scenario' described by the presenter.

At the moment when the speaker is uttering the warning that terrorists look for 'a place where they can pass *undetected*', a motorcycle engine begins to rev up, although no bike is visible. What follows is a series of reaction shots, as our host responds to an invisible threat. As the soundtrack gets louder, and as the presenter looks more alarmed, the audience is meant to assume that some terrible event will ensue: in one shot he is observed from the perspective of an imaginary rider as the non-existent motorbike bears down upon him. Just as the unfortunate victim warns that, having found a target, 'it wouldn't take much to make a big bang', a rather minor crash is heard, followed by a vigorous puff of wind. The man dusts himself down, before delivering the less than stirring line, 'your institution may not be a *primary* target, but believe me it's an opportunity' (NaCTSO *Higher Education* video, www. continuityforum.org, 2009). In this video, university managers have been told that they may face a major catastrophe, but this cautionary tale is undermined by the appearance of that strange representational category – the 'non-event' (see Chapter 4). The ARGUS videos fail at many levels, but one inadvertent effect is to make masculine authority appear ridiculous.

The bunker mentality

Not all the preparations made for the 'worst case' are quite so peculiar, although those conducted during periods of crisis are usually more alarming. During the Cold War, preparation for an armed confrontation with the Soviet Union included the revision of a secret document known as the 'War Book', which described 'how Britain would be governed in the event of a nuclear war' (Bates, 23 June 2009). The Book, which remained in use until the 1990s, consisted of sixteen chapters and envisaged the creation of twelve regional centres, each based in underground bunkers. These facilities were supposed to be occupied by a cabal of essential personnel (overwhelmingly male and upper-middle-class in composition), and were to be led by cabinet ministers endowed with extensive discretionary powers and a supporting cast of 'senior military officers, chief constables and judges' (Bates, 23 June 2009). In addition, the most important members of the administration, including intelligence chiefs, were meant join the prime minister in a large subterranean shelter at Corsham. This refuge, built far beneath the limestone hills of the Cotswolds in south-western England, was codenamed TURNSTILE, and had been designated as the seat of government in the event of war (Andrew, 2010: 327).

Despite their formal pre-eminence, the extent to which politicians would really have been in charge during such a crisis is rather doubtful (see below). The likelihood of any authoritative collective surviving an attack on the scale imagined is of course debatable, but the intention behind the War Book is clear – to isolate the upper echelons of the patriarchal Establishment from the rest of the population, in an attempt to preserve a functioning 'command structure'. This meant in effect that representatives of the elite group responsible for conducting – perhaps even initiating – a nuclear war would have been given the best chance of surviving it.

The ordinary inhabitants of the UK, meanwhile, would have faced the prospect of annihilation: at some periods it even seemed as though plans to reduce casualties by dispersing the population had been abandoned. At the height of the Cuban Missile Crisis, for example, when it appeared that a nuclear war with the Eastern bloc could break out, the UK's national 'evacuation plan' – supposedly designed to remove '19.5 million people from nineteen major cities' – was 'never considered or activated' (Wilson, 2008: 169). Certain individuals, however, would have been given special attention, and arrested as part of a strategy to 'round up subversives' (Hennessy and Berg, 23 June 2009).

Although the actual consequences of a nuclear exchange would probably have invalidated any attempt to impose order, even if there had been a few survivors, the fact is that repressive measures had been planned long before the prospect of such an eventuality. This decision indicates an ideological predisposition to use violence not only in this, but in any other situation that could be regarded as a serious threat to 'the rule of law'. It is notable that, during periods of social unrest, rumours concerning the use of military force always begin to circulate. In 2009, for example, one journalist reported 'talk in the officers' mess of possible "civil disorder"' because of the financial crisis, with the suggestion that the army would be asked to repress any outbreak of dissent (Ingrams, 21 March 2009). This task, he noted, would prove difficult, since the armed forces were already overstretched because they were engaged in the Afghan war.

The historical context

Whenever examples of official preparation for a 'worst-case scenario' come to light, the historical context of their composition should of course be borne in mind. This does not, however, mean that war plans from an earlier period become entirely irrelevant. While it is true that they no longer provide the practical rationale for modern emergency planners (who are absorbed in promoting the theory of 'resilience' in the face of threats that fall far short of Armageddon), many of the same practices have reappeared. When, for example, the government of the UK was faced with a series of nationwide fuel protests in 2000, Sir David Omand, then permanent secretary at the Home Office, adapted existing plans and 'built from scratch a crisis management machine' (cited in Hennessy and Berg, 23 June 2009).

Omand, who later chaired Whitehall's Security and Intelligence Committee from 2002 to 2005, revealed that 'we took over a bunker, and installed a chief constable, and representatives of the oil companies, and some civil servants' (Hennessy and Berg, 23 June 2009). It is hardly surprising, considering the nature of the dispute, that the choice of personnel should so closely resemble the model used during the Cold War, but equally it does not suggest the growth of a more democratic political environment. This is an important point because the practices of the past are often excused on the basis that they belong to a less egalitarian era, implying in turn that the current system is more equitable. The depiction of life in the final days before a general nuclear conflagration – marked by a combination of official neglect and selective repression – may no longer provide the 'master narrative' for the worst-case scenario, but this alone does not prove that the welfare of the citizen is now the primary concern of that entity sometimes known as the 'new protective state' (see Hennessy, 2007).

The persistence of secretive, high-handed practices in the contemporary period was underlined when Omand resurfaced to give evidence during the 2010 Chilcot Inquiry into the causes of the Iraq War. The matter he was asked to address was the infamous 'dodgy dossier' drawn up by the UK's Joint Intelligence Committee, which was intended to substantiate Britain's complaints about the military capabilities of Saddam Hussein's regime. Published in February 2003, this document had, Omand testified, been doctored by officials in Downing Street, and eventually contained the assertion that Iraq's non-existent missiles could be used within 45 minutes of an order being given. Omand revealed the 'natural queasiness' that some intelligence officers felt about putting any information into the public domain, but felt that the 45-minute claim was 'at least … something [that] the secret service would allow to be used' (Norton-Taylor, BBC News online, 20 January 2010). In other words, the essential falsehood of the claim meant that the intelligence community was relatively happy to allow its dissemination, whereas the release of accurate information would have been much less satisfactory. 'With hindsight', he said, adding what he called 'a bit of local colour' had been asking for trouble, but 'we didn't spot it at the time' (Norton-Taylor, BBC News online, 20 January 2010).

Hierarchy, governance and communication

Conceived as a form of crisis management, planning for catastrophe may appear to have little in common with the routine administration of everyday life. The emergency scenario is meant to exemplify an extraordinary and temporary arrangement, in which representatives of the security state organise the efforts of the corporate and public sectors so that they are able to meet a particular threat. The ordinary process of government and the 'exceptional' intervention are, however, both based upon legal mechanisms, and in this regard share a number of attributes. There is, therefore, nothing illicit about the recourse to special or discretionary measures as such.

Yet, by its very nature, the formal apparatus brought into being to deal with a crisis supplants the normal conditions of rule. In Britain, for example, the regulations contained within the Civil Contingencies Act of 2004 can be used to 'suspend, modify or override' any other Act of Parliament, with the exception of the Human Rights Act (Head and Mann, 2009: 85). Another, closely related, difficulty arises because the institution of this kind of authority leaves a powerful impression on the political system. It is the *normalisation* of exceptional measures which poses a significant danger, based both on their duration and on the appealing simplicity of the command structure they sustain. This gives rise in turn to the suspicion that supposedly extraordinary practices 'infiltrate the *ordinary* legal system, becoming regularised as a technique of government' (Neocleous, 2008: 67).

When concern is expressed about the possibility of Western nations 'sleep-walking' into a totalitarian condition, it is as though the anxious citizen is supposed to concentrate on one possibility only – that a number of supposedly liberal countries might, almost inadvertently, *pass a point at which* they will have turned into police states, and begin to display all the physical and ideological trappings that such entities are meant to reproduce. The material appearance of paramilitary capacity and the regular expression of authoritarian values are not, however, the sole indications that 'much is rotten' within the contemporary state formation. An equally important and substantial challenge is presented by the creation of extra layers of unelected authority, which adds to the specialised but parallel system of oversight that is described in this book as the 'security regime' (see Chapter 3).

An auxiliary structure

Established under the rubric of emergency planning, underwritten by the security state, and presented as a form of 'masculinist protection' (Young, 2003), an auxiliary structure is being extended throughout the domain of formal authority – which is to say, in every place where the largely unelected leaders of hierarchical organisations are committed to the process of internal surveillance and oversight. This form of rule, associated with the concept of governance, is brought into effect through the obligation placed on managers and supervisors to carry out risk assessments and exercises. Instead of following an obviously oppressive model of administration, however, the rationale behind the diffusion of the 'anti-terror' principle throughout the social order is posited on the notion of creating defensive networks.

The values, ways of life and physical well-being of the democratic nations are supposedly under attack, and therefore require political leaders not only to 'think the unthinkable', but to create flexible, responsive structures that reflect the imagined capabilities of an insurgent enemy. This development is not unique, nor is it found solely in the Western hemisphere. It is rather a feature of those formal democracies, the legal traditions of which enable the production of 'extraordinary' measures without their having to remove the rights their citizens expect to enjoy, and without the visible symbols of constitutional legitimacy being overturned.

Although, for example, there may be restrictions placed on the mainstream media, the outright banning of publications or programmes would be a sign of the weakness of the executive, rather than its strength. Equally, this type of restraint does not mean that political rights are not subject to a degree of erosion – for example, the notion that public protest is illegitimate if it involves violence represents one element of an ongoing project that aims to restrict the freedom of public assembly – but the contemporary liberal state cannot ignore the inconvenient fact that electoral politics alone does not constitute a democratic system. Political legitimacy, on the other hand, is useful because it allows the forces of repression to be properly funded and built into a powerful bloc – the fact that there is rarely any occasion to deploy such force can be seen in the overkill used whenever there is thought to be an armed challenge to the authorities (see Chapter 7).

The upsurge of interest in contingent threat is therefore a means of demonstrating the necessity of centralisation, but this power is not a unique attribute of the constitutional state. Administrations are in fact composed of an alliance between public and private sectors, underpinned by naturalised cultural assumptions about workplace behaviour and gender roles (the assumption that there are 'masculine' and 'feminine' mindsets or capabilities). Government itself becomes a profitable transnational enterprise, bringing in its wake a self-replicating industry of emergency planners, private security firms, public relations experts and academic pundits. Meanwhile, those designated as 'first responders' – local authorities, police, firefighters, medical personnel and minor state officials in general – are obliged to anticipate the range of possible risks and to carry out exercises based on what is often described as the 'worst-case scenario' (see above).

However serious, engagement in simulations and role-play, conducted in a town hall or shopping centre, may seem at first sight to have little to do with the grander designs pursued by leading members of the security state. The rather homely approach adopted by a number of British local authorities when giving advice to the public does little to dispel the suspicion that the security roadshow is run in a slightly amateurish fashion. In an attempt to draw attention to the virtues of emergency planning, Devon County Council has tried to enliven its address with cheerful exhortations, like 'Don't be scared, be well prepared!', emblazoned across a photograph a mournful-looking firefighter (Devon County Council, Local Resilience Forum, 2009). Other local organisations have made an effort to mimic established rhetorical techniques, using references to the future to motivate their audiences. This does not always, however, produce a reassuring message. The website of Tandridge District Council portrayed a group of happy civilians ranged below the puzzling and faintly sinister slogan, 'Prepare now – Know later' (www.tandridge.gov.uk, 2010).

Military procedures: intelligence preparation operations

It is, however, the establishment of structures modelled on the example of police and military operations that should underline the seriousness of what is not simply a response to a contingent event, but an attempt to introduce a useful mode of social control. In the United States, this kind of development is openly discussed, though not necessarily in the terms just described. One pertinent example is the appearance of a system known as 'Intelligence Preparation for Operations' (IPO), described as 'a civil analogue to intelligence preparation on the battlefield' (Sullivan and Wirtz, 2008: 16). IPO is concerned with preparing the environment within which *an armed conflict* is to be fought. It is a 'four-step process that provides a standard toolset' for planning and 'response rehearsal' (16).

Translated into a civic context, this programme infuses the civilian mindset with military procedures, and thus with social attitudes that can be applied beyond the confines of the exercise. In Los Angeles, the IPO system is played out across a specific period of time – or, in the jargon of the planner, an 'event horizon' – but it also attempts to define and therefore control the 'operational space' of the incident (Sullivan and Wirtz, 2008: 16). The ease of translation from the domain of the armed forces to that of civil contingency may of course be attributed to the greater 'militarisation' of life in America, but also to the possibility that this circumstance has led to a less secretive approach than that espoused by many of its allies. Certain nations are, however, increasingly interested in valorising their martial inheritance; in Britain, for example, the institution of an Armed Forces Day, the parading of soldiers returning from Afghanistan, and the statements made by politicians encouraging off-duty troops to wear their uniforms, provides evidence of a gradual decline in the traditional belief that civilian values should predominate in the visible constitution of public life.

The appearance in the UK of new bodies like the Civil Contingencies Secretariat, the 'Resilience Forum' and, under the coalition government of 2010, the National Security Council,[1] also lends weight to the proposition that governmental authority is being reinforced through the use of the 'crisis' paradigm, typical of a country engaged in a war. The recent British initiative is, of course, a rather anaemic version of the United States' NSC, which was formed in 1947 and then moved into the Executive Office of the President in 1949. The US body now contains a subgroup called the 'Committee on Transnational Threats', the purpose of which is to 'develop policies and procedures' so that information about perceived dangers is shared among 'Federal departments and agencies ... and the elements of the intelligence community' (Brown, 2008: 114-15). The British use of this model (which is supposed to be advisory, not executive, in nature), follows the principle that the wider goal is to increase cooperation between the respective systems of different governments – to create, in effect, that type of transnational relationship (through collaboration or rivalry) known as a 'security regime'. The strength of this perspective is analysed in the work of Jervis (1982), Crawford (1994) and Dörfer (1997), among others.

Increased international collaboration is, in addition, a major goal of the emergency planning community. One event held in 2005 – known in Britain as Atlantic Blue – involved coordination between senior figures in the UK, the USA and Canada. The objectives of this simulation were to 'test the existing procedures for domestic incident management of a terrorist event', to improve 'top officials' ability to work together across the affected countries', to 'practice the joint response of the UK, US and Canadian governments to *media handling and public information*', and 'to test the flow of operational time-critical intelligence among US, UK and Canadian agencies' (Cabinet Office, cabinetoffice.gov. uk/ukresilience, n.d.; my emphasis). This does not, however, mean that such countries are moving towards some form of political integration, because, as Croft notes, the idea that security is simply 'a field of interdependence' ignores the very real antagonisms and differences that exist between allied nations (Croft, in Hay, 2010: 189).

Ideological motivation?

Of course, where the participants are not security professionals, it is possible that some will not take the emergency exercise to heart, remaining quietly unconvinced by the various propositions advanced by an already overbearing managerial class. The point, however, is that such an attitude does not necessarily interfere with the successful conduct of a simulated crisis. Since much in the workplace is done on sufferance and not through conviction, no one has actually to believe in the possibility of a genuine connection between the table-top drama and the messy reality.

Narrow models of the ideological function, found for example in Couldry's repetition of Thompson's dictum that ideology is the study of the ways in which 'meaning serves to establish and maintain relations of domination' (cited in Couldry, 2000: 8), reinforce the assumption that the goal of ideology is to *persuade subordinate groups* of the rightness of a particular activity. More developed studies of this subject[2] demonstrate, among other points, the distinction between negative and sociological definitions of ideology, the rhetorical qualities of utterance, and, most crucially for the present discussion, the rejection of the idea that subordinate classes are controlled through the promotion of some form of doctrinal orthodoxy or unitary belief. As Abercrombie and his co-authors have argued, the repetition of an ideological position is, more often than not, designed to support the efforts of the ruling alliance to maintain *its own* expressive cohesion (Abercrombie et al., 1980).

In the current era, no particular dogma needs to be expressed in order to hasten the slide into a technological dystopia, if this is really the trajectory of the 'advanced' nations. It is, in fact, possible to hold any number of views while reproducing, through everyday behaviour, the prevailing structure of the system.[3] If ideology is no longer credited with the power to make the crucial difference in the composition of the social order, the question is, how are hierarchical class and patriarchal relations reproduced? It would be easy enough to argue that it is, after all, the economy – in all its discursive, material and virtual glory – that determines the fate of the human animal.

This, however, is a little general for an enquiry focused on the re-creation of security structures. If the question is confined, for the moment, to organisational issues *within* the broader structure of corporate rule, the reproduction of the system requires the contribution of an active, rather than an entirely repressed, subject. The success of the ubiquitous hierarchical form depends, therefore, on achieving an alignment between a number of qualities.

These are the *attitudinal, behavioural, practical* and *discursive* contributions made by the individual worker or bureaucrat. This is best summarised in the idea that subjects must strike a cooperative *attitude*, display appropriate forms of *behaviour*, demonstrate *practical* aptitude, and reproduce the dominant *discursive* code. Compliance, therefore, relies on the use of techniques, and the occupation of positions, rather than the reproduction of belief. Avoiding the tiresome challenge of having to follow a particular doctrine, but by the same token denying the inspiration that can come from having faith in a set of principles, the consequence is a choice between two alternatives: upward movement through the hierarchy, or the default position – simple resignation to practical necessity.

Normative habituation, the command structure and hierarchical form

As noted above, an important feature of those new formations of authority – the 'resilience forum', for example – that are supposed to enable the practical articulation of the security exercise is that *civilian* bodies are made to adopt a modus operandi that replicates the command structure of military organisations. The more subtle distinctions between the different roles that are evident within civic planning departments are discarded in favour of a basic division between three tiers of responsibility. Gold, or strategic command, directs the operation; the Silver or tactical group implements policy; and Bronze works at the operational level.[4]

Although the notion of ideology as an attempt to impose belief has been questioned (see above), and is supplemented in this book by an account of instrumental necessity, part of the utility of the command structure is to remove the civilian from an environment that might tolerate less rigid distinctions between hierarchical roles, and to demonstrate the virtues of a streamlined, top-down approach. The official line is that, in order for all participants to be able to reproduce similar behaviours in a 'real' situation, the 'game' of security must be taken seriously. As the UK Cabinet Office contends, 'all organisations are at some form of risk': therefore, if they are to recover from a disaster so that they can again 'provide satisfactory goods and services', their emergency plans must be tested 'in regular exercises to assess the validity of the arrangements' (Cabinet Office, cabinetoffice.gov. uk/uk/ukresilience, n.d.).

This requires, in effect, a type of *normative habituation* over and above the nonetheless useful socialisation undergone during the individual's formative years. Habituation depends not only upon the generation of specific assumptions about the nature of the task, but a repeated encounter with a general attitude about the world, in which for example the civilised West is threatened by irrational terrorist enemies. It is this condition – the combination of established points of view with an activity (emergency planning) that helps to maintain these assumptions – which constitutes the contemporary force of the 'ideological'. Participants are therefore given practical opportunities to reproduce a set of assumptions which can ultimately be traced back to a ruling elite (see Introduction).

In addition, the gradual composition of a parallel structure of command, drawn from the upper and mid-echelons of the semi-privatised social order, creates a more effective means of bypassing the inconvenient provisions of formal democracy than the traditional perspective that imagines the possibility of a dramatic 'seizure of power' or the gradual institution of a formal police state. This rather more bureaucratic circumstance requires the usual organisation of material resources and the control of subordinates, but in an essentially political cause. Based on (i) an analysis of standard institutional behaviour, and (ii) a particular conception of power as it is exercised within the patriarchal capitalist state, a number of further propositions about the purpose of emergency planning can be made.

Habituation at work: or, 'why exercise your disaster response?'

UK Cabinet Office document (cabinetoffice.gov.uk/uk/ukresilience)

The first of these arguments is relatively simple: that the various forms of preparation, rehearsal or simulation associated with the conception of risk, including the communicative and mediated behaviour produced by these projects, are (i) the product of hierarchical structures, and (ii) constitute acts of *governance* and oversight which can be applied to both internal and external constituencies (see Chapter 2). In other words, the point of creating, representing and 'playing out' a scenario is to help maintain a series of structural relationships: those established among the different grades of participant engaged in the exercise, and those reinforced by the distinction between this group of 'experts', the 'general public', and the leadership of the security apparatus. Drawing attention to the existence of hierarchy may not be regarded as a very profound revelation, since most activity pursued within contemporary institutions is based upon the assumption that an unelected but experienced and professional executive body must take responsibility for the final form in which policy is cast and decisions are made.

The point is not just that this condition exists, which must be apparent to all, but that it is reinforced through practice. One interesting contribution to the analysis of hierarchy goes so far as to argue that 'regardless of intentions, governing ideologies or norms', it is organisational form that is the most important factor in the development of political institutions (Cooley, 2005: 44). According to this perspective, the 'shape' of an organisation provides a more compelling explanation for the way in which an act of governance is actually carried out, than 'ideational factors, even in cases of empires and states heavily infused with a governing ideology' (44). In response to this argument, two important qualifications should be made.

First, where an authoritative organisation assumes a hierarchical structure, this *epitomises* the material and discursive character of 'a governing ideology'. As a reflexive mechanism that reproduces various aspects of the social order, hierarchical organisation is the expression of the dominant (ideological) principle. As Poulantzas realised, 'the enterprise itself reproduces political and ideological relations', so that ideology should be seen as 'an ensemble of material practices' rather than a 'system of ideas' (Poulantzas, 1978b: 32/17).

This observation provides a useful corrective to the idea that ideology is confined to the realm of ethereal speculation or manipulative address, already discussed above. It is essential nonetheless to remember that the formal composition of a consistent narrative (the basic 'rationale' provided for action) is an important element in the repertoire of any coalition of interests that tries to pursue its goals within a competitive political environment. To those in authority, the advantage is that this story-world can be supported as a distinct activity that need bear only a tangential relationship to either the actual practices of the organisation concerned or the beliefs of those who operate within it.

Ideology is, therefore, *the congruence of structure, socialisation and activity* expressed through everyday pursuits and workplace activity, and not simply the kind of 'exceptional' practice associated with scenario planning. If the whole point of the emergency exercise is to promote (as argued above) a form of normative habituation, then the experience will be repeated by the authorities in order to train its subordinates. The UK's Cabinet Office explains that 'exercises are an important management tool for informing and motivating personnel' but are also an opportunity for the self-promotion and validation of the individual, since they can give 'confidence to those who may be required to respond in a crisis' (Cabinet Office, cabinetoffice.gov.uk/uk/ukresilience). This passage seems to confirm the perception that it is better to produce active subjects than resentful or dysfunctional operatives.

The next issue concerns the ways in which contemporary institutions (government departments, corporations, etc.) distance themselves from the accusation that they are only interested in the reproduction of hierarchical power. Although the provision of career opportunities is not necessarily the hallmark of an enlightened organisation (since it is also an important means of reproducing structure) the contemporary institution seems to place a high value on flexibility, openness and interpersonal exchange, and creates a basic and economically convenient division between workplace roles based on the promotion of 'gendered' capability. Its external activity is characterised by an apparently inclusive form of address, while its internal structures are said to encourage the development of positive collegiate relations and successful individual careers. Within the 'advanced' societies of the (relatively) prosperous nations, the existence of hierarchy is therefore not only regarded as *a chain of command*, but also, by many of those who inhabit its structures, as a model of progressive modernity.

As an amalgam of authorisation and discipline, the system appears to provide the chance for individuals to make progress, and its 'fairness' is measured against the extent to which it meets this expectation. In addition, there is no doubt that, despite the sometimes rigid demarcation between roles within an organisation, these barriers sometimes count for little when moral authority is valued above obedience to the rules. This is an important point, because one of the features of the genuine emergency is the fact that the earliest of the 'first responders' are often not the officials designated by the authorities, but the victims of disaster themselves.

The actions of the public, usually imagined by those in power as a largely ineffective entity waiting for direction, can disrupt established protocols, which assume that the people will be 'acted upon' by both state and non-state actors. It is, however, the social, political and psychological impact of hierarchal relations – and particularly the effect of the 'command structure' on acts of communication – that provides the immediate context within which the composition of the 'scenario' should be analysed.

Reasons to be fearful?
Contingency, social control and 'secular prophecies'

The production of a 'scenario' is not simply intended to *meet a particular contingency*, but rather to preserve and reproduce the capacity and right of the institution concerned to *continue to make successful intercessions* within the social order. This, of course, is a difficult process, because any shared appreciation of social reality is partly determined by normative frameworks that are themselves subject to further development and change, particularly as certain events come to be regarded as more significant than others (see the discussion of '9/11' in Chapter 6). Nonetheless, despite the host of unintended consequences that any 'rational' project can produce, the same impulse to control not just the immediate environment, but the potentialities of the future, continues to characterise the behaviour of the powerful.

The timescale imagined may be the next quarter, or the coming year, or even a full decade, but the fundamental belief remains the same: an act of projection is thought to be a necessary mechanism for the reproduction of a favoured agenda. Contemporary organisations, at least those that constitute centres of influence, do not however concentrate exclusively upon negative conceptions, but appear to engage in the routine production of *secular prophecies*. These are often, of course, designed to increase awareness of the possible materialisation of hazardous events, but many also try to set out a positive vision of the future.

Such references to a 'better tomorrow' are particularly common in political discourse. The UK's general election campaign of 2010 provides a number of examples: 'real change comes when ... millions of us are fired up to play a part in the nation's future' (Conservative Party, 2010: iii); 'to deliver a future fair for all we need to rebuild our economy [and] protect and reform our public services' (Labour Party, 2010: 3); 'the future must be built on a different foundation: fairness' (Liberal Democratic Party, 2010: 8); and 'dare to dream the better future and ... work with us to make it happen' (Green Party, 2010: 4). With the exception of the Green Party, which advocates a future that, studied in detail, seems qualitatively different from that offered by the other three institutions mentioned here, these references provide the ideological supplement to more negative references to social discipline that appear in the discourse of the political class. In other words, exhortations to make steady progress towards a rosy future and doom-laden warnings about the appearance of existential threats should both be considered as contributions to what Neocleous calls 'the fabrication of social order' (Neocleous, 2000).

This type of 'pre-emptive' discursive activity, both positive and negative, lies at the heart of a number of contemporary practices, and is not the sole preserve of the political organisation. The strategic behaviour of every major institution seems to reveal a general, systemic obsession with the projection of events and the need to invest in mechanisms of control: financial markets, governments, security agencies, oil companies and armed forces all 'invest in the future', presenting this impulse either as a positive endeavour, made on behalf of progressive humanity in general, or as some kind of exceptional intervention designed to ward off an otherwise inevitable catastrophe.

The problem, however, is not simply the suspicion that these groups are not sincere about their intentions, but rather that they really *do* intend to shape the future composition of the social order. However it is presented, this type of forward investment is based on the seizure of both the ideological initiative and material resources. It is, therefore, an exceptionally oppressive gesture, one which tries to channel what is to come into the narrow preconceptions of a present that has already created a number of social, political, economic and environmental disasters.

The composition of a *scenario*, whether positive or negative, represents an opportunity for a particular interest group to create a premeditated intervention in the composure of the social, entailing the manipulation not only of the future but of the 'three dimensions of phenomenological or lived time' – the standard conceptions of the past, present and future (Osborne, 1995: ix). Accounts of previous experience, selective descriptions of current circumstance, and the imagined contours of the future are combined to produce a narrative which reflects contemporary preoccupations. These forecasts and predictions, not all of which are intended for public consumption, are therefore essentially *strategic* in character.

The strategic apprehension of disaster: presenting the 'worst case'

If historical examples of the 'worst-case' scenario are cited in order to demonstrate the need for vigilance, just as the appeasement of dictatorships in the 1930s was afterwards used to draw attention to a supposedly identical danger presented by leaders like Iraq's Saddam Hussein, then the conception of a particularly virulent threat is intended to provide a valuable form of training that can be used to meet the challenges thrown up by an unstable world. This does not mean that such conceptions are entirely misconceived. In some cases, making detailed preparations for an archetypal event does seem to prove worthwhile. The London bombings of 7 July 2005, for example, reminded many Whitehall officials of 'the desktop exercise Atlantic Blue', a transatlantic simulation run with the Americans and Canadians (see above), based on the premise that a number of 'catastrophic explosions' had taken place (Hayman and Gilmore, 2009: 28). When the real bombers struck, the authorities were able to base their response on the experience gained during the exercise (though see Chapter 7 for a contrary account).

Despite the manifestation of actual attacks, wholehearted acceptance of the prevailing discourse on the effects of terror is not universal. This is not only based on the feeling that the degree of threat has been exaggerated, which is a fairly common position, but is also produced by an opposing conception, which contends that many scenarios may fail to meet the expected level of severity. A gloomy synopsis can, after all, usually be made even more foreboding with a little narrative embellishment. It is difficult, in other words, for those in authority to argue that a particular scenario really does represent the most dire of imaginable outcomes, without being challenged over the accuracy of their predictions.

It is only when a particularly horrendous incident takes place that the inadequacy of the 'worst-case' scenario is made apparent. So, for example, when the head of 9/11 identifications at the Medical Examiners Office, New York, saw the 11 September attack on television, he realised that 'every single worst-case scenario that we had ever thought about … until this moment, was inadequate' (Ribowsky, cited in *9/11 Crime Scene Investigators*, 2010). This man, who used DNA testing to identify the remains of the people killed in the Twin Towers, noted that this was 'the biggest mass fatality *that we had never prepared for*' (Ribowsky, cited in *9/11 Crime Scene Investigators*, 2010; my emphasis).

From an institutional viewpoint, however, the purpose of making 'forecasts' is not that they should be fulfilled in every respect. They are instead supposed to enable the production of decisive interventions. It is, therefore, the deliberate conjunction of certain *practical* arrangements, rather than the quite distinctive rhetoric of terror, which leads to the suspicion that the actual or imagined management of an extreme scenario has more in common with the *everyday process of governance* than those in positions of authority would like to admit.

Once again, this perception emerges from the argument that every hierarchical structure is devoted to the maintenance (and extension) of the dominant order, and that as a consequence it will draw upon established models of social rule. The collaborative nature of the emergency exercise (which brings together a variety of official groups) cannot disguise the divisions that are made between a number of social categories: the principal actors, the functionaries who put plans into effect, those regarded as 'stakeholders', and finally *a largely undifferentiated public*. This seems, moreover, to replicate the model of authority that appears in supposedly *progressive* theories of administrative and corporate regulation, enshrined in theories like governance (see Chapter 2).

The 'scenario rehearsal' as the exercise of privilege

In summarising the argument that it is the material/ideological form assumed by authority which determines the type of hazard that is imagined and the kind of measures that will be used to mitigate undesirable effects, it seems that preventing the loss of human life is not always the top priority. Before it was revised after the events of '9/11', the United States' National Security Strategy, for example, was divided into three categories – 'vital, important, and humanitarian' (cited in Lansford et al., 2006: 23). Vital concerns were defined as the survival of the nation; important interests included challenges such as the maintenance of overseas bases and the avoidance of crises; while humanitarian issues encompassed responses to 'natural and manmade' disasters (23).

However it is envisaged, the anticipatory commissioning of the 'emergency' event is marked by contradiction. It is in practice the rehearsal of a response to an incident that will never happen in the form envisaged by participants, creating questions about what it is that would actually constitute a real event (see Chapter 5). Once again, it must be stressed that the purpose of these rehearsals is not simply to promote the proposition that 'the unthinkable' could really occur, but to demonstrate that public authority intends to retain the privilege, *whatever the circumstances*, to determine what the 'national' response should be, and how the public should behave. The 'worst-case scenario' is therefore only a more radical development of the usual procedural and discursive mechanisms through which the leadership of the state and corporate sectors attempt to maintain their right to govern.

The fact that 'governance' could survive as a general principle, even when there might be no one to govern, demonstrates the deliberate refusal of the ruling alliance to imagine anything other than the established model of political legitimacy. It is the act of projection itself (used as a means of securing the rule of a transnational bourgeoisie), rather than the promotion of the 'worst-case' alone, that constitutes the real challenge to any form of rational, egalitarian social project.

This apparent determination to preserve the current hierarchical order at all costs should not, therefore, be regarded as a simple wish to overcome challenging circumstances. The extreme end of the spectrum of risk is certainly used to justify the posture adopted by the Establishment, but the real intention of the dominant power is to use the 'worst case' to demonstrate that it will defend its own position *under any circumstances*. One of the consequences of this dangerous attitude is the application of the most severe and repressive 'template' to situations that would seem, to the casual observer, not to merit such a response. The *overproduction of force* is a central element of this form of rule, and is examined in Chapter 7.

Bureaucratic power and the neutralisation of elected authority

The scenario is thus a useful template for the active administration of the social order, and an alibi for the consolidation and extension of power during 'ordinary' periods. It does not, however, necessarily assume the standard form of political authority, enshrined in the notion of representative democracy. In other words, it has a tendency to bypass or incorporate elected officials, who are relegated to a subordinate role. In the case of the War Book, mentioned above, it is clear that it was the *'civil servants'* rather then the politicians (my emphasis) who 'used to rehearse the end of the world' (Hennessy and Berg, news.bbc.co.uk, 23 June 2009).

In practice, therefore, the idea that *politicians* should provide the essential leadership in these situations was no more than a formality. According to a former civil servant who had once, in the early 1970s, played the part of the UK's Defence Secretary, government ministers 'were not encouraged to take part' in exercises, because they would be 'disinclined to play by the rules' (cited in Bates, 23 June 2009). The bureaucrats were concerned that the politicians might show 'a reluctance to do what the military believed was necessary' (Bates, 23 June 2009). Another reason given for the exclusion of elected representatives was that their presence would weaken the deterrent effect of the exercises, since they were partly intended to impress the Eastern bloc with the robust character of British strategic planning.

The sense that members of the political class have little to offer during times of crisis, or even get in the way, has persisted over time, and reappears in later accounts of national emergency. On 7 July 2005, the day of the London transport bombings, a meeting of the UK government's crisis management committee was convened: held in the Cabinet Office Briefing Room (and therefore known by its acronym COBR or, if described as briefing room 'A', as 'COBRA'), it was attended by the various secretaries of state, together with the heads of MI5 and MI6. Chaired by then home secretary Charles Clarke, it also included Assistant Commissioner Andy Hayman, representing the Metropolitan Police.

During the briefing, Hayman became embroiled in an argument with one of the government ministers, Patricia Hewitt, who contradicted his view that there had been no more than four attacks. She seemed convinced that there might be as many as eight crime scenes to investigate. Recalling her intervention, and that of another politician who insisted that the Underground should be reopened, Hayman recalled in his autobiography that he had 'wondered if politicians should be making these key decisions about terrorism', and complained that there was too much 'jockeying for position and attention' within their ranks (Hayman and Gilmore, 2009: 30).

This belief, that senior ministers could not be relied upon to concentrate on the matter in hand because they would always be motivated by self-interest, represents more than the expression of an individual opinion. It is the standard perspective of the professional operative. Hayman, seeking to reinforce this point, drew an analogy between the expertise of the senior personnel who directed COBRA's response to the London bombings, and the situation faced by a patient who needed an operation. 'Would you', he asked, addressing his readers, 'want the chief executive of a hospital to operate on you, or the surgeon?' (Hayman and Gilmore, 2009: 30).

With this remark, Hayman clearly intended to highlight the difference between those professionals who were supposed to display useful practical knowledge and the shortcomings of politicians. The political class certainly makes an easy target, but part of its role is to provide the visible facade of the ruling elite, with the inevitable consequence that many systemic failings are laid at its door. Acting as a lightening rod for public dissatisfaction, it allows whole swathes of the dominant class to pursue their interests undisturbed. This condition is reinforced by the fact that there is much confusion about where the divisions between the powers of government and state actually lie (see English and Townshend, 1999: 4), and a near pathological ignorance concerning the true strength and influence of the corporate sector.

Dispensing with democracy?

Hayman's criticism, implying that politicians are simply too self-absorbed to concentrate on public security, hints at the existence of a more fundamental reservation. Such expressions of discontent, common among civil servants, security officers and military personnel, reveal a certain impatience, not only with one supposedly dysfunctional group, but also with those impediments to efficiency that many identify with formal (democratic) procedures in general. The ranks of the security apparatus are not, however, filled with identical individuals. Whereas an officer like Hayman will have forged a career within a field that still retains a public character, before gaining partial entrance into the world of the secret state, successful career bureaucrats are, while not openly inimical to the democratic system, not usually the product of its (limited) egalitarian or meritocratic precepts.

Occupying the upper ranks of a hierarchical structure, the bureaucratic elite is the product of a system based on an unhealthy combination of patronage, calculated subservience and ruthless self-determination, rather than the collaborative agency associated with the more optimistic models of democracy. Confronted with the foibles of elected representatives, professional functionaries, of whatever grade, find that their reservations about the political system are confirmed. It is the 'emergency', however, that provides them with a rationale for placing efficiency above democratic accountability. For security professionals in particular, temporary manifestations of the so-called 'exceptional' state (Agamben, 2005), confirm the sense that they should be operating as a dedicated, expert and unsentimental elite.

This contention, that the emergency planners would, if possible, dispense with the contributions of many of those who are supposed to represent the will of the electorate, is supported by an event that occurred during the Cuban Missile Crisis of 1962. Despite the categorical denials made at the time, issued through the press by the Ministry of Defence, Britain's nuclear missiles, supplied by America, had been placed on a greatly enhanced state of alert. In other words, nuclear bombers were waiting to take off, and the Thor missile system was ready to launch. What, then, was the role of the politician during this period? Apart from senior members of the executive, which includes a preponderance of unelected officials, the political class was by and large excluded from the decision to put the missiles on standby. In the words of Denis Healy, one of the members of the Labour opposition in the House of Commons, 'Bomber Command was able to prepare for a massive raid on the Soviet Union, without even letting the Ministry of Defence know, let alone Parliament' (cited in Wilson, 2008: 163).

The seriousness of the situation was described by Squadron Leader Bill Young, who was in command of the missile launch pads at Shepherd's Grove, Sussex. He described how all the weapons were 'brought to readiness, and to save launch time, kept fuelled and "on hold"' (Wilson, 2008: 148). He went on to illustrate just how close he had come to the point of no return. He recalled that 'it would have taken only another two or three minutes to complete Phases Four and Five, ending with ignition and lift-off' (148). Although tension was high throughout the UK, the exact depth of the crisis was known only to those most directly concerned with the preparations for war.

Some individuals, in line with the quiet fatalism alluded to earlier, refused to believe that anything much would remain after the first exchange. The director general of MI5 during this period did not think it worth contacting his own staff to explain the service's role during a nuclear standoff, since he thought that 'it was no good envisaging an organised Head Office existing anywhere' in the event of an actual war (Andrew, 2010: 327).

According to the testimony of Air Marshal Sir Michael Beetham, who in 1962 was stationed at the RAF's Bomber Command Headquarters, Prime Minister Harold Macmillan also wished to play down the whole situation, since he insisted that all planning arrangements must be carried out in secret. Obeying the instruction to exercise the utmost discretion, senior airforce officials could not use the BBC to put out a general call for the return of those personnel who were on leave, or away from their stations on other business. Flight crew had to be contacted by telephone. In the event, Beetham felt that the RAF had been so successful in its subterfuge that *nothing ever seemed to appear in the press*, despite the fact that we had generated the entire V-force [Vulcan bombers] to a very high state of readiness' (Wilson, 2008: 50; my emphasis).

Whereas many elements of the crisis scenario are deliberately publicised for maximum ideological effect, serious preparations for war are usually kept hidden from public scrutiny. The strategic management of 'nuclear Armageddon' (see above) is a case in point, removed from the public realm until such time as it can be represented as a 'historical' phenomenon. In the case of nuclear war, the principal goal of executive power is perfectly evident: the survival of its own administrative apparatus. Yet the point of using emergency powers is to establish a mechanism of command and a repertoire of techniques that can be used in any circumstances. So, for example, the British war plan, originally conceived in the 1960s to prosecute a conflict with the Soviet Union, was as we have seen above, 'adapted for use during other, domestic, emergencies since the cold war, including the fuel protests in 2000' (Bates, 23 June 2009).

TWO

Governance, technology and the state

> The basic supposition of capitalist ideology [is] the sharp separa-
> tion between political and economic or social spheres ... the very
> separation that makes possible the development of liberal-democratic
> forms while leaving capitalist production relations intact.
>
> Ellen Meiksins Wood (1986: 135)

> Today's great question is not the critique of capitalism, but ...
> the critique of the democratic form as we know it.
>
> Alain Badiou (cited in Engelmann, 2009: 89–90)

Theories of governance

Before the growth of 'managerialism'[1] as a fully fledged ideological
practice, the semantic range of the term 'governance' encompassed the
act or process of governing or regulating a particular entity, whether
political (e.g. a state or district or canton), religious (such as a holy
order) or individual (the exercise of discretion over personal conduct).
This notion of governance, in use from the fourteenth century, suggested the existence of an ethical purpose, since it was applied to the
legitimate and therefore supposedly judicious use of power within a
hierarchical social order.

In recent years the concept has reappeared, ostensibly in a more
democratic form, having retained some of its original connotations as
a type of morally conscientious administration. 'Governance' is now

employed to refer to a form of collaborative power, in which the authority of government is increased by the inclusion of partners drawn from civil society. The spheres of activity covered by this practice include the management of public administration, the bureaucratic activities of private corporations, the organisation of states and empires (Cooley, 2005),[2] the regulation of cross-border security (Kirchner and Sperling, 2007) and the technical supervision of international economies (Grieco and Ikenberry, 2003).[3] The establishment of 'good governance' in weak or 'failing' states is even cited as one of the primary goals of the West's (informal or non-territorial) neo-imperial wars.[4]

Examples of the use of this practice in the context of warfare are not difficult to find. Describing the British 4th Mechanised Brigade's 'Operation Black Prince' – which took place at the end of July 2010 in Afghanistan, and was portrayed as an attempt to disrupt the concentration of Taliban forces in the Saidabad enclave – Lieutenant James Carr-Smith, the spokesperson for 'Task Force Helmand', described the broad aim of the mission. It was intended, he said, 'to clear the insurgents … into less populated areas', an action that had received, he claimed, 'the full blessing' of the local population, which wished to see 'some governance, some Afghan governance coming into that area' (Carr-Smith, ITV news, 30 July 2010). Holding the ground would, he argued, provide the opportunity to help 'economic development' and would allow 'governance to flourish' (Carr-Smith, ITV news, 30 July 2010). References to governance have clearly, therefore, gained an important place within the discursive repertoire of military officers, but this is because its use was already established among civil servants, policy analysts, executive directors and politicians.

The regulation of the social order

Many of those who advocate the virtues of governance present it as an enlightened approach to the regulation of political and economic life. In order to substantiate this claim, they characterise older methods of managing human and material resources as hierarchical, inflexible and unadventurous. As a doctrine and a modus operandi, governance is supposed to mark a departure from the authoritarian model – which offered universal benefits through the paradigm of 'command and control' – by fostering 'indirect relationships with dispersed and diverse entities' (Heinrich et al., cited in Ingraham and Lynn, 2004: 3). The avowed purpose of this emphasis on collaborative networks is that they are capable of increasing the legitimacy and responsiveness of public institutions, while also promoting efficiency 'in the provision of public goods and services' (Lane, 2000: 95). An interest in these supposedly more flexible approaches to the management of social and economic life is not, however, confined to theorists of government. The 'implications for military doctrine and practice' have also been considered, partly because groups like al-Qaeda have been credited with the ability to operate as diffuse entities: the response of the security apparatus of the 'advanced' nations has been to examine the advantages of 'information superiority, adaptability, the flattening of management structures, increases in speed and, above all, networks' (Bousquet, 2009: 206).

The expression of such principles – at least among civilian institutions – might suggest the emergence of a less rigid mode of regulation, while the active engagement of the voluntary sector,[5] and the involvement of other non-state actors, may seem to indicate a welcome rejection of the 'regulatory state' that is supposed to have become undemocratic and overbearing. According to some of its intellectual sponsors, therefore, governance allows the 'cultures, incentives, structures and other capacities' of the state to be re-directed towards the goal of 'finding solutions to the problems that citizens worry about most' (Perri 6 et al., 2002: 34).

The accuracy of this last assertion would, of course, depend in the first instance on how these concerns and fears are identified, because certain perceptions are often *attributed* to the public, in line with a set of precepts already held by those in authority. So, for example, the emergence of government policy devoted to making services 'more flexible and responsible to the wants of [its] clients' (Self, 1993: 278) is often based on the assumption that the principal wish of the populace is to be given greater 'choice' between different 'providers'. Of course, this raises the suspicion that such an aspiration has been identified as the heartfelt wish of the citizen, precisely in order to justify the multiplication of private influence.

Nonetheless, the emphasis placed on choice, horizontal partnerships and adaptability means that theories of governance (and to a lesser degree the parallel analysis of Foucauldian 'governmentality'⁶) feature strongly in the work of those academics who analyse power as a form of association. Instead of discussing the formal 'chain of command' that is supposed to have characterised the traditional exercise of state and public control, they examine networks, relationships and procedures, in an attempt to 'map out the multiple centres of calculation and authority that traverse and link up personal, social and economic life' (Miller and Rose, 2008: 20). These remarks provide a useful starting point for an enquiry into contemporary administrative mechanisms, and suggest the need to examine three closely related issues.

Authority, hierarchy and the state

The first is the reference to authority in Miller and Rose's description of the 'centres' that connect different aspects of human activity. Authority is in practice a source of influence, in whatever form or combinations of form – moral, coercive, normative, intellectual – it assumes. The second is the absence in this brief description of hierarchy and the institutional career path, both of which underpin the structures that constitute these 'multiple centres' of power or influence. The proliferation of institutions should not, however, of itself be equated with democracy; nor should it suggest that the various centres are necessarily different, beyond the basic distinction between the variations in hierarchical structure that they display (see, for example, the unitary and multidimensional models mentioned in Cooley, 2005).

The third issue is the demotion of the state as the object of study, expressed by Miller and Rose as the pursuit of analysis 'without necessary recourse to the state' (Miller and Rose, 2008: 20). Their attitude to the state may be attributed to a number of causes: the sense that the 'practices of governing' should constitute the primary concern of sociologists, the feeling that 'the hierarchical images and explanatory schema' used within the social sciences are unproductive (21), and the conviction that the state has been studied as an instrument of compulsion rather than as a more complex phenomenon.

Where the state does appear in recent social theory, it is presented in a variety of altered guises. The 'strategic-relational' model outlined by Jessop (2008) is one of the most successful and thorough of these reworkings. In other hands, however, the contemporary state is sometimes softened in appearance to support the idea that there is a distinction between the arcane practices of the past and the progressive attributes of the present. In the work of some security analysts, for example, it emerges as the 'new protective state' (Hennessy, 2007). This represents an attempt to answer the accusation that the 'repressive' apparatus has been built into a separate and unaccountable monolith.

The theorist of social risk Ulrich Beck also seems to place his faith in the notion of transformation, arguing that 'the authoritarian action state has given way to the negotiation state, which sets up stages and conversations and directs the show' (Beck, 1997: 140). Yet, as Ayers notes, the notion that 'good governance' consists of the creation of a more progressive, 'minimal, 'neutral' and accountable state' is exactly what needs to be subjected to scrutiny (Ayers, 2009: 12). Reluctance to do so explains the reversion to historical comparisons and the notion of improvement over time, so that some writers seem to attribute bad authoritarian practices to traditional state formations, and good modes of regulation to the art of governance.

Governance and the 'reform' agenda

The widespread popularity of governance as a description of virtuous organisational behaviour might, however, require some explanation, since it may not be immediately obvious that it operates as a key concept within a larger agenda of political, economic and psychological 'reform'. An overview of the economic debate, and of the relationship between public and private spheres, is covered in the discussion of marketisation (see below).

In the meantime, as a description of a prescribed activity that is conducted by authoritative institutions, 'governance' has, as already noted above, gained an important place within the discursive practices of civil servants, policy analysts, academics, military officers, executive directors and politicians. However, unlike more familiar tropes (such as democracy and freedom), which are circulated in an attempt to reinforce a general political consensus about the nature of the contemporary social order,[7] regular use of the concept does not seem intended to create any popular enthusiasm.

This is because it is articulated in contexts that make it clear that it is meant to describe the serious (though benign and cooperative) exercise of power, reinforcing the perception that its origins lie in the rather exclusive domains of public management theory or foreign policy. When deployed in media interviews by authoritative figures, it is this apparent solemnity that predominates: talk of *governance* does not necessarily seem to represent an actual invitation to participate in government! Audiences are called instead to witness the fact that they are part of the class that is meant to be governed. The increasing propagation of governance as both a theory and an account of a desirable state of affairs may therefore represent an increase in distance between rulers and ruled, and the growth of discrimination between those who are and are not targeted for inclusion as active participants in the project.

The fact that some of the partisans of governance do not try, or have tried and failed, to facilitate the entry of the notion into everyday discourse suggests that its real worth lies in the opportunities provided for ambitious functionaries to adopt an ascendant mode of thought and expression, and thus to associate themselves with a supposedly enlightened, serious and above all modern account of the relationship between the state and its various 'stakeholders'. This is not to deny that there is never room for improvisation or development, but any script that is produced by public officials or corporate managers must remain faithful to the key assumptions that have already been established through the circulation of various government and corporate edicts.

The bureaucrat or entrepreneur is thus provided with an opportunity to deploy a performative code that can both *refer to* and *mobilise* a host of associated activities. There is no need for an exact correlation between every public use of the term, because the commonality lies in the obligation placed on those using it to observe the basic spirit of the concept. In speaking of governance, those engaged in the process have made an investment in the moral discourse it is meant to animate.

Linguistic interventions are not, however, necessarily made in an attempt to discipline the speaker or the listener by restricting what can be said or heard, but can be used in order to provide the ruling alliance and its intellectual servants (see Abercrombie et al., 1980) with the chance to improvise on a theme. This means, in effect, that individuals are allowed to expand, restrict or consolidate an avowed policy as long as it does not obstruct the central goal of authority – which is to maintain and reproduce itself. Individual procedural behaviours often include actions that might not at first sight appear to have much connection with the 'moral' goal of equitable administration and the creation of new partnerships. So, to take an extreme example, the distribution of money by the West to the Kabul government in Afghanistan can be regarded as part of a strategy designed to encourage 'good governance', whereas it might be seen in another context as the provision of bribes.

The context of governance: power and social control

The primary concern of this chapter, however, is to study governance as one (supposedly advanced) explanation for an apparently contradictory feature of modernity: the imposition of forms of consent on the political subject. This process is exemplified by the tax system, in which a 'consensual' act takes place within a context where there are sanctions for non-compliance. This form of subjectivity does not require the individual to feel a real attachment to the state, or to believe anything about the circumstance in which they must (willingly) subsist, other than the fact that it is an inescapable part of the real.

Social control is not, therefore, simply a means of 'producing conformity through socialization or repression' (Sumner, cited in Bergalli and Sumner, 1997: 4), but is renewed through everyday encounters with 'authoritative' structures, which are empowered to demand various kinds of economic and behavioural responses from the subject concerned. These exchanges are, significantly, not simply the collision between a citizen and an authority figure, as delineated in Althusser's famous fictive account of the process of 'bringing the subject to order' through a form of address produced by a police officer who hails a subject (Althusser, 1971: 174). For the most part, the reproduction of subjectivity is automatic, in the sense that it is achieved through a process of technological verification. In other words, interaction may still be conducted between human beings but, from the perspective of the regulatory state and its corporate associates, this is of less importance than the constitution of individual identity through the composition of an extensive electronic footprint. Precise in the provision of detail, but cumbersome in terms of the huge amount of data it generates, oversight becomes a universal principle, which can be applied to any individual for commercial as well as supervisory purposes.

Some of the clearest accounts of how people are tracked as they make their way through the 'surveillance web' (McCahill, 2002), are provided by those who have directed criminal investigations. As ex-Metropolitan Police Assistant Commissioner Hayman noted, 'every time someone uses a credit-card or hole-in-the-wall cash dispenser' they reveal 'lots of information that helps the investigator build a picture of them' (Hayman and Gilmore, 2009: 281). He went on to reveal that 'sixty pounds withdrawn from a cash-point will give a location', together with a 'specific time at which the suspect was there' (281). This, in turn, enables the police to obtain the 'relevant CCTV footage from the local cameras' and thus to get hold of an up-to-date photograph of the subject (281).

Hayman, for one, is perfectly clear that such measures are applied to the population in general, emphasising his own disagreement with the extension of the powers that, in 2005, he helped to consolidate. He described how surveillance had been used to 'target fly-tippers, tax and housing-benefit dodgers and trading-standards swindlers' (Hayman and Gilmore, 2009: 272), though he was careful to list individuals engaged in criminal rather than political activity (see the Conclusion). The lesson that should be extracted from this example is not, however, that one particular 'misuse' of technology should be questioned, but rather to ask why this mode of supervision is universal.

The explanation is largely economic, in the sense that the prevailing logic of the social is one of commercial exchange, underwritten by the conviction that this must be conducted honestly – at least on the part of the consumer.[8] One of the features of bureaucratic control in the contemporary period is the long reach of the state and corporate power based, as argued above, on the use of technologies that can track the consumer-citizen. This individual may enjoy formal political rights, but is charged or taxed for a host of facilities, goods and services that are impossible to refuse if a full engagement with the real is to be embraced. Unless the subject becomes rich, he or she leads the life of a virtual debtor, who always stands on the verge of criminality.

Technological governance

Despite the electronic duress under which the subject is placed, it is the paradigm of *illegal*, anti-social activity that motivates many complaints about the dangers of new technology, organised under the heading of cyber-crime, Internet fraud, identity theft, and so on. Steve Boggan, a journalist working for the *Daily Mail*, tried to demonstrate the vulnerability of the average consumer by hiring two security experts, one of whom worked for a multinational corporation. Boggan gave these men no more than the name and address of his girlfriend, and from this sparse information they produced a fifteen-page report that described 'virtually every aspect' of her life, 'past and present' (Boggan, 11 September 2010: 34). The thrust of the article he produced about this experience was how easy it had been for 'fraudsters' to hack into people's private lives. The material had been collated in this case by studying applications on Facebook, LinkedIn, Flickr, Friends Reunited and TripAdvisor, all of which provided a wealth of electronic data (the date and time a photograph is taken, for example, is entered by the digital camera that is being used, rather than by the photographer concerned). Once again, Boggan drew attention to the hazards posed by 'organised criminals' using this information 'in increasingly sophisticated ways to target victims' (34). The material he had been given, however, was not assembled by the inhabitants of the underworld, but by security operatives. They, however, are regarded as entirely innocent, and supposedly concerned with nothing more than a desire to rid the digital marketplace of illicit activity.

It is clear, in the meantime, that all the publicity generated by Western governments, corporate bodies and the cyber-plutocracy about identity theft and personal security has nothing to do with attempting to reassure the citizen that he or she can protect him- or herself through the use of the latest security procedure or 'firewall'. Its purpose, instead, is to encourage individuals to participate in the technological governance of the social order, through forms of *self-expression* as much as through self-identification. Individuals distinguish themselves through the seemingly innocuous decisions they make about lifestyle and purchasing choices, but also through their enthusiastic participation in social network sites and other modes of personal display.

To the individual consumer, this may feel like entering a domain of personal freedom, while to the advertising executives who analyse such behaviour in order to understand the composition of 'niche markets', it reveals the behavioural characteristics of entire groups. The herds may be smaller, but the 'herd instinct' is still meant to prevail. It is a specific 'demographic', therefore, which is important, rather than the uniquely sensitive individual to whom commercials seem to be addressed. If the definition of coercion is the persuasion of an unwilling subject, then the key term in the contemporary lexicon is freedom of choice. As Bergalli and Sumner explain, 'the discursive currency of regulation, conformity, assent, participation and balance' has replaced 'the register of repression, pacification, conquest, censure and censorship' (Bergalli and Sumner, 1997: 7).

This contradictory attitude has a political dimension, which can be observed in the disquiet displayed by papers like the *Mail* when 'respectable' citizens are monitored by local councils, a perspective that is much less in evidence when subordinated social groups or 'trouble-makers' are placed under observation. This problem is compounded by the fact that the media themselves contribute to oppressive scrutiny, printing images of protestors and on occasion calling for their readers to identify malefactors. It is this kind of practice which gives support to the theory of 'mediated surveillance', in which the media appear as discursively complicit in the reproduction of an authoritarian mindset, yet also as an instrument of limited critique.

One way of avoiding the accusation that power is exercised for repressive purposes is to present the growth of technological oversight as a beneficial development. Such was the case when the creation and use of a small surveillance drone was described *in the context of military operations overseas*. It was supposedly designed to provide military personnel with an overview of the battlefield and was presented a means of saving the lives of soldiers (see Savage, 20 August 2008: 11). When, however, the same equipment was deployed a year later within a domestic context, it turned out that it was being used to spy on protestors who had gathered to oppose the pitiful antics of the far-right British National Party (Barrett, 16 August 2009b: 12).

The flying craft of Team Tumbleweed featured six propellers, thermal imaging and laser technology JOHN LAWRENCE

The techie challenge to save the lives of soldiers

By Michael Savage

IT'S NOT a sight you see every day. A team of hi-tech robots – some trundling along on caterpillar tracks, others hovering in mid-air like flying saucers – hunting down enemy snipers, lookouts, criminal gangs and road-side bombs. And all in the middle of Wiltshire.

The robots, designed by teams of businesses, universities and schools, were taking part in The Grand Challenge, a Ministry of Defence (MoD) competition to find a device that will help soldiers spot potential enemies and hidden hazards during urban warfare. The designs included mini-helicopters, a hovering flying saucer, gliders and even a moon buggy. The oddest-looking invention came from team Tumbleweed. Its craft comprised a central hub mounted on six propellers.

All contained the latest surveillance, thermal imaging and laser technology designed to help locate threats before soldiers are put in harm's way. The army hopes the technology could help troops locate improvised explosive devices (IEDs), which have killed troops in Iraq and Afghanistan.

The event, which culminated yesterday, has taken place over five days at Copehill Down, on Salisbury Plain,

the MoD's purpose-made village used to test soldiers in an urban environment. For the duration of the competition, it has been infested with jeeps, mock-explosives and gunmen.

Though 23 teams submitted entries for the competition, only seven made it through to the finals. They had to complete a "golden hour" in the hazard-laden village, in which they had to spot gangs, bombs and snipers while identifying innocent civilians.

In appalling weather, all the teams had problems with wet equipment. Before the announcement of the winner yesterday, the pits were [...] speculation about who had m[...] to spot the most threats. Team[...] with their two mini-helicop[...] two hefty, bright yellow gro[...] cles, were quietly confident.

Others admitted they ha[...] gled to navigate their v[...] through the wind and rain. Th[...] inative Team Swarm saw t[...] ing device, powered by four [...] crash out. The remarkabl[...] saucer-like craft designed [...] Projects also fell before the [...]

The eventual winner wa[...] Stellar, made up of six bus[...] and a group from Cranfield [...] sity. Their robot, which loo[...] Disney's Wall-E character [...] called Eugene, won the una[...] judges' decision. Eugene t[...]

along on caterpillar tracks rather than flying over enemy territory but won because its high degree of automation meant it could operate independently on the battlefield.

"We are a big team, but we have gelled very well – and it's been a lot of fun," said Julia Richardson, the team leader, after picking up the trophy from the television presenter Philippa Forester.

But while the occasion was heaven for the techies, Major Matt Kelly, an urban warfare specialist at Cope[...]

AUG 17, [...] 2008 | The Sunday Telegraph

Sounding off Neil McCormick's blog on how to write a perfect pop song telegraph.co.uk/culture

SPY IN THE SKY FLYING CAMERA TRACKS PROTESTERS

Demonstrators at a rally against the BNP in Codnor, Derbyshire, right, are watched by a hovering CCTV camera, above, operated from a control panel, left

IT IS the face of modern policing: a hovering CCTV camera – labelled the "Flying Saucer" – which can hover above a demonstration filming every movement of the protesters below.

The remotely-controlled device was used by police yesterday as anti-fascist protesters assembled at the BNP's annual Red, White and Blue festival in Codnor, Derbyshire.

Similar to a mini-helicopter, the device has four pairs of carbon-fibre rotor blades which support a camera. An operator on the ground controls the flight using a hand-held control panel with two joysticks.

The drone – which is based on

military unmanned aerial vehicle (UAV) technology – feeds live images back to a screen on the control unit, enabling the "pilot" to operate the machine even when it is out of sight.

Merseyside Police was the first force to use the drones, launching them for a number of campaigns to against gun and gong crime, as well as tackling anti-social behaviour.

The aerial cameras have also been deployed to deter crowds at pop festivals.

Yesterday was the first time one was used at a demonstration.

Their capacity to provide extra video evidence could prove useful to police

forces which face allegations about their public order tactics, and about differing versions of major events such as London's notorious G20 protests in April.

A Derbyshire Police spokesman said: "A photographic drone plane will be used to record evidence at the Red, White and Blue festival.

"It will be used by a trained operator from the manufacturing company.

"It will record any incidents of disorder for evidence-gathering purposes.

The drone is about 3ft in diameter and can be configured together with night-vision cameras. Unlike full-scale police helicopters it is virtually inaudible. Derbyshire Police is believed to have rented the drone from a rather force for the day at a cost of £300.

Police have been told to change the way they control public protests after the G20 demonstrations saw the death of Ian Tomlinson, a newspaper seller, was pushed to the ground by a police officer.

Earlier this month it emerged that a woman may have suffered a miscarriage shortly after being manhandled by officers at the G20 protests.

DAVID BARRETT

Surveillance equipment for domestic use introduced as a military necessity

Governance and power: oversight, distribution and control

While the standard investigation of consensual forms of authority begins by trying to determine the degree to which they can be distinguished from coercion, it might be more productive to ask how contemporary existence is determined by the integration of coercive measures – as 'unexceptional' forms of personal security – into the routine modes of existence. The person who uses a credit card agrees to make a purchase, but does not give active consent to a process that allows their decisions to be used to generate an electronic profile. In a technological environment, approval of the system is not required – just a readiness to participate in activities that appear entirely normal. Forms of coercion, therefore, appear to lie just beneath the surface of modern life.

If the argument made in this chapter had to be summarised, it would be that the proliferation – within various centres of authority – of the term *governance* can be explained by its usefulness as a paradigmatic code: as the expression of an official stance on the question of political control and public representation, it has the advantage of seeming to advocate a liberal approach to the administration of peoples, territories and resources. Its appeal to those who occupy positions of executive power lies in exactly the fact that it retains a certain moral distinctiveness, based on its apparent commitment to 'participatory' forms of rule, combined with the positive aura it retains among those blue-chip businesses which seek to publicise their post-crash commitment to regulation and oversight.

The question, however, is whether the coercive or 'repressive' principle of hierarchical power has actually disappeared, or whether it has only been subsumed within a more liberal discourse, to re-emerge through the simple, apparently 'non-ideological' expedient of economic necessity. Approached in this way, the appearance in authoritative speech of references to 'governance' may achieve two closely related goals: to circulate the impression that progressive modernity is the hallmark of a particular institution or of powerful organisations in general, and *to establish a common language in order to integrate the functions of disparate groups.*

The use of the word in military circles (described above) testifies to the extension not just of a single term, but of a general *thesis*, from the civilian context in which it is supposed to make sense to a sphere of activity in which it might at first seem anomalous. This is why the armed forces do not argue that they are directly responsible for creating good governance, but that they are instrumental in setting the conditions under which it can take place. The business operative, by comparison, seems able to cut directly to the chase, appropriating the term and employing it within the larger context of 'good citizenship' and 'corporate social responsibility'.

Governance, *in common with all propositions about the character of rule*, relies on the strategic management of public perception, which, as this book seeks to demonstrate, includes the use of public diplomacy, inclusive and intimate modes of address, and an orientation to the future that entails the use of forecasts and the staging of events. Theories of governance must therefore be seen within larger administrative frameworks of managerial power.

These include (i) *social oversight*, a practice based on the principle that the supervision, surveillance and documentation of national and transnational 'publics'[9] are a legitimate and necessary exercise; (ii) *social distribution*, the provision of goods, services, qualifications and rights to deserving recipients; and (iii) *social control*, which is usually associated with attempts to coerce or oppress the political subject. This is sometimes described as a form of ideological manipulation, but (as I have argued repeatedly) it actually works as much through economic compulsion, negative acts of disqualification like the removal of benefits and privileges, and (in the workplace at least) through positive regimes such as 'staff development' and individual appraisal and training. By attending to the relationship between the three activities of oversight, distribution and control, the regulation, sustenance and repression of public energies can be discerned. As a practice, governance is understood, therefore, as an intervention in the management of the social order, one that seeks to combine a critique of rival formations (particularly 'statist' models of rule) with an often rhetorical account of bureaucratic modernity.

Marketisation and governance

The conflation of distinct interests that occurs within unreflexive models of governance may actually suit the purposes of those practitioners

– politicians, academics and business gurus – who agitate for 'public choice'. This perspective, which stands accused of having collapsed citizenship into consumerism, has been criticised for regarding 'the whole political system' as a 'gigantic market for the demand and supply of "public goods"' (Self, 1993: 3). There is, however, nothing particularly new about the validation of market-oriented practices, or the proposition that private endeavour is the natural predisposition of the individual. Every discussion of the social order that identifies 'self-interested market-based activity' as the 'operating principle behind civil society' emanates from the growth of liberalism in the eighteenth century, specifically the conviction that an effective society depends on 'the commercial freedom and independence of its citizens' (Neocleous, 2000: 37).

The problem, of course, is that genuine economic liberty is not the universal condition of all, while extra rights and privileges can be accrued through the concentration of wealth. Doubts about the extent to which most citizens – at least those who hold capital for use rather than accumulation[10] – are actually able to identify and secure their collective interests suggest a structural imbalance in the powers exercised, not only by individuals, but by the various institutional partners nominated for inclusion in the project of governance. Outright discrimination between various groups is not, of course, a novel practice: Hood and his co-authors note that 'rulers of all kinds have long used mechanisms that pit individuals and organisations against one another', in order to 'exert control over their executive apparatus and public service systems' (Hood et al., 2004: 8).

The perception that a form of 'divide and rule' continues to operate under the aegis of governance, in both domestic and international contexts, has reinforced claims that the real aim of the process is to allow business interests to make profitable incursions into the public realm, ensuring in effect that public resources are turned into capital assets. Ayers, in her work on the international dissemination of Western political practices, shares this reservation, arguing that the reconstitution of the 'public and private domains' can only mean a 'greatly enhanced role for the private sector' (Ayers, 2009: 12).

This development is not, however, regarded as controversial by all those engaged in the analysis of governance. Miller and Rose, for example, take a much more dispassionate view of an issue that has been presented by some as no less than the 'restructuring of economic and social life' (Newby, in Newby et al., 1985: 2). These authors insist that sociologists should not 'accept at face value the distinctions' that have traditionally been made between the public and the private, in order then to 'ask to what extent the boundary has been inappropriately transgressed' (Miller and Rose, 2008: 19). From their perspective, the controversy seems artificial, and the movement of private interests into the public realm no more than a minor incursion into territory that should never have been conceptualised as an absolute division.

The target of critique: neoliberalism or capitalism?

Many academic commentators have questioned the supposedly unfettered role of 'the market' in determining the form of the contemporary social order. Yet, besides the fairly mundane observation that it is wrong to exalt free enterprise as a civic principle, it is not always clear if this is based on a more fundamental objection. Is it, for example, the dominance of the economic sphere over the social that is not to their taste, exemplified perhaps by the moral degeneracy of the financial sector, or are there more general reasons for their discontent? Is it 'neoliberalism' as a practice, or the existence of capitalism as a social relation, that they find most objectionable? After the peak of the financial crisis, which built up from 2007 into a general economic conflagration, a great deal of critical attention has been devoted to a single target – neoliberalism. Expressions of hostility to this creed are often, in addition, accompanied by calls for a more vibrant, inventive or expressive democracy (Couldry, 2010; Fierlbeck, 2008; Harvey, 2005).

One author in particular has focused on the negative effects neoliberalism is supposed to have on the ability of the citizen to engage in forms of public engagement associated with the concept of 'voice' (Couldry, 2010). In his opinion, the 'offer of effective voice is crucial to the legitimacy of modern democracies' (1). Voice is described by Couldry as both a process and a value, and he charges neoliberalism with making the assumption that 'for certain crucial purposes voice as a process does not matter' (2). His main concern is to define voice as value, since voice as a process – which neoliberalism is meant to disdain – is in his opinion 'already relatively familiar' as a concept (1).

When, therefore, Couldry examines 'voice as a value', he is referring to 'the act of valuing, and choosing to value, those frameworks for organising human life and resources that *themselves* value voice (as a process)' (Couldry, 2010: 2). In order to establish what it is exactly that this author is trying to say, this explanation should be examined step by step. Broken into stages, Couldry's argument appears in the following terms.

First, voice as a value is described as an elective 'act', which means that it represents a deliberate choice; second, this conscious action accords value to certain 'frameworks for organising human life and resources'; third, these frameworks, which are valued by the act mentioned previously ('the act of valuing' that marks voice as a *value* in itself), are frameworks that value voice as a *process*. If the first two parts of the argument are taken on their own, and if 'voice as a value' can be expressed as a, and a is equivalent to 'the act of (choosing to) value' frameworks for organising life and resource then, where this act of valuation can be expressed as b, a must equal b. At this point, it would seem as though voice as a value is the *act* of valuing certain frameworks, or $a = b$.

However, the third and final element of the definition needs to be introduced into the equation. Although a is supposed to be the same as, or at least can be defined in relation to b, b is also a framework that values voice, not necessarily as a value, but as a process. Voice as a process, however, is not defined at this stage because it has been described as 'already relatively familiar' (Couldry, 2010: 1). This means that a definition of voice as a process must be sought elsewhere. In a later passage, this is explained as the act of 'giving an account of one's life and its conditions' (7).

So, voice as a value is an act that values frameworks, which in turn value voice as the process of giving an account of the self. This can be expressed as a (voice as value), is b (the act of valuing frameworks), which in turn is c (the act of valuing voice as process). In effect, therefore, if voice as value is equivalent to frameworks that value process, voice as value is ultimately the same as voice as process. If so, this would mean that value or worth is the same as process or procedure. Couldry describes this as 'a value about values or what philosophers sometimes call a 'second order' value' (2010: 2).

Couldry then asks how use of the term 'voice', in conjunction with other concepts, such as 'democracy and justice', could help in conceiving forms of political change, and provides a response that draws attention to a 'historically specific situation' (2010: 2). This is the existence of 'a particular discourse' called neoliberalism, a force that has 'come to dominate the contemporary world', and that 'operates with a view of economic life which does not value voice and which imposes that view of economic life on to politics, via a reductive view of politics as the implementing of market functioning' (2).

Rather than go through the type of formulaic analysis used with the previous example, it is enough to note that the argument is similarly constructed. In this case, the 'view of economic life' that is expressed by neoliberalism is a view that 'does not value voice'. If we remember that 'voice' is an act which, rather unsurprisingly, values those frameworks that champion its own production of individual narratives, neoliberalism is in the wrong because (i) it does not value this process of individual self-evaluation, (ii) it imposes this negative perspective on the political domain, and (iii) reduces politics to a market function.

The symptom and the disease

The act of nominating one condition, neoliberalism, as the universal paradigm of market oppression – dominating the realm of the vocal, the narrative/confessional and the political – has two effects. First, it obscures the central purpose of any market operation, which is to influence the economic base of the social order. This obviously entails a major assault on alternative paradigms of conduct, because economic restructuring must be accompanied by an aggressive rationale. Neoliberalism exerts, therefore, a considerable psychological and discursive pressure on the individual. It is not, however, based entirely on the suppression of 'voice', because this is not an essential precondition for the success of neoliberalism as a practice. The second problem associated with Couldry's position is that it makes no sense to confine the critique to neoliberalism, as though it is a particular aberration rather than a development of an underlying condition.

Jessop, by contrast, begins by setting out the meaning of the economic/political formation that pre-dates the later development that is the subject of Couldry's complaint. It is liberalism which, according to Jessop, is 'a polyvalent conceptual ensemble in economic, political, and ideological discourse', and also 'a strongly contested strategic concept for restructuring market–state relations' (Jessop, 2002: 106). When describing liberalism, Jessop provides a useful lesson for those commentators who load all their opprobrium onto one, supposedly all-powerful phenomenon – he notes that '[liberalism] is better seen *as one set of elements* in the repertoire of Western economic, political, and ideological discourse', than as 'a singular, univocal, and internally coherent discourse in its own right' (106; my emphasis). If liberalism is 'one set of elements', then it may be that neoliberalism, as a development of the previous form, must also be part of a larger catalogue of economic and discursive strategies. In Jessop's opinion, liberalism is 'a more or less significant principle of economic, political and social organisation' which is placed within 'a broader institutional configuration', and is not therefore 'a self-consistent, self-sufficient and eternally reproducible principle' (106). What, then, of the neoliberal order that absorbs the attention of Couldry?

This condition, according to Jessop, is an extension of the principles that animated the older configuration, involving 'the liberalisation and deregulation of economic transactions, not only within national borders' but also 'across these borders' (Jessop, 2002: 107). Neoliberalism also required 'the privatisation of state-owned enterprises and state-provided services', together with 'the use of market proxies in the residual public sector' and the treatment of public welfare spending 'as a cost of international production, rather than as a source of domestic demand' (107).

Neoliberalism was thus, from its inception, not only designed to escape democratic management but, in ideological terms, quite openly presented as a harsh variant of international capitalist expropriation. Kiersey, drawing on the work of Foucault, argues that the latter contended that 'neoliberal capitalism has *a consciousness of itself as a theory*' which seeks to 'incite entrepreneurialism to the point of crisis' (Kiersey, 2009: 365; my emphasis). Instead of an aberration that can be overcome through the resurgence of 'voice', however that is eventually defined, neoliberalism is 'the *resurgence* of liberalism', the effects of which are 'rooted in the nature of *capitalist* social formations' (Jessop, 2002: 108; my emphasis). To imagine that neoliberalism is the worst expression (or the 'unacceptable face') of capitalism is to forget just how miserable existence could be under the previous economic regime. As Harvey argued, the 'drive towards neoliberalisation after 1980 entailed little material change in [the] impoverished condition' of much of Africa (Harvey, 2005: 11). Ultimately, it makes no sense to separate neoliberalism from capitalism.

The devolution of power?
Governance and the 'market state'

Part of the reason for the enthusiasm with which governments greeted the prospect of the 'devolution of power' was that it was in fact a response to the ubiquitous power of the market. 'Governments', in Leys's view, tried to escape this pressure by ' shedding responsibilities downwards' through tactics like 'devolution and "subsidiarity"' (Leys, 2001: 2). Considered as the political expression of an essentially pragmatic impulse – one that establishes a form of social peace on the terms of the strongest faction – neoliberalism is no different from other forms of economic stricture. Concentrating on this admittedly poisonous social proposition is to feign ignorance of a host of mechanisms that are employed by governments, including the manipulation of an (often ambiguous) electoral mandate to underpin executive power. Liberal democracy may well be an efficient system for the concentration of resource, currently organised under the signs of consent and 'networked' governance, but it was never the untainted source of democratic practice. When a simple distinction is made between the various currents that make up the strategic repertoire of capital, making one variant only the target of disapprobation, then the danger is that other configurations appear unduly benign. Keynesianism, for example, can be imagined as a kind of proto-socialist redistributive panacea for the ills of capitalism, ignoring the development of hybrid forms of social organisation such as 'privatised Keynesianism' (Crouch, 2009), which can act as a supplement to the dominant mode of capitalist enterprise.

From the overview of governance set out above, it should be clear that rhetorical pronouncements about the devolution of state functions to subordinate partners should not be confused with the actual delegation of political powers to, for example, regional or national assemblies. If the actual goal of 'partnership' is to reduce the budgetary commitments of the state,[11] circumvent local elected authorities, shift the administrative burden to the citizen, move resources to the private sector, and establish direct control over atomised groups that are unable to make autonomous decisions, then governance has become an alibi for the post-democratic manipulation of a deliberately fragmented public realm. This perception has led some critics to offer a critique of the larger rationale that they believe shapes the political environment in which governance operates: one of the most salient of these perspectives refers to the development of 'the market state'.

Hall, for example, identified the 'marketisation' of administrative practices, drawing attention to the 'adaptation of the machinery of the state to the 'mission' of 'entrepreneurial governance' (Hall, 2003: 16). Referring to the principles enshrined in the British New Labour project, he discerned a 'concerted drive to introduce corporate business leaders into every sector of public life' (17). This process, in Hall's opinion, was not based on the simple, piecemeal introduction of advisers, but was part of a larger strategy to transform the values and practices of the public sector, to such an extent that the 'the corporate enterprise itself becomes progressively *the new model of the state*' (17; emphasis in original).

This does not mean that all programmes of governance necessarily tend towards this outcome. Hall recognised, for example, certain contradictions in New Labour's conception of public management. This was the combination of economic liberalism with a 'subaltern programme, of a more social-democratic kind', which he believed was geared to satisfying the demands of its basic constituency and thus maintaining its electoral base while the grand strategy of privatisation was pursued (Hall, 2003: 17).

Clarke and Newman, on the other hand, begin their analysis by examining New Labour's commitment to the rhetorical and practical pursuit of modernisation, a project designed to initiate a series of reforms across the entire spectrum of government activity. Instead of giving priority to one particular tactic, Clarke and Newman base their approach on the notion that the reform agenda had to be pursued through the use of different models of governance. These included collaborative processes, conformity to external standards, and the use of innovation and 'entrepreneurial' models (Clarke and Newman, in Steinberg and Johnson, 2004, 55). The point is that the various modes of institutional behaviour described here do not stand in mutual contradiction, since all have in practice been deployed within a structure that encourages 'private–public partnership'.

Another perspective is offered by Self, who was an adviser to the Australian and British governments: he argues that the turn to models of governance can be explained by the growth of economic constraints. A shortfall in funding for civic development projects meant that assistance had to be sought from 'the private sector, voluntary bodies and public opinion' (Self, 1993: 278). Although the reasons for this shortfall need further discussion, this author is even-handed enough to make a distinction between the possible benefits of devolving power to 'microinstitutions such as schools and hospitals' – the prospect of securing a greater variety of provision – and the disadvantages of a decision that could amount in effect to 'state endorsement' of 'oligarchic institutions with some resemblance to private clubs' (278).

Ultimately, the extent to which governance has become an alibi for a form of retrogressive social engineering, rather than an authentic attempt to democratise the political process, depends on the evaluation both of the intellectual assumption that power has been 'competitively distributed through post-liberal democratic governance networks' (Nickel, 2009: 383), and of the individual initiatives that have emerged from the practice of governance itself. More focused, empirical studies are often helpful in providing evidence of the actual outcomes of policy, since it is clearly useful to compare the concrete effects of governance with the propaganda disseminated on its behalf, just as Cameron and Palan – in a discussion of the 'reality' or otherwise of globalisation – tried to distinguish between the material impact of the phenomenon, and the manifestation of 'communal story-telling' that promotes and perhaps distorts its significance (Cameron and Palan, 2004: 1). Thompson is equally cautious about the wisdom of allowing a general myth of the global process to overcome a more rational depiction of the phenomenon, when she argues that 'there is no *a priori* or plausible theoretical reason to suppose that [global] interdependence will … translate into transnational structures of governance to address the problems [globalisation] generates' (Thompson, 2010: 142).

An empirical enquiry

A useful empirical enquiry was carried out by Sager, who examined the relationship between governance and coercion by analysing how the Swiss cantons (individual states within the larger national confederation) chose to implement alcohol control policies (Sager, 2009). Noting the common assumption that the use of coercion, as the special prerogative of central authority, is not usually attributed to policy networks – which are supposed to operate through the employment of 'softer instruments' – he discovered that a preference for 'strong governance' actually reinforced the appeal of using restrictive or authoritarian methods. As a result of this bias towards direction and control, the junior partners in governance had to call for *the intervention of the state* to secure the desired outcomes (Sager, 2009: 552). In other words, if they wished to achieve certain instrumental goals, members of the network were forced to rely on the power invested in formal state authority, rather than the use of more subtle, persuasive techniques.

This does not mean that the absolute dominance of the state is always evident in these relationships, since some investigations draw attention to the importance of 'transnational private governance systems' (Cashore, 2009: 504). Cashore's argument, which is based on an analysis of global markets in food, fisheries, tourism and other services and commodities, turns on the proposition that the state's decision-making authority can in some cases be bypassed in favour of what he calls 'non-state-market-driven (NSMD) governance', a form of power that gains compliance over those 'audiences' it 'seeks to rule' through the use of market incentives (504). However, just as the notion of an all-powerful state is unconvincing, so the role of the market can be misunderstood: in the case of Cashore's research, for example, the new private governance system relates to sustainable forestry certification, which he calls 'arguably the most advanced case' of NSMD governance in the world (503).

This does not provide much ammunition for anyone who might argue that the power of the state is being eroded. In the words of one economist, who writes in opposition to 'conservative and pro-market ideologies', markets will never be able to replace state functions, or act without government direction when it comes to 'making strategic choices, organizing solidarity over a given territory' and providing institutional frameworks for the practices of capitalism (Boyer, 1996, 110). There is no doubt that certain international initiatives, particularly with regard to the environment and security cooperation, require the acquiescence of national polities, but this should not suggest that individual states will be prepared to give up power in those areas regarded as essential to their national integrity: just such an example can be found within the contours of the 'security state' (see below).

The study of governance, meanwhile, demonstrates some degree of devolution and the creation of new relationships, but it is a mistake to assume that this means that power has been 'competitively distributed through post-liberal democratic governance networks' (Nickel, 2009: 383). Nickel argues that such groups and associations actually converge with neoliberal precepts promoted by the state, because they are 'dependent upon the state *seeming to do less* in order for the network and the market *to seem to do more*' (390; my emphasis).

Retreats from governance: holistic governance?

The sense that the actual process of governance has little to do with the goal of enhancing democratic accountability, and is more concerned with the imposition of economic liberalisation by the state, has led to the appearance of less ambitious arguments about its purpose. One such adjustment can be identified in the notion that 'joined-up government' should be the real aim of policymakers.[12] A prime example of this tendency can be found in the rather overwrought introduction to the determinedly optimistic concept of 'holistic governance' (Perri 6 et al., 2002).

The aim of this particular variant is described as an attempt to offer 'a grounded assessment of the possibilities and limits of moving substantially further to establish a new form of holistic governance centrally focused on delivering integrated policies and practices delivering genuinely desirable outcomes to meet real needs' (Perri 6 et al., 2002: 1). In making an assessment of this passage, it must first be said that it makes a substantial contribution to that obscurantist practice known as management-speak.

The absence of punctuation seems designed to propel forward a set of propositions at such a rate that they slip past the barriers of reason. If, however, the statement is treated as a series of related claims (even though they do not make up a coherent argument), they can at least be assessed according to their overall contribution to (or retreat from) the theory of governance.

In the first place, the notion of making a 'grounded assessment' seems calculated to suggest the empirical validity of the exercise, though some uncertainty is created when the declared intention is to test the 'possibilities and limits' of making progress towards the goal of holistic (presumably consistent and unified) governance. Although the pairing of possibility and limitation generates a faint air of redundancy, it does at least suggest the tension between latent energy and structural restraint. However, it is difficult to know what it means to move 'substantially further' from a position that is unspecified, and impossible to come to a conclusion about the extent or value of such a development if no earlier state or condition has been identified.

The purpose of 'holistic governance' is described as the delivery of 'integrated policies and practices', yet the absence of clear definitions reduces the impact of this assertion. A number of beneficial but obscure 'outcomes' are also mentioned, a set of effects that are supposed to be necessary for the fulfilment of unnamed but fundamental necessities. Once again, it is not clear who decides which outcomes are 'genuinely desirable', nor how or by whom 'needs' should be described as 'real'. The advantage of discussing governance in such abstract terms is of course the fact that any number of conditions or circumstances can be grafted onto a general model. In this case the concern must be that such a formula allows governments and their business associates, rather than the nebulous group known as 'the public', to decide how the common good should be described.

The paragraph under discussion reflects many of the techniques associated with 'language in the new capitalism' identified by Fairclough and his followers, and examined in the analysis of New Labour's linguistic performances (Fairclough, 2000). When a declaration imbued with such ambiguity appears, the best way of understanding its true purpose is to place it within a more precise political setting. Later in their argument, the proponents of 'holistic governance' provide this context by offering an insight into the dominant attitudes and precepts followed at the time by the UK government and its assorted collaborators.

Noting that centrism in government, which they define as an attempt to 'institutionalise social peace between capital and labour', has produced 'successive waves' of rationalism (the revision by incoming governments of a previous administration's policies), these authors describe – with apparent equanimity – the downward revision of ambitious political goals. 'Today', they note, the agenda has changed from the earlier preference for more substantial reform: 'this means', they say, 'combating social exclusion rather than achieving equality' (Perri 6 et al., 2002: 17). In retrospect, the tortuous explanation of 'holistic governance' begins to resemble an attempt to adjust expectation.

More exalted, though supposedly unattainable, social goals – like equality – are abandoned in favour of a much more circumscribed though essentially unmeasurable conception. Although it is clearly not the case that these calls for 'holistic governance' are responsible for the evasive language of the political class, the whole perspective is essentially determined by the agenda set by the political executive. The practice of linguistic equivocation employed by leaders like Blair is replicated in the discourse of those academics who see their role as the fine-tuning of formal policy. Just as there is no way of evaluating a statement that seeks, without solid points of reference, to 'establish a new form of holistic governance' (Perri 6 et al., 2002: 1), so it is impossible to calculate how 'social exclusion' can be reduced without understanding how it is defined, who suffers from it, and how it might be eradicated.

One description, which is presumably authoritative because it was expressed by former UK prime minister Tony Blair, described the policy as directed at 'a hardcore of society outside its mainstream' (cited in Johnson and Walkerdine, 2004: 126). This revealed nothing about the precise composition of the group that occupies this supposedly un-orthodox position. The deficiency was resolved by the Social Exclusion Unit set up within the Cabinet Office at the end of 1997, which defined both the central idea and the scale of the problem. An early publication produced by the Unit described 'what can happen when individuals or areas suffer from a combination of ... unemployment, poor skills, low incomes, poor housing, high crime environments, bad health and family breakdown' (in Fairclough, 2000: 53). In terms of numbers, the Unit identified 'the five million people who live in households where there are people of working age but no one in paid work', together with the 'three million people' who were thought to inhabit 'the worst housing estates' (51).

There is, however, a sense in which talking about social exclusion, a concept which emerged from the European Union, does more than identify a problem. It reconceptualises the whole notion of poverty and deprivation, avoiding the use of terms that might imply that hardship is the inevitable product of capitalist exploitation. In Fairclough's words, it is presented as 'a condition people are in, not something that is done to them' (Fairclough, 2000: 54). It is perhaps no accident that the form of exclusion identified is 'social' rather than economic or political, since social carries with it the suggestion that the type of discrimination is based on outmoded, retrogressive attitudes (often attributed to the 'excluded' themselves) that may perhaps be resolved by a technical adjustment in public policy.

There is also something unsatisfactory about discussions of exclusion that do not articulate a common understanding of its opposite, as though the point is to distract attention from the possibility that it is not some form of oversight but the product of the 'legitimate' process of *inclusion*. Concentrating attention on those denied the fundamental benefits of the social order (which must encompass economic, cultural and political rights) means that the systemic composition of class society is not subjected to scrutiny. It also guarantees that the heightened degrees of privilege made available in a class patriarchy to the national elite are rendered even less visible. These advantages, it must be noted, are not on offer to the bulk of the population, let alone to those who are supposed to occupy the lowest strata.

It is ultimately as though the concentration of resource associated with the capitalist system is uncontroversial, while the wider moral problem can be solved by designating certain groups as underprivileged and then orchestrating permanent government campaigns aimed at addressing (rather than actually resolving) the deficiency. A similar development can be observed when the goal of eradicating inequality is abandoned in favour of projects devoted to 'lifting' individuals and groups out of a state of poverty that is nonetheless maintained as the corollary to wealth. Perhaps the whole purpose of using such language is to train policymakers and apparatchiks in the reproduction of an ideological perspective that reduces the need to identify specific commitments.

Governance and trust

The growing perception that there is a deficiency in the conception of modern governance has led to more than one adjustment in expectation. Lane, in his sympathetic assessment of the 'new public management' (a philosophy closely aligned with theories of governance and 'public choice'), seems also to be aware of the drawbacks, suggesting that, at least in the case of public-sector professionals, the mechanisms used to oversee their activities should be founded on trust rather than the use of bureaucratic commands or competitive economic tendering (Lane, 2000: 159). It seems that even those who advocate the dissemination of 'good governance' realise that it appears to rest on authoritarian precepts.

Quite how trust can be enshrined in hierarchical relationships is, however, unclear.[13] When decisions are made, the judgement of the dominant partner (also usually responsible for allocating economic resources) will override the opinions of any weaker associate. There is also of course the fundamental question of how trust itself is defined: as Fisher and his co-authors point out, a 'trust-judgement' is not a simple unitary concept (Fisher et al., 2010: 162), but is used to indicate a number of forms of human association, taking for example *strategic*, *moral* and *deliberative* forms.[14]

Although those in positions of influence may well raise the issue of trust (in an attempt to demonstrate their commitment to reform), this does not extend to the equalisation of relations between the dominant group and its junior stakeholders. Such a move is not necessary in order to gain consent, and networks of governance are not created in order to hasten the dissolution of formal power. Reluctance to accept this basic truth seems to emerge from the assumption that governance is a form of egalitarian pluralism, based on the goal of establishing a 'deliberative' democracy.

In such cases, pluralism is made to serve as a synonym, not only for the (mythical) openness of discursive exchange, but also for the existence of progressive forms of power-sharing. This position emerges from a refusal to pay attention to the 'inherently conflictual nature of modern pluralism' itself (Mouffe, cited in Dean, 2009: 13), and the ways in which its conception of independence has been assimilated into the administrative order. Belief in the pluralist argument also relies on the denial of simple distinctions between the forms of power exercised by the partners that make up the network of governance: Cawson identifies 'its refusal to recognise fundamental structural differences' in the 'organisational capacity' of competing interests (Cawson, 1986: 33). Yet the notion of pluralism is still used as a justification for the defence of contentious public policy. In 1982, for example, the Council of Europe declared its opposition to 'the assault by terrorism on the values and institutions of pluralist, parliamentary democracy and on human rights' (Council of Europe, 2007: 425).

The governance of inequality?

Furthermore, the interests of the private sector are usually enshrined within the overall rationale of governance, while coalitions of prosperous citizens usually find that their class interests can be advanced through collaboration with a powerful patron. In these circumstances, there is thought to be no harm in encouraging contributions from those less exalted groups, composed of 'ordinary' people, provided they do not make uncomfortable demands or pursue autonomy. Their views are sometimes sought within the framework of a national 'debate', which is actually no more than a period of consolidation that follows an executive decision. This process contributes to the 'institutionalised fiction' of public opinion to which Habermas referred in his work on the public sphere (Habermas, 1991: 237).

Seen from the perspective of those who exercise authority, civil society is composed of groups that possess different degrees of power and influence: in the case of those drawn from the public, the less robust they are, the greater the willingness of the political elite to describe them in positive terms. The purest example of this can be found in expressions of concern for 'the poor'. Evident within the speeches of bourgeois politicians, this ritual utterance serves a practical purpose – the ruling class promotes a view of deprivation that fulfils its need to make a public demonstration of compassion, directed in this case towards a group that is only regarded as deserving because it is deliberately maintained in a state of penury and then imagined as politically impotent.[15]

To those politicians who inhabit the 'leading corporate-government coalitions' (Nitzan and Bichler, 2009: 315), and who pursue the goal of viable governance, it is the relative strength of their principal associates that is of more importance. A simple division exists between those commercial interests that hold capital assets – used to enhance wealth and exert influence – and those collectives unable to wield this kind of authority. It is this distinction, between the comparative power of the real economic 'players' and the modest role assigned to representatives of public institutions, which demonstrates that the interest in govern-ance – as a practice which promotes a connection between central government and special interest groups – does not necessarily mean that some form of progressive decentralisation is an inevitable outcome. Nor, however, does it signify the unambiguous return of corporatism as a political and economic strategy.

Corporatism

Corporatism has been defined as 'a system of interest representation' in which the various contributors are 'organised into a limited number of 'compulsory, non-competitive, hierarchically ordered' categories recognised by the state (Schmitter, 1974, cited in Cawson, 1986: 26). Established models of corporatism may, in some respects, appear similar to theories of governance, since they also depend on the state licensing 'controlled systems of interest representation' and incorporating 'key functional groups' into the management of the social order (Cox, 1988: 32). If it is true that, in the last analysis, successful acts of governance allow or even encourage the imposition of central authority, then another key similarity to the corporate model has been identified. There is, however, an important distinction between governance and corporatism that should be considered. Systems dependent on the former do not need to integrate powerful constituencies into a system of rule, simply because the contemporary state does not have to take account of institutions that are, compared with their condition at the height of the corporatist experiment, relatively weak.

This is particularly so in the case of those bodies representing the organised working class. When used as a tactic to achieve instrumental goals on behalf of the neoliberal state, governance appears not to require any contribution from trade unions or other forms of 'labour interest' (Cox, 1988: 32). The preference is for the creation of relationships with groups that represent no political or structural threat to the state, either because they already occupy the heart of the project, or because they are kept in a position of dependence or subservience, having little independent strength of their own. The structural distinction between governance and corporatism should not disguise the fact that they share a similar impulse: both seek to draw their associates into the hierarchical order of the state. The difference lies in the relative weakness and ideological instability of many of the civil associates that enter the realm of governance.

THREE

The security regime:
state, governance and contingency

In Whitehall, the internal operational security regime, in which only very small numbers of officers and officials were allowed to become involved [in Iraq invasion preparations], constrained broader planning for combat operations.

R. Norton-Taylor (*Guardian*, 23 November 2009)

[The military] would be justified, without special power, in dealing with spies or other persons actively assisting the enemy, and even in shooting such persons without trial were it necessary to do so for the safety of the ~~regime~~ realm.

Home Office Departmental Conference, 26 June 1940
(PRO HO 45 20245, correction in original document;
in Townshend, 1999: 174)

Theories of power: regime or government?

A full eight months before the website WikiLeaks released thousands of US military files, describing combat operations in Afghanistan, the British press obtained a number of 'post-operational reports', compiled by UK field commanders in the wake of the Iraq war (Norton-Taylor, 23 November 2009: 5). The leaked material, first circulated by the *Daily Telegraph*, reveals the chaotic nature of the Blair government's preparations for the conflict, a situation that was caused, according to the officers who produced the documents, by the executive's reluctance to publicise the fact that it had decided to give full support to an American invasion. At a time when a peaceful resolution to the crisis was still supposed to be the primary goal of the US/UK coalition, any suggestion that a decision had already been made to attack Iraq would have caused considerable disquiet. A thorough, systematic mobilisation would, of course, have alerted 'Parliament and the UN' to the fact that 'Blair was already determined to go to war' (5). A similar form of subterfuge had been employed, for the same reasons, during the UK's response to the Cuban Missile Crisis (see the Introduction) and, before that, in the run-up to the Anglo-French invasion of Egypt in 1956 (Thomas, 1970: 145).

When it came to the Iraq deployment, everything had to be prepared on a rushed, ad hoc basis. Some of the British soldiers were flown out to their bases aboard civilian airliners, carrying their equipment as hand baggage: 'dangerous' items, like penknives and nail scissors, were confiscated before they entered the aircraft (Norton-Taylor, 23 November 2009: 5). Besides the usual stories of logistical confusion (one officer claimed that a container full of skis had been flown to the desert), the *Guardian*'s report of these events contained a rather curious reference. The documents, headed 'Operation Telic 2.5, General Staff Analysis', also complained about the Army's lack of access to Whitehall's 'internal operational security regime', into which only 'very small numbers of officers and officials were allowed to become involved' (5).

'Internal operational security regime' is an unusual phrase, which appears to describe a previously unheard-of subdivision within the UK's state apparatus. This may be, of course, because an informal and irregular term, unfamiliar even to many of those who inhabit the darker recesses of government, had been applied to a mode of organisation that was itself nebulous and impermanent. If this is the case, then a variety of expressions could be applied to this, or any other apparently eccentric political arrangement. Such an assumption, however, might reinforce the rationale supplied by senior officials, whenever they are pressed about the existence of secret factions, either to the effect that such groups do not exist, or that they do not operate in the way portrayed by those who would use them to provide evidence of conspiracy.

It might be tempting to dismiss the whole issue out of hand, on the basis that a single remark cannot substantiate the notion that an unaccountable Whitehall cabal was able to direct UK foreign policy. When, however, it is possible for a former head of MI5 to declare that the UK's political leadership was content for the population to 'live in fear under a police state' (Rimington, cited in Norton-Taylor, 11 July 2009), then it is perhaps worth trying to understand what references to an 'internal operational security regime' might actually mean.

No details are supplied as to its membership or function but, despite this paucity of information, it is still possible to imagine its purpose and composition (see below). It seems obvious, in the meantime, that this structure is not a formally recognised and thus *publicised* element of the British system of government. It provides a dramatic counterpoint to conventional depictions of political authority in democratic nations, which rely on a range of fairly standard and largely reassuring concepts, such as governance, public administration, civil society, and so on.

Part of the explanation for such a dramatic difference between the two modes of expression is the fact that the contemporary state is based upon a conscious though unacknowledged division between two types of conduct: a highly rhetorical and almost flamboyant attachment to openness and transparency, accompanied by an intensely secretive and ruthlessly functional pursuit of the 'national interest'. Some may argue that this is less evident in a culture where networks and other more 'progressive' forms of association lead to the diffusion of agency, but this does not necessarily apply to those agents working 'within policing institutions' who act 'to preserve the already existing principles of hierarchical organisation' (Sheptycki, 2009: 374) – nor does it interfere with the functions of the political executive.

When the leadership of particularly powerful nations is still able to take momentous steps – such as the decision to remove Saddam Hussein from power – this demonstrates the weakness of those alternative sites of influence so often lauded as the guarantor of rational argument and political diversity. It was not only the Iraq debacle that illustrated the subordinate position occupied by those excluded from the 'inner circle' of power. Thomas notes how, during the Suez Crisis, the government's 'law officers' insisted 'on placing on record the fact that they had not been consulted' about the drive to war (Thomas, 1970: 139).

At this point, the fact that the standard vocabulary used to describe authority should remain so broad and uncritical begins to look like a rather convenient feature of formal discourse. In other words, the use of a number of normative categories makes any enquiry into the precise composition of individual factions seem unreasonable and peculiar, as though the analyst is trying to find pathologies where none exists. There are, of course, some categorical precedents for identifying the various centres of power that appear to operate without licence or accountability, which do not begin by assuming that they presage the development of a police state. These alternatives, however, have rather comfortable, domestic connotations. Anyone interested in the internal machinations of the political elite will have heard of ideas like 'kitchen cabinet' and 'sofa government', which are used to describe the informal arrangements that are such a notable feature of modern political administration.

The term 'regime', however, is usually reserved for a national or sub-national entity that lacks a legitimate mandate, and that exerts power through the use of authoritarian measures – it is not often applied to the directive capacity of democratic states. In fact, the secret diplomatic, espionage and surveillance activities of Western countries are still defended as though they are not inimical to the rule of law. Assigned to the domain of 'national security' it is as though, in serving a higher principle (reminiscent of MI5's contention that it acts in 'defence of the realm'), secret agencies are automatically credited with an essentially ethical world-view. The insistence, however, that the security services avoid engaging in any form of outright repression is not always supported by the facts. MI5's lack of candour over its role in the interrogation of suspects by American officials is a case in point.[1]

From the security state to the security regime

In recent years, as the 'repressive apparatus' of the Western state has accumulated extensive discretionary powers, and some of its operatives have been accused of engaging in torture, assassination and acts of rendition, the moral integrity of the whole political system has been called into question. In such an atmosphere, the use of the term 'regime' seems increasingly apposite: there are, nonetheless, still reasons why it has not become a universal feature of public discourse. There have, for example, been some unhappy precedents, when the adoption of radical and uncompromising language could not provide a useful insight into the mechanisms of the state. One example is the way in which, during the social unrest of the 1960s, many on the American left identified the system as 'fascist' (Varon, 2004).

Indulgence in inadequate forms of description remains, however, a minor reason for the failure of subsequent attempts to identify the 'deep' state, and to study its authoritarian impulses – the main cause is the determination of secret agencies to maintain near pathological levels of discretion. If some of the critical language used by the left borders on the abusive, then it is equally the case that the political elite can, in their determination to demonise their enemies, use terms that come back to haunt them. The popularity of the phrase 'regime change', for instance, employed by the US authorities to describe the forcible removal of an entire ruling structure, marks the re-entry of the term 'regime' into general consciousness. Opponents of the Iraq War lost no time in using 'regime change' to call for political reform in their own countries.

Dissatisfaction with the ruling alliance's reluctance to come clean about the illicit practices associated with the exercise of power will therefore continue to lead to questions about the extent to which the system is 'truly' democratic. One way of determining the degree to which the secret agency (and, by implication, the state that it inhabits) has evolved towards an authoritarian condition is to map the development of the state's secret capacity against a general typology of the security apparatus. Using the concepts *autonomy* (the resistance of the agency to the encroachment of other state institutions) and *penetration* (the extent of its ability to supervise and monitor other groups), the academic Gill examined the characteristics of various organisations and created a graph that recorded the extent both of their relative independence, and of their influence.

Gill described the four types of agency as: the *domestic intelligence bureau*, which is given a government mandate to gather intelligence, typified by bodies like the Canadian Security Intelligence Service; the *political police* agency, which operates on a more aggressive footing and is less dependent on the state, represented by Britain's MI5; the *security state*, which has wide powers to suppress dissent; and the *independent security state*, which pursues its own policies without reference to other groups within the ruling elite (Gill, 2009: 476–8). Gill demonstrates that immediately after '9/11', based on the perception that a number of secret agencies had failed in their basic duties, all these organisations were reined in. Then, as the 'war on terror' became more aggressive, there seems to have been a renewed drive to act with greater autonomy and thus a greater propensity to employ the 'independent' approach.

This useful model depends, however, on an assessment of the individual agency. Although Gill is clear that he is not attempting to study the much larger intelligence networks to which they belong, there is another possibility that should be considered. This is the existence of smaller units that can be called into being to meet particular contingencies, on the basis that (i) national security is not solely the business of elected representatives, (ii) the larger configurations of state power are too cumbersome to mobilise, and (iii) the wider security state must be protected from association with nefarious activities.

While most writers continue to analyse the trajectory of the intelligence apparatus as a whole, using terms such as 'security control society' (Sheptycki, 2009: 371) and in some cases the rather less convincing notion of the 'new protective state' (Hennessey, 2007), there has also been a modest increase in the use of more critical designations, such as 'security regime' (Young, 2003; Price, 2010; Grusin, 2010). These authors attempt to indicate the existence of both internal and technological modes of secret governance, and not just the regimes of cooperation between states outlined by Jervis (1982). In one instance, which went to press before the *Guardian* report had appeared, 'security regime' was used to refer to the cross-departmental coordination of operatives dedicated to the secret work of intelligence-gathering and surveillance, pointing to the existence 'in mainstream democracies' of structures that 'do not require popular sanction' (Price, 2010: 67).

It should be noted that this author makes no attempt to classify the *entire* state as a regime, but that he is, nonetheless, quite explicit about the fact that authority, formal or otherwise, prevails because it finds ways of undertaking authoritarian projects without tainting the entire state system. References to the 'security regime' also occur in Grusin's exploration of pre-mediation, securitisation and the growth of social networks. His concern is with the ways in which communication technologies 'help to maintain the security regime ... by enabling and encouraging mobility' (Grusin, 2010: 125). In effect, people are tracked by the electronic signatures they leave as they pass through actual and virtual space: it is their transition from one location to another which ensures that they become part of the regime's general function. Once again, it would seem that no 'ideological' collaboration with the security apparatus is necessary. Young, on the other hand, argues that the 'logic of masculinist protection', which she identifies as the core of the regime, is used to conceal the growth of authoritarian government and, furthermore, that those who live within its domain are forced to tolerate 'an oppressive protection racket' (Young, 2003: 223).

Compared to these sources, which describe an apparatus that exercises considerable autonomy from the formal and legal constitution of the state, the military officers who contributed to the reports mentioned in the *Telegraph* and the *Guardian* used an even more focused and refined concept to describe the subdivisions of the democratic state. The '*internal operational security regime*' (see above) is a precise enough designation to point in the direction of collaboration between existing structures, like the Joint Intelligence Committee, the Cabinet Office, MI5 and MI6, and so on, but it does not provide an exact description of the organisation that was actually formed at the time.

In addition, therefore, the existence of bodies that are not widely advertised, but are nonetheless vital to the maintenance of the contemporary social order, must be examined to see if they might contribute to the undeclared regime that becomes visible in times of emergency. An example is found in references made within the UK's 2004 Civil Contingencies Act, in which the 'Civil Power' can ask for military aid to suppress dissent. The Civil Power is supposed to include 'government ministers … police forces … the security and intelligence services, the Government Communications Headquarters (GCHQ), customs, coastguard and serious crime agencies', as well as 'maritime, rail and air accident investigation branches' (Head and Mann, 2009: 85).

By 2006, the British refinement of the security state was based on the TIDO system (Terrorism International Defence and Overseas), a 'machine' staffed by 'civil servants, the intelligence community and the military' and overseen by two committees led by ministers (Hennessey, 2010: 378). The operational element of the whole 'crisis management structure' would be directed by COBRA, and would include a 'Gold' strategic coordination centre, served by Silver and Bronze subordinates (378).

The clue to the actual constitution of the internal security regime lies in the term 'operational'. An *operational* security regime is 'task-oriented' and will change its form according to the resources it needs to mobilise. Senior personnel are recruited into what appears to be a temporarily constituted centre of power, but one that is based on a set of *permanent* structures and principles that allow it to be activated without delay. The tendency in the current period, ostensibly in response to 'jihadist' terrorism, has been to create new bureaucratic mechanisms that are able to coordinate the activities of a number of different agencies.

This means that additions are made to what Hennessey calls the 'inherited institutional armoury' of the secret state, the most significant of which has been the 'cross-agency, inter-departmental, multidisciplinary' Joint Terrorism Analysis Centre in June 2003 (Hennessey, 2010: 374). JTAC, as it is known, does not wield executive power as such, but depends on the efforts of some 130 staff and sixteen 'partner organisations' drawn from 'Whitehall departments and agencies, the military and the police' to provide intelligence assessments that can be passed on to the COBRA planners (374).

JTAC, according to Hennessey, 'gives every appearance of being a permanent fixture of the UK secret state (Hennessey, 2010: 376). The other recent innovation, besides the formation of JTAC, was the institution of a National Security Council (NSC) by the coalition government in May 2010, which replaced the Brown government's National Security, International Relations and Development Committee (NSID). The NSC represented the political or ministerial wing of the security state, consisting of the prime minister and six colleagues, served by a National Security Secretariat (384).

The successful mobilisation of state authority, however, depends on the degree to which a particular interest can be advanced within existing structures. A sense of how this might work in practice was given during Jack Straw's evidence to the Chilcot Inquiry, which examined the causes of the Iraq conflict. Straw, who was foreign secretary at the time of the invasion, and justice secretary when he spoke to the Chilcot panel, though clearly interested in making his own role appear less venal, claimed that he had drawn up a 'contingency plan' in which the UK would provide the American military with intelligence and logistical support, but would take no part in the invasion (Wintour, 21 January 2010). The purpose of mentioning this incident is not to discuss the plausibility of the tale itself, but to illustrate the practical configuration of power. Straw's plan was not, he said, discussed in cabinet, but instead presented to a smaller group of key figures, including members of his own private office, Prime Minister Blair, Chancellor of the Exchequer Gordon Brown, intelligence chiefs, Blair's foreign policy adviser Sir David Manning, and US Secretary of State Colin Powell (Wintour, 21 January 2010).

There is no doubt that decisions are reached because a particular faction within a ruling alliance manages to exert a form of influence that cannot be discerned by an outsider – in this case, Straw did not occupy a strong enough position (or was not sufficiently committed to it) to see his proposal come to fruition. In addition, the whole point of creating hierarchical structures is to lessen the tendency to take a course of action that departs from the dominant ideological perspective.

Regime and regimen

Another, often neglected, feature of the 'regime', besides its supposed informality and impermanence, is the fact that it involves what can only be called the consensual imposition of a coordinated *order*. A regime is based on the ability to enjoin or direct modes of conduct, of discourse, of movement, of events. It will entail, therefore, the production of a prescribed 'regimen' or set of practical procedures. These are simple techniques that allow individuals to achieve a set of goals. A regimen governs the delivery of anything from a course of treatment to a way of life: it not only lays down rules that should be followed, but identifies a collection of approved activities. It does not, however, need to 'force' its adherents into performing any particular action, because they have agreed in advance to abide by its rules. A regimen cannot be brought into being without the active involvement of the human subject, both as administrator and as subjective participant.

As a form of structured regulation, a regimen is therefore based on the expectation that people will submit to its requirements for their own good, and will perform the functions that are supposed to enable them to emerge from the programme chastened, qualified, cured, strengthened or reformed – or eligible for entry to the next level of engagement. They are, in effect, disciplined by their own attempts to 'achieve their full potential', and by the reproduction of those behaviours and attitudes thought appropriate to the situation in which they find themselves.

The internal cohesion of the security agenda, therefore, does not require the dissemination of authoritarian beliefs, because the structural demarcation between role functions demonstrates the advantages of pursuing a career path within a hierarchical structure. All the standard managerial practices designed to integrate a workforce into the company system – SWOT analyses, working parties, informal networks and bonding exercises – have become standard practice, and are replicated in the language of the security state. One source describes the training exercise as an opportunity to 'establish and reinforce relationships between those taking part', and to bring together 'people from different areas together to work as a team, to realise clear goals and to get to know and respect each other's strengths and weaknesses' (cabinetoffice. gov.uk, n.d.).

This is not necessarily a recent development: during the Cold War there was an awareness that participants in civil defence exercises would have to be motivated through the provision of rewards as well as the exercise of discipline. Guidance produced by the Home Office in 1964 described the need to 'accustom the individual volunteer' to working 'as a member of a team', and noted that a 'sense of purpose' could be instilled in people by encouraging them to qualify for 'the silver and gold stars' (Civil Defence *Handbook No. 3*, 1964). Those involved in the exercise would also be subjected to the critical scrutiny of umpires.

In comparing the present era with the 1960s, it is clear that a fairly rigid demarcation between roles has remained in place. In the earlier period, distinct 'Divisions' were created, which would include 'fully-trained members of Class A, members of Class B' and of 'the Reserve who are trained to a lower standard' (Civil Defence *Handbook No. 3*, 1964: 11). Based upon the expectation of cooperative behaviour from their subordinates, the 'senior directing staff' could meet in private to set out the main principles and goals of the emergency exercise (11). The contemporary exercise, in a similar fashion, distinguishes between

Gold, Silver and Bronze functions. Supposedly designed to meet an actual contingency, the integrity of the regime depends, nonetheless, on its strict separation from the everyday, and its removal from the domain of the real.

Two types of authority, or the despotism of structure

In a study of state power, Mann distinguished between two types of authority: the 'despotic' command that could be exercised by a national elite, and the 'infrastructural power' belonging to more sophisticated systems. Mann attributed the first sort of rule to those historical formations, like the ancient Chinese Empire, that could exercise absolute discretion over life and death; he also associated it with the political leadership of the Soviet Union. Infrastructural power, on the other hand, was in Mann's opinion able to 'penetrate civil society, and to implement logistically political decisions throughout the realm' (Mann, 2003: 54). In addition, as a feature of the modern capitalist system, this type of institutional restraint prevents the dominant political faction from assuming absolute operational control over state policy. In other words, again according to Mann, the existence of multiple centres of influence stops the ruling group from becoming 'an *autonomous* state elite' (55; my emphasis).

This model, however, gives rise to certain problems, beginning with the separation of despotic force and infrastructural influence. The assignation of the first to some historical hinterland and the second to the more enlightened practices of modernity comes close to caricature. This is not to deny that it is possible to observe the *relative* ascendancy of either mode of rule, depending on the circumstances, but only as long it is remembered that totalitarian power requires some kind of infrastructure, just as the apparently more consensual form of liberal democracy uses executive measures without necessarily observing all the niceties of the legal process.

This is not simply a matter of democracies responding to *exceptional* circumstances, since powers introduced to 'answer' an emergency tend to remain on the statute books. Equally, more liberal procedures (which are sometimes cited in an attempt to validate the progressive intentions of bourgeois democracy) provide a useful means of regulating the social order. Jessop argues that democratic systems are successful partly because they 'bend under the strain and therefore provide more flexible means to organise political class domination' than the rather less malleable structures of dictatorship (Jessop, 2008: 130). In practice, of course, some dictatorships can be adaptable enough to use less onerous forms of regulation for those spheres of activity that are not considered to be an outright political threat. 'Democratic' elites conduct themselves in a similar fashion, separating the political realm from the (monitored) space where the citizen-consumer is allowed to engage in the consumption of leisure and material goods.

This brings the discussion back to the question of just how much autonomy the 'elite' has in pursuing its goals. Theorists of the state like Mann are right to observe that the dominant faction in complex societies is not an entirely free agent, because there are a large number of other bodies that have a role to play in the constitution of authority. It should not be supposed, however, that just because contemporary executive power is not entirely at liberty to do as its dominant figures please, that it is not *decisive*. Its whole purpose is to 'act as [the] final arbiter of conflict between different parts of the government machine' (Rhodes, 1995: 12). As such, its authority must be recognised.

One solution to the problem of the state and its multiple functions is to see it as the legitimate facade behind which each branch of authority tries to construct its own particular regime. It is therefore important to be aware of both the 'hybrid' nature of the state system – in the sense that some national entities contain a mixture of centralised and networked functions (Robinson, 2008: 566) – and the variety of organisations that make up the totality of the state 'machine'. The political executive is itself, in the words of Rhodes, made up of 'the complex web of institutions, networks and practices surrounding the prime minister, cabinet, cabinet committees and their official counterparts', together with 'less formalized ministerial "clubs" or meetings, bilateral negotiations and interdepartmental committees' (Rhodes, 1995: 12).

Of special interest here is the roll call of bodies that is tagged on to the end of this list: Rhodes notes that the executive also includes coordinating departments, such as 'the Cabinet Office, the Treasury, the Foreign Office, the law officers, and the security and intelligence services' (Rhodes, 1995: 12). These structures, particularly influential in matters of 'national security', should perhaps have come at the top of this compendium, but the more significant issue is again the degree of manoeuvrability available to the security regime.

These organisations and subgroups do not simply 'set limits' to the unbridled exercise of power, since they also provide the necessary mechanisms through which executive initiatives are mediated. It is worth noting, for example, that even a cursory reading of the recollections produced by famous political leaders shows that they describe not only how their wishes were sometimes frustrated by the tenacious opposition of established interests, but also how the same institutional forces often helped to determine the form and content of those interventions that were successful.

Once again, the political advantage of maintaining this complex relationship between the executive and other parts of the Establishment is fairly obvious: it is a useful means of ensuring that various contributions are recognised, and of retaining the support of individual power blocs for the decision that is eventually reached. Of course, this should not be used to suggest that interdepartmental strife is actually no more than a form of shadow-boxing, or that conflict is merely a way of making the public think that it is witnessing a real political event, when the real business of the state is carried on elsewhere. The *constitution* of the state, however, should be understood as the active, 'antecedent' production of doctrine that, once recognised as a set of precedents, contributes to the subsequent resolution of the general form eventually assumed by state power. This means, for example, that a state may be a 'constitutional monarchy' or a republic without disturbing the overall category in which it is placed.

The vital point is to distinguish between those bodies that retain some broadly representative function (bearing in mind the difference between securing an electoral mandate and then feeling free to manoeuvre as circumstances dictate) and those organisations that operate at the heart of the state without the pretence of any connection to the popular will. It was not until the Security Service Act of 1989, for example, that Britain's MI5 was placed on a statutory footing (Andrew, 2010: 767; Pythian in Andrew et al., 2009: 338). Its purpose was not only to combat threats from terrorism and sabotage, and to counter 'actions intended to overthrow or undermine parliamentary democracy by political, industrial or violent means', but also 'to safeguard the economic well-being of the United Kingdom' (Andrew, 2009: 767). This reference to the economy, listed among the other elements that constitute the 'bottom line' and are non-negotiable, may explain the rather rigid postures that are adopted when Britain's industrial and financial systems are subjected to any form of disruption, however mild.

Whatever the exact priority of the security agencies, the existence of an uncompromising power that is able, to a large degree, to determine its own agenda should make the analyst think carefully about the role of those organisations – officially recognised or not – that have always existed comfortably within the bounds of democratic legality. If there is any point in trying to understand capitalism as a system, then it is useful to remember that one of the major functions of 'representative democratic institutions' is to provide the means of securing stable rule (Jessop, 2008: 129). This stability, however, allows the development of several perfectly legal forms of antagonism to flourish. These include competition between capitalist enterprises, between rival political parties, and between nation-states. There will always, however, be areas of activity where democracy is regarded as an impediment to the efficient pursuit of the 'national interest', but there is also the formal provision of spaces within which 'class and factional conflicts' can be played out (129). This means that a safety valve is provided so that internal disagreements do not undermine the viability of an administration. In addition, the 'democratic' structures are *physically separated* from the security institutions and, in the words of ex-prime minister Callaghan, the latter are 'run as separate departments' (cited by Pythian in Andrew et al., 2009: 338).

This observation is not meant to reinforce the notion that the secret divisions of the state are necessarily efficient. British news reporters accompanying the UK's Falklands task force in 1982, for example, were made to observe 'operational secrecy' by submitting their despatches to censorship (Cockerell et al., 1985: 170). Reports were first subjected to scrutiny and alteration by civilian 'minders' from the Ministry of Defence, then underwent the same procedure at the hands of military personnel, before being censored by as many as four more groups of officials, once the copy had reached London (170).

Using the media

Of course, not all the serious arguments that take place between official bodies are revealed at the time of their occurrence. The failure of the UK's Home Office, for instance, to prevail in the 1972 confrontation with the National Union of Mineworkers – together with the deterioration in the relationship between the prime minister of the day (Ted Heath) and his home secretary (Reginald Maudling) – provide a case in point, and are cited as reasons for the Cabinet Office's seizure of responsibility for emergency planning during that period (Jeffery and Hennessy, 1983: 236). Of more significance, at least in terms of their ability to reveal the machinations of the powerful, are those controversies that are played out 'in real time', when institutionally situated participants use all the means at their disposal to promote a particular point of view.

This means that the spectator can expect a more open and unguarded exchange of views, divulged on a daily basis within the media, as opposed to the more subtle uses of backroom influence associated with the work of 'special advisers' and spinners (see Cockerell et al., 1985, for a useful early account). In such cases, the workings of the state apparatus can be observed in detail, as the various antagonists respond to one another's (rhetorically volatile) positions with pointed interventions that prompt a new round of exchanges.

Although considerable emphasis may be placed on the structural context of these disputes, this should not imply that human agency counts for nothing. Structure does more than set certain limits – it also supports and enables the production of effects. Institutional behaviour is the product of collective energy, directed through established channels, and shaped by rules or *sanctions* that either provide official approval for an action, or prevent its development by the imposition of penalties. The meaning of 'sanction', although it appears to embrace two opposing conditions, is useful because it demonstrates that power can be both positive (encouraging certain behaviours) and negative (preventing the pursuit of others). These should be seen, therefore, as two faces of the same process, which is the exercise of organisational discretion through the application of rules and procedures.

Interdepartmental conflict

Writing about the Westland affair (a dispute about the correct government response to the market failure of a UK helicopter manufacturer), which erupted in 1985 during Margaret Thatcher's premiership, one analyst drew attention to a model of structured activity that 'stresses the openness and indeterminacy of much core executive decision making, especially under *crisis* conditions' (Dunleavy, 1995: 189; my emphasis). The Westland controversy set the Department of Trade and Industry, supported by the Cabinet Office, against the secretary of state for defence, Michael Heseltine. The exact details are not relevant to the present discussion, but Dunleavy's analysis of the tactics adopted by the various participants (based on the application of four different interpretative perspectives to the case) provides a number of useful insights.

Of particular interest is the observation that 'the normal closed and private intra-party channels for balancing conflicting capital interests' broke down, so that 'government had to become overtly involved in resolving the issue' (Dunleavy, 1995: 197). Members of the administration therefore made extensive use of the media, employing press and television to make points that would usually be exchanged within the confines of Whitehall. The open antagonism between members of the same government, so much in evidence during this period, was not because the various individuals concerned had decided that free, democratic debate would resolve the issue; nor was it intended to mark the beginning of a new, more 'transparent' relationship with journalists and the public. Ministers used the media as a weapon. Subterfuge, spin and the timely release of information from unattributable sources continued to suffuse the practices of the political class.

In sum, therefore, considerable emphasis should be placed on the fact that, however complex, multifaceted and interdependent contemporary state factions might be, their existence should not be used to support the notion that bourgeois politicians have encouraged the development of more responsive democratic structures. Procedural complexity and the existence of competing networks do not amount to egalitarian pluralism. Instead, the diffusion of certain powers within the more important branches of the state is a testament to its *systemic* flexibility.

In other words, the proliferation of influential centres is not the result of carefully refined checks and balances, but the consequence of the slow growth of structural complicity between different social actors, brought together in a process of mutual dependency that can manifest itself in either conflictual or consensual forms of association.

Democracy and security

The impulse to employ the term 'democratic' to describe the operation of bureaucratic systems is ultimately based on the powerful contemporary myth that 'democracy is a primary, *a priori* good', so that 'if a state qualifies as 'democratic', then it and its policies cannot be legitimately be contested by other actors' (Fierlbeck, 2008: 31). According to this perspective, 'the fundamental attraction of democracy' as a system is that it 'permits the diffusion of power within a relatively ordered social environment' (2).

In Fierlbeck's opinion, if it is true that democracy is devoted to egalitarian rule, it is also 'even more manifestly' about the exercise of power (2008: 39). The question is how this power is actually deployed, and who is responsible for deciding to use it. Any issue that relates to 'national security' falls within the remit of the security state, and the distributed fields of authority identified by Fierlbeck seem to be irrelevant. The only question is to what degree the security regime should be regarded as a semi-autonomous centre of power that can be found within not just the democratic order but the larger apparatus of the security state itself. Rather than a formal element of state power, the regime appears to be a mechanism of variable size, activated within the 'deep' state when decisive interventions are required. Democracy, while discursively ubiquitous, is confined to a particular sphere and exercised within a limited period of time, while the majority of the activities that underpin the system are based on forms of collective effort directed by hierarchical authority.

As described above, one of the most notable features of the loose but influential structure sometimes known as the 'contingency planning community' (Jeffery and Hennessy, 1983: 230) is that it works unashamedly as a 'command structure'. The top-down structure of the 'emergency' collective also demonstrates the existence, within the ranks of the bourgeoisie and its allies, of a considerable degree of impatience with the scope, albeit limited, of democratic exchange that takes place in the public sphere.

Licensed by the state, new structures like the 'Resilience Forum' receive direct guidance from elements of the security apparatus and become part of this parallel form of authority. Perhaps the most remarkable aspect of this development – besides the circumvention of the democratic practices that are, in other circumstances, praised as the source of political legitimacy – is the attempt to turn existential uncertainty into political and financial capital.

The spectre of cataclysmic threat is used to build authoritarian structures that are supposed to provide a defence against a set of hazards that are never attributed to the rapacious activities of capital. Leading politicians responsible for foreign policy and security, often in opposition both to their own intelligence agencies and to the more 'civic' conception of emergency, refuse to accept the proposition that the state is complicit in the production of public hazards. Wars and counter-insurgencies, for example, are supposed to undermine rather than incite terrorist violence, and do not appear on the list of threats drawn up by state agencies. The intense and ceaseless production of uncertainty is therefore assigned to the deliberate machinations of an alien insurgency, one that is supposedly driven by an apocalyptic religious delusion. In turn, according to the security state, an otherwise contented or neutral subject is in danger of being 'radicalised', turned in effect against the governing precepts of Western democracy.

Radicalisation is no longer described as the growth of political consciousness, but as the 'process by which [sic] people come to support violent extremism and, in some cases, join terrorist groups' (NaCTSO, *Pursue Prevent, Protect, Prepare*, 2009: 11). This interpretation of the term has created the opportunity for any manifestation of 'radical' behaviour to be linked to the pursuit of 'terrorist' objectives. Radicalisation is supposed to have 'a range of causes', including 'perceptions of our foreign policy' (11). In the strange world of the security operative, the problem is not the invasion of foreign countries, but the supposedly mistaken *perception* of Britain's overseas adventures.

Of most significance, however, is the combination of new attitudes to the disaffected 'radical' and the assumption that extremism (and by extension terrorism) can involve activity directed against the industrial base of the nation. In the UK, for example, the growth of a small but vibrant group of 'direct action' environmentalists, dedicated to making physical interventions against the spread of nuclear energy, coal-fired power stations and airports, has seen their forced assimilation into categories that were supposed to apply only to the most dangerous opponents of liberal democracy. A host of other activists has been similarly targeted. So, for example, once Sir Richard Dannatt, then chief of the general staff, had declared that government ministers must assume 'a war footing' in order to secure victory in Afghanistan (Norton-Taylor, 31 July 2009: 15), and it had been decided that the conflict must be linked to security within the borders of the nation itself (Sengupta, 3 August 2008: 13), then action against anti-war protestors could be justified on the general grounds of security.

In 2009, a *Guardian* report revealed that senior police officers were using a category, 'domestic extremist', that had no legal basis but that included those who might get involved in direct action or civil disobedience (Evans and Lewis, 26 October 2009: 1). The 'terrorism and allied matters' committee of the Association of Chief Police Officers was responsible for overseeing the work of three national police units, and received a total of £9 million from the Home Office and other police forces, in order to pursue its goals.

Similarly, a whole crop of headlines seem to attest to the extension of powers that encompass groups that would be difficult to imagine as a major security threat: one article with the title 'Police stop and search two-year olds' revealed that sixteen police forces in the UK had stopped and/or searched 4,000 children under the age of 10 (Barrett, 16 August 2009a: 12). The headline 'Met used anti-terror laws to stop and search 58 under-10's' covered the same story from a different perspective (Dodd, 19 August 2009: 13), while the banner '"Problem" children to be monitored for signs of criminality' referred to one of the initiatives attributed to Tony Blair, who, according to the report, went so far as to suggest that 'health visitors could intervene before the birth of children judged at risk of falling into a life of crime' (Morris, 28 March 2007: 20).

Habituation and ideology

It is worth noting that the 'amplification of risk' (Pidgeon et al., 2003) has a role to play in recomposing public authority along authoritarian lines. This is not just because emergency planning provides the opportunity to draw a number of innocent people into a network of criminality, but also because the use of 'non-traditional' actors in the realm of crisis management offers access to ready-made structures of social control. While it is true that the recruitment of a local bourgeoisie is of great value in securing practical expressions of consent from an influential part of the community, it also allows the security state to use their subordinates as cheap labour.

This is achieved not through the difficult process of persuasion or the pursuit of hegemony, but through the more direct route of 'habituation' (see Chapter 1). This is a process that depends on the promotion of forms of practical endeavour, the adoption of norms and shared attitudes, and communicative exchange (and thus mutual alignment) between various elements of the workforce. All this is overseen by a class of managers that issues orders to a subgroup of functionaries, which is in turn accustomed to carrying out instructions in a variety of mundane contexts.

The goal is therefore to expand the normal duties associated with work on the shop or office or factory floor, so as to include the preparations and drills that are much more useful in materialising threat than any overtly ideological intervention. PR experts, civil servants, CEOs, emergency planners, security officers and police come together in these new centres of influence to manufacture uncertainty, building an 'ideology' of unpredictability into the system.

Although this may seem to reinforce the perception that the system is built on fear, and thus to exemplify a mode of popular control through 'emotional governance' (Richards, 2007), the idea that the general public is actually in a state of perpetual dread is absurd. The extent to which rule can be achieved through the creation of anxiety is doubtful, because a state of trepidation cannot be maintained when there is very little everyday evidence that fear is justified; equally, it is impossible to maintain the same level of preparedness when there is no emergency in sight. The promotion of 'terror' is, therefore, a useful but temporary ploy.

The real purpose of contingency planning, though it does involve the production of discipline, is to try to create a form of stasis that increases dependence on the 'expertise' of the planner and the authority of the managerial class. The emergency simulation does not discourage innovation, of course, provided it takes place within the bounds of the exercise. The event itself obeys the unity of time and place – as is fitting for something that most resembles an improvised drama – and pays particular attention to media management techniques in order to cope with the demands of 'breaking news'. Meanwhile, the division between those who serve as members of the contingency teams and a public that is the subject of its 'protection' leads to some marked contradictions between the ideological messages promoted within the same arena. The shopping centre or mall, for example, is presented as both the epicentre of leisured consumption and, as a 'crowded place', one of the prime targets of the terrorist. A walk through such a precinct is therefore conceived as both an excursion into a realm of consumer luxury and an incursion into the domain of extreme risk (see Chapter 8).

Power and regulation

Unfortunately, there is a distinct tendency, observable within the analysis of state power, to assign the repressive, despotic or totalitarian features of authority, if not to ancient cultures or ailing autocratic regimes (as did Mann, above), to those polities that can be described as particularly offensive, or that exist at the periphery of the state system, or that have simply failed to align themselves with the West. In many instances, the accusation that such countries are dictatorships is accurate, but the problem is that dictatorial methods are then assumed to be their special preserve. The study of 'advanced' democracies, on the other hand, is predicated on the assumption that any authoritarian practices or 'excessive' use of executive intervention must represent an unusual deviation from liberal norms.

Whereas the 'constitutional' left might interpret the process as evidence of a threat to established values and freedoms, a traditional right-wing perspective could represent them as entirely desirable, on the grounds that they will reinforce the ability of the state to protect its (legitimate) citizens against extraordinary threats. Neither position offers a particularly useful insight into the true composition of demo-cratic power. As English and Townshend (1999) note, there are many separate functions at work within the modern liberal state, and these can be invested with all kinds of emotional resonance.

Government, so often used as a means of identifying the centre of power, is only 'one component' of the state, performing 'its executive function' while other organisations deal with its 'military, legislative, administrative, or judicial work' (English and Townshend, 1999: 4). Where a crisis of some sort arises or is imagined, then the standard approach is to examine the 'balance' between the influence of these various centres of authority.

This gives rise either to approaches which argue that iniquity must be redressed (in an attempt to bring the system back into a mythical state of equilibrium) or to interpretations that see the development of particular trends as the inevitable growth of a structural imbalance in favour of the repressive state. Poulantzas, for example, was one of those who believed that power was being accrued by the executive and its coercive apparatus (see Dunleavy, 1995: 196; Jessop, 2008: 131–2).

This fairly persuasive theme has continued to appear in recent times. According to one *Newsweek* journalist, writing about the United States, the government had in the nine years since the 11 September attacks 'created or reconfigured at least 263 organisations' dedicated to dealing with some aspect of the 'war on terror', while $75 billion, according to (rather low) government estimates, had been spent on intelligence-gathering (Zakaria, 13 September 2010). In addition, 'thirty-three new building complexes' occupying no less than 17 million square feet had been built for security bureaucracies, and 30,000 individuals were employed to 'listen in on 'phone conversations and other communica-tions' within the borders of America itself (Zakaria, 13 September 2010). The Department of Homeland Security had by this time acquired a workforce of 230,000 people, while the whole apparatus produced 50,000 intelligence reports a day.

Although this seems to support the argument that the security state is expanding, there are certain features of its growth that should be mentioned. It is not, for example, entirely dependent on government resources, because some of the increase in size can be attributed to private (or privatised) capacity. The other question is how the whole development should be regarded, since it can be interpreted as either an extraordinary or an essential and permanent feature of the neoliberal social order (Bonner, 2007; Neocleous, 2008).

The character of power: structural complicity

It is clear that the appearance of the 'worst-case scenario' is often used as a ploy to distract attention from the suspicion that everyday administration and oversight are the real problem. The context of any such enquiry into the nature of the state remains particularly challenging, because the most dramatic evidence can be drawn from exactly those periods of 'exception' that may or may not characterise the system as a whole.

There are two conditions that are usually associated with the question about the degree to which capitalism is ultimately dependent on the production of coercive force. The first is when such states are prosecuting a war, and the second is when they engage in internal repression. The conjunction of war and domestic emergency may also lend weight to the radical argument that extreme times call for equally uncompromising countermeasures from the oppressed. The Vietnam War, for example, and the accompanying social unrest that, policed with an exceptionally heavy hand, produced a generation of Americans that distrusted the motives of the state, also gave birth to groups like the Weather Underground and the Black Panthers, which assumed positions modelled on examples of insurrectionary revolt (Varon, 2004).

Yet, if they are understood as *exceptional* events, any study of the two conditions could only be applied to the 'temporary' situation itself, and to the specialised forces deployed to suppress dissent, leaving the larger question of the *formal* state's responsibility out of the equation. In the end, therefore, not much would have been learned about the constitution and capabilities of state power, other than to discern the apparent growth of 'authoritarian law and order ideologies' within the 'core control agencies of the liberal democratic state' (McLaughlin, 2007: 61).

The problem facing those who engage in a critique of authority is therefore the unfortunate opposition between two highly restrictive questions: (i) do current developments represent the increasing pre-eminence of the security regime, so that its values and characteristics begin to infect the body politic as a whole, or (ii) is the 'relative autonomy' of police and secret agencies always bounded by structural practices that cannot be subsumed within the security agenda (the 'rule of law' for example). Rather than submit to this frustrating dilemma, it might be more productive to conceptualise the problem in another way.

Although it may be the case that, as the power of patriarchy and authoritarianism increases, egalitarian practices grow weaker, this does not mean that the latter will disappear altogether. Instead of a struggle in which one quality threatens to overcome another, the alternative practices should be considered according to their strategic value. In effect, this means that the overall function of the state, as a collection of structures and an alliance of interests, should be the focus of analysis. If this larger perspective is considered, then internal conflicts within the state can be seen not simply as territorial disputes or as the expression of ideological differences, but as the standard means of producing specific outcomes. The power of the state, dispersed among a variety of branches and agencies, is underwritten by the capacity to produce effects, though the exact nature of these 'end products' cannot be predicted. It is, therefore, the structural complicity between functions, like the sometimes 'antagonistic' contributions made by police, probation officers, judges and lawyers to the material conduct of the legal system, that should be understood.

This does not negate the observation that the process of control seems to be on the increase. It means instead that it is the product of the system as a whole, rather than of some imbalance within it. So, for example, the fact that the use of surveillance is everywhere in evidence is not really because previously 'private' spheres of existence have been invaded and sullied by the state and its corporate allies. It is rather that new modes of urban existence have *brought into being* a technologically dependent way of life that *cannot be private*, because the economy depends on identifying the niche markets and political tendencies to which the citizen belongs. The high visibility of the individual, as he or she is tracked across the street or in the shopping mall, is only the most obvious example of this *political* pursuit of economic knowledge. Another form assumed by this project is the popularisation of the idea that the consumer is a free, digital-savvy agent, liberated by the opportunities presented by a 'networked' environment.

Boltanski and Chaipello examine what they call 'the generalisation of the *network* form of representation' (Boltanski and Chaipello, 2007: 139; my emphasis), noting that the use of the term, originally a simple reference to technical facilities like the telephone system, began to spread into management studies and thence to some branches of the social sciences. According to their research, before it entered the lexicon of organisational discourse, *network* was 'nearly always used pejoratively to characterise clandestine, illegitimate and/or illegal' links between social groups (141). They argue that the growth of what they call 'the connexionist imagination' is partly attributable to developments in communication and transport (140) and, in particular, by the existence of sophisticated media forms and technology such as the office computer, which has 'conferred concrete existence on the abstract notion of network' (140). Accompanying this apparent materialisation of a new communicative order, 'network' began to be used to conjure up a vision of positive developments in human relations, suggesting the existence of free association, rather than the standard depiction of life within a rigid hierarchical structure.

Appreciating the significance of the whole regime of commercial security means seeing the 'consumer' as an individual who exercises rational choice within an irrational framework. The shopper-labourer has become completely reliant on the goodwill of a plethora of public and private agencies for his or her very survival. This may sound like a rather dramatic statement, because the standard representation of modern city life is one of abundance and choice. The individual is, however, trapped in the only environment that he or she can navigate, which suits the free-market ideologist who believes the ideal urban dweller to be essentially apolitical. This attitude is linked to the recent emphasis on emotional intelligence, aesthetic sensibility and the acquisition of soft skills. 'Practically' useless in the sense of being unable to carve out an independent economic existence, the individual is supposed, nonetheless, to be highly adept at following trends, devoted to play as the central principle of life, and able to display a high degree of technological competence (so that the latest electronic toy will make an impact on the market).

While the citizen-consumer is monitored as a potential source of income (or trouble, if they are dilatory in paying for the various 'services' on offer), the political executive continues to reproduce the notion of democratic accountability. Yet, under the general rule of suspicion, it is the public that is made to account for its activities. The discourse of egalitarian (or 'meritocratic') life pretends that authoritarianism is the foundational principle of permanent dictatorship, separating this notion from the idea that it is actually the default position of all those hierarchical systems that present themselves as liberal democracies. While there has never been much misunderstanding as to the real meaning of *liberal* in this formula (it is an economic category), the true definition of democracy as a form of flexible, strategic rule receives less attention.

Forms of authority and internal dynamics

The determination to intercede in the conduct of everyday life is not the unique characteristic of structures devoted to surveillance and security. Every form of executive authority, whether political, military, patriarchal or economic, will attempt to reproduce its own structures, precepts and values within the context of the social, practical, natural[2] and virtual environments it inhabits. Among the conditions required for success, three key internal features should be recognised. The first is the existence of bureaucratic procedures and rules, which provide a template for the pursuit of essential goals. The second is the provision of training, so that operatives can follow established practices without the need for constant supervision. The third is the right of senior management to issue directives. All contribute to the *practical* maintenance of an institution's ideological perspective, or its general *ethos*.

The last of these three points, which suggests that hierarchical power is maintained through the distribution of edicts, may seem a little crude. After all, theories of hegemonic rule, together with loose talk about the triumph of networked relations, have drawn attention to the semi-consensual and sometimes positively cooperative nature of contemporary organisational existence. It is fairly common, in addition, to argue that a 'top-down' approach is generally undesirable and unprofitable, and is confined to those bodies, like military formations, that are supposed to require obedience. Other collectives, meanwhile, are supposed to employ more flexible arrangements. The technological enterprise, whether state or corporate, is often used as an example of a more subtle approach to management: dependent on a relatively autonomous class of professional experts, it nurtures the impression of collaborative endeavour and the pursuit of common goals.

Arguing that internal authority (i.e. that exercised over a class of subordinates) is based on negotiation and agreement does not, however, undermine the existence of an overall 'command structure'. As White et al. point out, the development of 'human resource management practices', including training, job rotation and enhanced communication, 'does not mean that the organisation is relaxing control' (2004: 84). Indeed, the incentives that are given to employees to complete tasks commensurate with the needs and principles of the organisation should also be seen as forms of control, because 'they are always linked to some kind of system for checking that the incentives really are generating performance' (85).

The proliferation of specialised units and small-scale operational collectives, staffed by well-qualified and opinionated careerists, should not, however, be confused with democratic control. The subject of the address is still expected, if the occasion demands, to comply with an order *that has its origin* within a chain of command. Once again, it is important to emphasise that instruction is not the only technique at the disposal of an administrative elite; nor does it always assume an explicit (and thus potentially offensive) form. The point of bringing this use of direction and instruction to the fore is simple: it is important to redress an imbalance in the conception of power.

The problem is created by the assumption that an increase in personal, expressive communication – engendered by a greatly expanded media environment – must indicate the rebirth of deliberative democracy. Whatever its virtues or shortcomings, this thesis cannot be applied to the functional operations that must be completed within the workplace; nor can it explain the way in which the 'scenario narrative' is composed by security agencies and reconstructed using the same discursive materials by local forms of management. Equally, there is no need to go to the other extreme, arguing that the vocational environment is bound to be oppressive and unpleasant – the lesson here is that hierarchical structure and the ability to set internal agendas go some way towards explaining why the myth of the 'worst case' is so easily perpetuated, but so difficult to substantiate.

'Commanding' allegiance

The ability to direct operations is not, however, the 'last resort' of the hierarchical system, but the defining characteristic of any organisation thought capable of exercising power. When, for example, reference is made to the fact that a specific hierarchical form *commands the allegiance* of its subordinate departments, or that a manager *commands the respect* of his or her employees, the correct interpretation of the phrase is that the apex of a managerial or administrative formation secures obedience through instruction. Allegiance must be substantiated, requiring some concrete expression of the loyalty demanded by (and thus 'owed' to) the dominant faction. This literal meaning is currently obscured by the more subtle connotations that the term has accrued.

With the rise of perspectives that imagine the social order as a network of interest groups, subject to compulsions that cannot be explained as the simple antagonism between clearly delineated classes, these more nuanced meanings have come to prominence. The practices that lie behind them may, however, be subject to a range of interpretations. Moran, for example, notes that even where the emphasis is placed on regulation, rather than cooperation, there are differences of opinion about the meaning of such oversight. Moran argues that 'much discussion of the American regulatory state' assumes that it is 'too hierarchical', while in Britain and Europe the tendency has been to identify the same approach with 'the dissolution of government by command into uncoupled systems of self-steering' (Moran, 2002: 391).

Greater emphasis has indeed been placed, within European research, on the diffusion of power among various centres of influence, while external conflict between different groups, or internal antipathy within particular factions, is played down. An echo of this approach is found in the work of Latour, who, replying to the criticism that actor-network theory is indifferent to inequality, interpreted the disparity between classes as evidence of a more positive situation – this is the existence of multiple roles, exemplified by Latour as the 'various skills' possessed by 'scientists, politicians, artists, moralists, economists [and] legislators' (Latour, 2005: 254). Latour does not, therefore, consider social stratification to be a problem. He sees instead a useful and legitimate division between functions, allowing a range of contributions to be made to the composition of public life, just as 'electricians, carpenters, masons, architects and plumbers' can expend their energies on constructing a single building (254).

The proliferation of roles or institutions, and the cooperation between individuals engaged in specific projects, do not, however, explain how particular goals are actually achieved. Quite besides the question of class demarcation – an architect and a plumber not only fulfil distinct functions, but belong to different social strata – executive power does not appear in Latour's model. Yet no one builds a house on a whim, without direction, resources, assistance or reward. The stress placed on networks sometimes neglects another issue. How are individual centres of authority themselves constituted? The simple answer to this, already discussed above, is *as hierarchies*. This contention, in turn, is often countered by the observation that great strides have been made in reconfiguring corporate and state power along more democratic lines, at which point theories of public management and governance come into play (see Chapter 2).

If the precepts of governance are applied to the example used earlier – the act of *commanding* allegiance or respect within the workplace – it might be interpreted as the end result of a process in which consent is achieved by initiatives that build mutual trust and confidence. These supposedly enlightened approaches can include the creation of cross-departmental networks, the instigation of 'transparent' systems of management, and a greater engagement with the views that circulate within the lower ranks. In such a situation the emphasis is placed on the practical aptitude of the worker, on personal development and innovation, and on the rational exercise of communicative exchange between the various grades of employee. In other words, emphasis is placed on the positive value created by cooperative endeavour.

The fact that employees will tend to identify with an organisation that listens to their concerns and allows them to develop their careers has unfortunately no bearing on whether or not these bodies are run in an enlightened or considerate fashion. A sense of loyalty will arise whenever individuals undertake tasks that bring their own fortunes into positive alignment with wider institutional goals, as argued above. Equally, the opposite may occur if workers come into conflict with these aims. Unfortunately, progressive managerialism shares with its authoritarian counterpart a belief in decisive action and will adopt (if with less apparent enthusiasm) the same measures during periods of crisis.

The contention that contemporary organisational structures are not hierarchical, that orders are not given, and that there are no consequences for those who remain 'non-compliant' is untenable. The production of decisive interventions is essential to the success of any practical project. This does not mean that better modes of institutional conduct cannot be imagined, but rather that conventional patterns of (gendered) behaviour will persist for as long as a competitive struggle for power and resource is regarded as a form of virtue.

FOUR

The scenario:
imagining events

Exercises are scenario-based and are specifically aimed at testing key participants at either tactical or strategic level. All delegates will receive ... a detailed live briefing before the exercise commences. Scenarios will take delegates from the initial response phase through to dealing with recovery.

'Who are Phoenix?' Phoenix Resilience Training (phoenixresiliencetraining.com, 2009)

Britain is grounded tonight. Industrial action couldn't do this, and neither could the threat of terrorism. But a volcano 900 miles away in Iceland has created a menace that is not safe for planes to fly through.

Paul Davies, ITV News at Ten (15 April 2010)

The scenario as a device

The (often bogus) distinction between ordinary knowledge and professional erudition is exemplified by the routine manufacture of formal predictions. Where it is possible to use technological instruments to analyse the current condition of a particular phenomenon, such as the performance of shares, the fortunes of political parties or the state of the weather, a series of forecasts can be produced, reinforcing the notion that the use of specialist expertise can help to make uncertain circumstances seem less formidable. In some cases, such as the prophecies generated by the financial markets, this process can bring about the (profitable) outcome it pretends to foresee. In others, like meteorological analysis, the future development of a weather front is extrapolated from satellite pictures, based on the movement of spatial mass over time.

A five-day forecast, for instance, is dependent on the observation of the recent past, plotted against existing models of atmospheric behaviour. There is, however, some considerable difference between acquiring some foreknowledge of an event and being able to meet the actual contingency. The appearance of Hurricane Katrina (see Chapter 7) demonstrates all too clearly how a real incident can reveal the limitations of a system that is suffused with ideological posturing but incapable of coping with reality. The comments of the journalist cited at the head of this chapter show how the modern emphasis on state security can distort the perception of risk, which then needs adjusting according to collective experience: 'industrial action couldn't do this, and neither could the threat of terrorism' (Davies, ITV News at Ten, 15 April 2010).

The manipulation of eventuality for political gain is, however, based on a simple technique, and requires so little technical proficiency that it can be used by anyone familiar with the rudimentary principles of public relations (PR). It works through the deliberate conflation of the various meanings associated with the word 'scenario'. As Chapter 1 explained, a *scenario* is essentially a written script, or an outline for a story that will require further development before it is actualised. It is, therefore, a sketch for 'an imagined situation'.

This essentially practical measure, devoted to works of the imagination, has been extended in the following way: its status as a *synopsis* has been applied not just to works of fiction or entertainment, but to postulated developments in the realm of politics, the economy and security. In effect, this marks the transformation of a guide intended to help in the realisation or substantiation of narrative, into an instrument of governance. In the process, an authoritarian principle has been substituted for the more open, creative purpose of the original structure.

This comment should not be mistaken as an attempt to argue that the artistic impulse is never driven by a desire to create order or authority; rather, the security regime gains a particular advantage through the use of a device that few are likely to find objectionable. Equally, there is no suggestion here that those who participate in the emergency exercise are unable to contribute to its development. The fact remains that the scenario-event works backwards from its own (sometimes cataclysmic) conclusion. While the scenario is not a *useless* exercise, therefore, its purpose is not just to avert some future catastrophe, but to maintain the current form of the patriarchal-capitalist social order.

The event

If the scenario has become a form of imposition disguised as an insight into risk, then the term *event* (drawn from the Latin *eventus*) is usually understood as an accomplished fact. It has, indeed, been defined through variations on this theme, as 'anything that happens' (*Cassel's New English Dictionary*, 1956), and the 'fact of a thing's happening' (*Concise Oxford Dictionary*, 1964). Of particular significance to the current enquiry, however, is an alternative definition that regards an event as 'anything that happens, or is *contemplated* as happening' (*OED* online; my emphasis). The notion of futurity, so prominent in the composition of the scenario-event, is therefore brought into focus.

The first description ('anything that happens') posits a broad, inclusive class of phenomena, in which membership of the category is assigned to all individual occurrences, irrespective of their particular character. This implies that a specific incident need not necessarily exhibit any special distinction or value to qualify as an event, beyond its own appearance. In this example an event could be any one of an innumerable but discrete series of manifestations or effects – very different from some contemporary uses that reserve the term for an outstanding or important occasion that is planned in advance.

The second of the three alternative definitions offered above ('the fact of a thing's happening') identifies a fundamental characteristic that anything designated as an event is supposed to display: the *certainty* of its occurrence. Construed in this way, as the *fact* of a thing's happening, an event would be the undeniable materialisation or actualisation of a state of affairs, with the strong implication that it takes place in the immediate present. The third classification ('anything that happens, or is *contemplated* as happening') distinguishes between an actual event (something substantial or real) and the act of thinking about the possibility of such a circumstance. This reference to contemplation suggests that, in order to determine if something qualifies as an event, both established and imagined phenomena must be subjected to some form of cognitive analysis. By concentrating on thought processes, another possibility is suggested: the *forward projection* of events into an indefinite future and, by implication, the idea that, in the fullness of time, they may manifest themselves.

The insights generated by the definitions given above suggest that six further arguments could be made. First, an event *emerges from or is produced within* a particular constitutive environment; second, it is either the product of a coincidence of forces working within that environment or the (intended or unintended) outcome of deliberate human intercession; third, an unmotivated or 'natural' episode can exist, a kind of event that does not depend on human manipulation or recognition; fourth, any successful 'evental' intrusion into the realm of social reality (composed of spatial, temporal, economic and political elements) must depend on the *registration* of an event and its symbolic reconstitution by an authoritative human collective;[1] fifth, any groups seeking to *organise* events must be able to command sufficient material/symbolic resources in order to achieve their aim; and finally, sixth, considered as *an object of contemplation* an event can be (i) an established phenomenon that is recognised as an event through an act of retrospective assignation, and would therefore be open to comparison with other events that may emerge in the future, (ii) a 'live' event that occurs in the immediate present and challenges classification, and (iii) a projected occurrence based on the notion of *potentiality*.

If an event is 'realised' or made real by the underlying (virtual or invisible) forces within a situation, then all that can be said at this stage is that this coincidence of separate energies or circumstances is not available for scrutiny (is hidden but still real). This suggests that there must be different *types* of events, of a greater or lesser magnitude than those that are more readily 'visible'. Such phenomena could be described as (i) proto-events (events that are yet to appear), (ii) sub- or non-events (incidents that do not meet the criteria for fully fledged events, but see below) or (iii) meta-events (those of a more advanced or superior or complex kind).

The inevitable consequence of thinking about any type of event is that attempts will be made to predict its imminent appearance or future character. Powerful interest groups will then take the opportunity to use this instinctive human procedure to create their own versions of the past, present and future, often based on the active anticipation of some malign outcome. This should be understood as the practical manipulation of contingency, for the purposes of repressive governance in the here and now, rather than some vague depiction which imagines a situation that is essentially much the same as the present.

Events and the integrity of form

So far, the conception of the event has concentrated on its status as an abstract phenomenon, and has not dealt with the process of classification or any reference to actual incidents (see the discussion of '9/11' in Chapter 6). It is notable that these more practical questions, concerning the exercise of judgement about what is and is not an event, and how it is possible to distinguish between different types, are sometimes cast aside in order to pursue an argument about the supposed convergence of two qualities: an actual event and its subsequent representation.

This either produces the argument that it is impossible to distinguish between an event and its reproduction in symbolic form (the use of language and other modes of depiction), or the even more immoderate insistence that the existence of an event depends entirely on its linguistic 'construction'. The role of the symbolic is certainly important, because it provides the currency in which formal knowledge of events can be exchanged, but it is possible to exaggerate the power of this function.

Instead of deciding that an event is only given substance through an act of representation, it might be more useful to see the relationship between description and the object of enquiry as a certain type of *constitutive process*. Rather than an act of creation, it would be more accurate to identify a procedure that is dedicated to the assignation of value or status. The contention here is that the role of the symbolic is to 'encode' an occurrence, so that it circulates as a sign within a system of representation. Such a process amounts in effect to the imposition of social significance or meaning on disparate events.

The essential challenge is to identify the source of this procedure, the principles upon which it is founded, and the social and political effects it is meant to produce. It is clear that some events – those that appear to be particularly dramatic, or unexpected, or beyond the control of human beings (including 'natural' exigencies) – seem to display an *autonomous integrity of form*, and are therefore difficult to classify or accommodate within the current system of regulatory oversight and classification. If this is true, then it goes some way to explaining the elaborate attempts of powerful interest groups to manipulate the general conception of reality that circulates within the social order.

The 'exceptional' event, which seems to disturb the dominant structure of representation, is often associated with the 'natural' disaster, as well as with industrial accidents and collapses in financial markets: it may also, however, include those unusual, deliberately engineered phenomena that are introduced into a situation, sometimes without warning, which would include revolutions and the type of spectacular assault discussed in Chapter 6. The peculiar aspect of this last condition – the eruption of dangerous events – is that those in positions of executive authority seem to make a sharp distinction between those intentional acts produced by official (state) actors and the activities of groups that are actively opposed to dominant interests. The rule of the bourgeoisie is presented as the measured application of regulatory power or, where it includes the 'illicit' or the extraordinary use of force (rendition, assassination, subversion, etc.), is regarded as an unfortunate aberration. The behaviour of their adversaries, even the more routine or conventional procedures such as economic espionage or political dissent, is by contrast often described as 'terroristic'.

Whether or not exceptional events are induced or organised by human beings, they share the basic characteristics of all dramatic occurences, including their sudden intrusion into human consciousness through the senses. They may not require independent acknowledgement or validation to exist, but the fact of this existence can only be known, and then conveyed to others, through the use of symbolic content.[2] A supposedly natural event (a volcanic eruption, for example) has to be *recognised* as a distinct phenomenon (as a particular *kind* of fact or happening). It owes its *qualitative status* or meaning, rather than its material form, to human intervention.

The subjective identification of a particular characteristic from among a host of related properties is, however, an uncertain and imperfect process. Although the imposition of meaning is supposed to be based on the essential qualities manifested *by* an event, human discrimination, which is prone to error and is sometimes dependent on ideological predisposition, may give some aspects of an event prominence, while downgrading the significance of others. Therefore, alluding to an event as a *fact* may not necessarily help in identifying all its important features.

The value, on the other hand, of retaining the factual as a standard of validation is that events can emerge from more than one source, provided they conform to the principle of *facticity*. This would mean that they would have to be, whatever their size or duration, truly 'indisputable'. The contrast that is usually made is between those 'natural' events (that have no identifiable human progenitor and must undergo a process of classification) and events that are organised by people, given a form and a purpose, and are therefore open to interpretation as social acts (see below). In most cases, the ability to determine the significance of either type of event depends on some form of agreement, often imposed by prominent groups, that it has either (i) presented enough of its 'essence' to satisfy the criteria required for entry into a particular category, or that it has (ii) reached a state of completion, and can therefore be assessed to see if it is a genuine example of its class.

It is more difficult to achieve a reasoned perspective when certain incidents are actually in progress (in the process of 'unfolding' or appearing), because although they might be acknowledged *to have the potential to be* events, they may seem to be of an uncertain (or prototypical) kind. They exist by virtue of their facticity rather than their place in an overall system, since they would have to be assigned a precise social (or nominated) form. It seems to be the case, therefore, that an event is often regarded as a stable, categorical object only when it has reached a point of stasis (the exhaustion of energy or the attainment of equilibrium), at which point it can be used (as was '9/11') to characterise all those incidents that can be forced into an association with its dominant qualities.

Facticity and significance

In making a distinction between types of event, especially where one example is regarded as more important than another, there is the possibility of confusing the state of *facticity* with the notion of *significance*. In such cases, the reality of an occurrence is either asserted or denied on the basis of its supposed magnitude or apparent value, so that for instance some incidents are regarded by certain social groups as real and therefore *valid*, while other occurences are designated as 'non-events'. A 'non-event' may seem to be a contradiction in terms, since it is clearly meant to refer to something that has actually happened while, at the same time, appearing to deny that the incident is important enough to be awarded full membership of the category. A 'non-event' is something that fails to live up to expectations and, rather than existing in a state of negation, is recognised as real but inferior.

This problem, the way in which relative value is assigned to different occurences by refusing to acknowledge their significance, can be traced to an underlying grammatical condition: as the beginning of this section noted, when 'events' in general are called to mind, the usual sense is of a collection of unremarkable incidents. The depiction of a single (and by implication *singular* event), on the other hand, suggests that the occasion under scrutiny is important, setting it apart from those other (plural or multiple) phenomena to which it may otherwise have been assigned. The application of the term 'event' to a particular phenomenon depends therefore upon some 'automatic' processes that help to make sense of the human environment, yet that also form the basis of deliberate and often highly contentious judgements.

In summarising the dominant ways in which events are designated, a number of principles should be considered. The first is the notion of *perspective*, or the fundamental relationship between the phenomenon and the observer. This is closely related to the second aspect of the controversy, that of *qualification*, both in the sense of what counts as an event, and in the sense of who determines that it is actually valid. This entails that some thought be given to a third concept, that of *significance* (why some incidents are regarded as of sufficient importance to qualify as events, and others are not), followed by a fourth issue, often associated or even confused with the previous category, which is *magnitude*, or how the scale of an event helps to determine its overall status. Once a number of events have reached the threshold of recognition (having been, for example, distinguished from 'non-events'), then a fifth process can be initiated, that of *individuation* (the process of distinguishing one event from another). The sixth notion that must be addressed is *duration*, or whether or not it is necessary for an episode to last a particular time before it can be regarded as a 'true' member of its particular category. The seventh challenge is to decide if an event has to reach a state of *completion* before it can be described, or whether – even if it appears to be in the process of unfolding – it has met enough of the conditions of significance to receive recognition (see 'The Event in Deleuze and Badiou', below).

The categorisation of events

Whatever its origin, the successful intrusion or 'advent' of a (natural or 'non-intentional') fact into the domain of social reality depends on its recognition and evaluation by *authoritative* social groups, which have the power to declare whether it qualifies as a genuine event. It is therefore subjected to a process of categorisation, in which attempts are made to place it within an established class of similarity or resemblance.[3] This is to be expected, since acts of discrimination are essential for the organisation of social priorities. Events are used to substantiate certain ideological positions. As Ricœur argues, 'by entering into the movement of a narrative which relates character to plot, the event loses its impersonal neutrality' (Ricœur, cited in MacKenzie, 2008: 5).

The real issue that must be addressed is not just that decisions about significance are made, but who is deemed capable of making them. Much of the existing literature on the 'event' as a philosophical concept seems to treat human intercession as an undifferentiated power, as though the crux of the matter is simply whether or not an average or typical individual is able to identify, and then define, a specific occurrence. Once social groups are brought into the equation, the essential problem concerns not just 'agency' considered as a general attribute, but the *distribution* of capacity, authority and resource among those collectives that are recognised as legitimate actors within a particular field.

Based on this observation, two further points can be made. The first is that some groups are entirely excluded from certain types of decisive activity. Although they may be able to comment on the assignation of an event to a particular category, their perception, even when undeniably correct, can be dismissed as irrelevant to the systemic operation of authority. So, for example, if a goal in a football match is disallowed, and it is clear to the spectators that the ball crossed the goal line, this perception, however widely shared, would not necessarily alter the official result. There is a general division, therefore, between classes of actors and an active discrimination between the types of power to which they are supposed to have access. A well-known explanation for such a fundamental demarcation between social functions is that it emerges from the concentration of authority in the hands of an elite, the allocation of administrative roles to a subordinate caste, and the delegation of any controversial matter to the indecisive realm of mediation (where debate is enacted between two, often quite limited, conceptual poles), or to those quasi-legal enquiries designed to 'white-wash' government activities.

This form of manipulation, however, offers only a partial explanation for the limited range of debate over the meaning of contingency, since there is a concomitant drive towards the destruction, the delegitimisation or (if they lie within the orbit of the state) the *depoliticisation* of alternative or supplementary modes of organisation.[4] Whereas during the height of the debates over the character of class and power it was possible to argue that the working classes were denied access to proper political representation, the current situation is marked by the movement of the political to the 'neutral' realm of the bureaucratic, and the provision to the public of a 'private life' focused on immersive entertainment.

This does not mean that established meanings are not contested, or that the population in general is incapable of political thought, but rather that formal politics, as a national activity at least, is 'ring-fenced'. It is constituted in such a way so as to prevent easy access to any individuals other than those who have made it into a profession and who therefore have the 'right' to be political. It is not just the relative strength of the various actors attempting to establish their point of view that matters, but where they stand in relation to the various centres of influence. This is pursued in more detail below, but for the moment the pressing question is how the intervention of formal authority leads to the categorical determination of 'important' events.

In the case of the 'terrorist event', the existence and multiplication of specialised agencies is central to the growth of an influential model of security and the more recent concept of 'resilience'. Organisations like the UK's NaCTSO offer a useful example. Although this body is the creation of the Association of Chief Police Officers, itself a private institution that is not directly sanctioned by the state, it is used as a conduit for a series of announcements and initiatives. These not only remind other organisations of their statutory obligations, but are also employed to generate a set of codes, propositions and protocols that are reproduced across the whole range of local and national official institutions concerned with 'public safety' and security. In all such transmissions, the central notion is that of 'responsibility' to clients, subordinates and the public. The very language used to describe the different social groups that compose the social order reveals the values inherent within a class hierarchy.

Occurrence and predictability: the meaning of events

Some of the earlier theorists working in this field treat events as 'properties of moments or intervals of time' (Pianesi and Varsi, 2000: 5). Montague, for instance, described 'the event of the sun's rising' as the property of the moment at which the sun appears (Montague, cited in Pianesi and Varsi, 2000: 5). Of course, two questions may follow from this illustration. First, whether or not a sunrise may be described as the same event no matter where in the world it takes place (wherever it is witnessed), even though it may seem to occur at different times for different people; and second, whether each sunrise that takes place should be regarded as a recurrence of the same occasion, or as a fresh event. Montague dealt with this problem by identifying 'generic' events. Of course, subjective human perception is central to this example, since the sun only appears to rise as a consequence of the earth's progress through space and around the sun.

The apparent substantiation of an event may therefore lend weight to particular theories about both the natural and the social environment. An event may, for example, confirm an observer's perception that it is the paradigmatic expression of a dominant political condition, and that it may represent an underlying state of affairs that was partly obscured until its appearance. The 'event' or 'coming about' of a specific episode may even suggest that this particular incident *was always likely to occur.*

The radical Irish politician Bernadette Devlin McAliskey expressed exactly this sentiment after the findings of the Saville Inquiry. This investigation produced a report on events that took place in Northern Ireland on 30 January 1972. It found that soldiers from the Parachute Regiment had opened fire on a civil rights demonstration and that, during the course of the incident (known subsequently as Bloody Sunday), thirteen unarmed civilians had been killed.

Devlin McAliskey, who had been present on the day, declared that, until this event, she 'had discounted any real belief that the British government would countenance killing the people in order to suppress the protests', but that 'now that it had happened, it made sense to me that it was always going to happen' (Devlin McAliskey, 16 June 2010: 7). In her response to the Saville Report, she asked if the killings were more than a simple testament to the indiscipline or viciousness of the British troops (the 'anonymous and brutalized soldiers', in her words) and whether they might not in fact indicate that 'the British government committed a war crime' (Devlin Mcaliskey, 16 June 2010: 7).

This demonstrates the common perception that visible or quantifiable incidents may actually represent deeper, perhaps less obvious, tendencies or structural conditions. It is certainly true that the study of individual episodes, without knowing their full context, might lead to serious misapprehensions concerning the true relationship between a political executive, the military leadership of any armed force and the discretion exercised by the operatives on the ground.

In the case of the British Army's use of lethal force, it seems as though the conclusions of the Saville Inquiry supported the original account provided by the marchers themselves, in that they agreed that the deadly assault had been entirely unprovoked. Thirty-eight years had elapsed before the official version of the shootings coincided with the accounts given by the surviving victims and civilian witnesses. Nonetheless, it is possible to argue that the agreed 'outcome' of any public event may never be entirely secure, in the sense that 'an event may come to acquire new properties as the result of later happenings' (Pianesi and Varsi, 2000: 16). In the case of Bloody Sunday, the question of government culpability, addressed by the UK's prime minister David Cameron when he apologised for the incident, might offer the most significant confirmation that it had acquired a near universal meaning. This does not mean that the full status of an event will be appreciated, even by those who profess to have an interest in politics. The case of George Watson, a fellow of St John's College, Cambridge, provides a useful warning to anyone who assumes that ignorance can be kept at bay by an expensive education. In an article defending the parliamentary system of government, Watson declared that 'this is the land where troops do not fire on crowds' (Watson, 16 September 2010, 28). It is only by assuming that Northern Ireland does not constitute part of the United Kingdom, or by choosing to ignore the history of Britain as a whole, that such a statement could be made.

The passage of time: event as an 'end product'

The notion of an event as the consequence or the 'end product' of a particular development (as in the 'upshot' of the inquiry into Bloody Sunday) conforms to one of the earliest English uses of the word, current in the sixteenth and seventeenth centuries. It can be seen, for example, in a passage written by the legal scholar William Fulbecke, who expressed his expectation that the *event* of a particular situation would be positive (*OED* online). He was using 'event' in this instance to signify an *outcome*. This meaning still appears in contemporary conversation, whenever a speaker uses the formulation *in the event* or *in the event of*. The first usage is employed to describe the conclusive result of a particular circumstance ('in the event, *x* turned out well'), and the second to recognise the possible materialisation of some future condition ('if *x* actually occurs [then *y* will follow or be proven]').

This range of connotation – from the depiction of a definite outcome to the anticipation of a potential state of affairs – is of considerable use to the political tactician. Comparison of the past with the future allows the rhetorical conflation of an accomplished categorical fact or object with the possible appearance of new phenomena. In other words, the way events have been characterised (or re-presented) in the past can be used to prepare the ground for the dissemination of new propositions about the manifestation of similar occurences in the future.

The projected materialisation of a 'threat event' is based on the common practice of making provision in the present for the *uncertainty* of the future. During the development of agricultural societies, for example, the 'increased control over the extended future' (Adam, 2004: 88) created 'long-term food security through practice' (88). It is the attempt to meet certain 'eventualities' – a term that refers to the *possible* appearance of phenomena – together with the knowledge gained from previous experiences that allows preparations to be made for the future.

The quality of an individual event – the extent of its impact and significance – is therefore closely associated with its contextual development and its temporal condition. One argument is that all events, 'finished' or not, are actually best understood as a provisional manifestation of some larger condition. Chisholm followed this line when he argued that an event is 'any contingent state of affairs which is not a proposition and which implies change' (1970, cited in Pianesi and Varsi, 2000: 6). In this example, an event is a potential manifestation, but one that does not try to contest a particular position or advance a thesis: like realist definitions of the truth, it is a phenomenon that lacks intentionality. If this perspective were to be adopted, an event would make 'no profession of any kind', and would have 'no intention', and would not 'stand for anything else' (Sheriff, 1994: 51).

Another approach to the event examines the idea of duration – and, by implication, the problem of how to distinguish between events – by making a distinction between an instantaneous event, such as 'two balls coming into contact', and a protracted event, like 'the American Presidential campaign' (Pianesi and Varsi, 2000: 5). This awareness of the *extent* of an incident was used as a strategic ploy by General Petraeus, US military commander in Afghanistan, when he described the official policy to withdraw American troops by July 2011 as 'a process, not an event', which seems to be a cunning way of saying that it might never happen at all (cited in Judd, 16 August 2010: 11).

The notion of process, however, would not satisfy those theorists who contend that an event is characterised by surprise and immediacy, in line with Badiou's declaration that the event 'is neither past nor future' but 'makes us present to the present' (Badiou, 2007a: 39). According to this perspective, the event alerts an individual to the quality of present circumstances and, in the case of a revolutionary disjuncture or break with the capitalist system, provides an opportunity to identify with, and become an advocate of, a new moral order. The virtue of this perspective is its ability to point out the immediacy of experience: the problem is that no 'ordinary' event would really qualify for inclusion in the overall category if the term is reserved for an exceptional conjuncture. In addition, some on the left regard the whole notion of a 'messianic *now-time*' as itself rather suspect, and perhaps as no more than a way of updating what was is in essence a form of 'reactionary thought' (Negri, 2003: 106).

Ricœur is also interested in the question of duration and temporality, writing about 'the fleeting character of the event as opposed to the stability of the system' (Ricœur, 1976: 9). This places emphasis on the idea that it is structure that is durable, while events are impermanent and less substantial. A theorist like Badiou would presumably find some worth in this position, since his own approach is to draw attention to the event as a 'vanishing mediator' and an 'intemporal instant' (Badiou, 2007a: 39). The question is whether such a brief occurrence might weaken this author's contention that the revolutionary moment is powerful enough to disturb the flow of history.

Ricœur's perspective also requires some further qualification. His depiction of the system as more durable than the event needs to be seen in the context of his belief that the system 'only has a virtual existence' (Ricœur, 1976: 9). This assertion is close to the position expressed in Chapter 3, where the system, structure or regime is brought about through operational necessity, appearing not just in language but through directed activity.

It is important, however, to recognise current definitions of the virtual: in computing, the term 'virtual' refers to something that does not have a physical existence, but that is made to appear as though it does through the use of software. In this instance, words appear on a computer screen (they 'present' a typeface or font) but they do not possess a solid, material depth. Similarly, in the case of the term 'linguistic governance', it can be argued – if one is allowed to adapt the insights produced by Ricœur – that it is only 'the message' or the *event* that 'gives actuality' to language' or to *structure* (Ricœur, 1976: 9). It is discourse that 'grounds the very existence of language' (9). Considered as a *timely* linguistic act carried out by a recognised authority, therefore, 'discourse is realised temporally and in a present moment, whereas the language system is virtual and outside of time' (9).

Authority, exercised through acts of 'directive address' (Price, 2007), depends on the fact that the sentence (a basic unit of language) is 'characterised by a single distinctive trait: it has a predicate' (Ricœur, 1976: 10). A predicate, of course, is that part of a sentence or a clause containing a verb and stating something about a subject. It represents an affirmation or assertion, which is the typical means through which the human subject attempts to attain material and social goals, or tries to justify a particular position. Ricœur distinguishes between the subject, which he says 'picks out something singular', and the predicate, which 'designates a kind of quality, a class of things, a type of relation, or a type of action' (10–11). With regard to the *structure* of discourse, he argues that it is formed by the 'interplay of the functions of identification and predication in one and the same sentence' (11). Placed in the context of state power, therefore, an utterance emerges from a 'place' within a hierarchical system, and both expresses a particular view about the singular value of objects and describes the possibility of action in response to the *contingency* of events.

The event in Deleuze and Badiou

In his contribution to the study of the event, Fraser describes 'event-thinking' as part of an anti-reductionist project that 'seeks to describe the relations between actual things, bodies and happenings, and the independent reality of these events themselves' (Fraser, 2006: 129). In examining the work of the French theorist Deleuze, Fraser notes that he distinguishes between two kinds of entities. These are 'bodies which exist in space and in time' together with their corresponding 'states of affairs', and 'incorporeal beings or transformations' which are 'not things or facts but *events*' (129; my emphasis). These events 'subsist or inhere' rather than exist (129). When something subsists, it lies below the surface, while a quality that is inherent is a permanent part of something's essence. Existence, on the other hand, refers to the objective fact of being, or continuous material presence. This distinction suggests a difference between the actual and the virtual, which in Deleuze's philosophy are 'two mutually exclusive, yet jointly sufficient, characterisations of the real' (Parr, 2005: 297). The actual is defined as something that is 'unfolded from potentiality' (10), while the virtual, which must be defined as 'a part of the real object', expresses its reality through structure (Deleuze, cited in DeLanda, 2002: 39).

In Deleuze's system, events are ' real inherent possibilities' and appear as they are 'actualised' in some 'body or state' (Parr, 2005: 87). An event is not, according to Deleuze, the apparent, visible occurrence, because this is supposed to be no more than the 'surface effect or expression' of its actualisation (87). In direct opposition to Badiou's contention that the event is 'a pure break with the becoming of an object' (Badiou, 2007a: 39), the Deleuzean position is that the event is 'the product of the synthesis of forces': as such, it cannot be 'a disruption of some continuous state' (Parr, 2005: 87). Stagoll gives the example of 'a tree's turning colour in the spring', arguing that this evident occurrence is merely 'a passing surface effect or expression of an event's actualisation', such as 'weather patterns, soil conditions, pigmentation effects and the circumstances of the original planting' (87).

Instead, therefore, of the dramatic break envisaged by Badiou, in which the event 'opens a space of consequences' (Badiou, 2007a, 40), the event is constituted by 'underlying' forces, and is therefore the 'expression of the productive potential of the forces from which it arose' (Parr, 2005: 87–8). It is an 'original and creative production' which, as 'pure effect … has no goal' and represents only 'a momentary productive intensity' (88). This idea, that an event has no intentional force, is actually close to Badiou's belief that the event does not possess 'the least sense, nor is it sense itself' (Badiou, 2007a: 40). Both authors, in fact, seem to be speaking of the event as though it is an essentially 'natural' manifestation of circumstantial energy, and thus one that is not produced by human intervention.

However, in Badiou's case, 'one feature of a political event is whether or not the individuals involved in the occurrence claim it as an event' (MacKenzie, 2008: 8). This is the act of nomination, when an event is identified as 'belonging' to a particular situation (Badiou, 2007b: 203). In Badiou's opinion, however, it is not enough simply to describe an event like the French Revolution, because this act also requires the observer to take sides and, if in favour of the Revolution's basic principles, to express 'fidelity' to the political cause of liberation (Badiou, cited in Engelmann, 2009: 31). Badiou is therefore interested in the universal, and in political truth, which he defines as 'a concrete, time-specific sequence in which a new thought and a new collaborative practice of collective emancipation arise, exist, and eventually disappear' (Badiou, 2010: 231).

Events that have a supposedly universal significance are those, according to Badiou, that can be used by anyone who wishes to advance the revolutionary project. This means that there are other incidents that are 'denied ... the status of events', such as 'the Nazi accession to power' (MacKenzie, 2008: 8), exactly because they are discriminatory and cannot provide a general template for social progress. MacKenzie is clearly dissatisfied with Badiou's position, arguing that his definition of a political event is too narrow, excluding not only the fascist 'simulacrum' of politics, but also any smaller, progressive incidents that might fail to produce 'a truly universal and militant political subject' (34).

Although MacKenzie does not perhaps recognise the value of notions like fidelity and the universal, used as tactical weapons designed to create a *strict differentiation* between the revolutionary principle and the bourgeois order, it is worrying that Badiou nominates as the paradigmatic examples of emancipatory activity certain revolts – like the Russian Revolution and the Cultural Revolution in China – that are essentially authoritarian in character. There seems to be no discussion of the libertarian tradition associated with events like the Spanish Revolution of 1936.

Ultimately, MacKenzie finds Deleuze's rather less inflected 'pre-occurrence' approach to events more persuasive than Badiou's strident 'post-occurrence' theorisation (MacKenzie, 2008: 2). In MacKenzie's view, Deleuze proposes 'an impersonal or non-subjective account of the emergence of significance' (2). This suggests, however, that Deleuze lacks interest in the power of human intervention to alter, or perhaps even recognise, the dominant political condition. Badiou's fault, by comparison, lies more in the fact that he has chosen revolutionary interventions that were disastrous for humanity. It is Badiou's analysis of the limitations of bourgeois politics, rather than his attachment to the principles that are supposed to lie behind authoritarian communism, which makes him a useful critic of the social order.

As O'Hara notes, the point of confronting 'the event of truth' is that it forces the use of terms, of names, whose referent *is not the situation as represented*' (O'Hara, 2008: 173; my emphasis). O'Hara is right to argue that 'the State neglects to represent' certain elements in a particular circumstance, while it is at the same time busy producing 'many more representative but essentially empty terms for the situation' (174–5). Badiou is aware of this form of political-discursive suppression: using the example of 'standard parliamentarianism', in which 'the majority and the opposition are commensurable', he argues that political conflict is a mere show of difference, and that the actual relationship between these formal opponents is 'a regular, law-governed' connection (Badiou, in Engelmann, 2009: 17).

This supports one of the contentions expressed in the present work and within the arguments set out in a previous publication (Price, 2010) that the apparent antagonism between formal enemies within the bourgeois political system should be understood as a form of structural complicity, in which both sides contribute to the perpetuation of a situation that is of mutual benefit. This sense of being forced to witness a ruling elite pretend that its eternal internecine wrangling represents the true domain of political activity is probably what makes Badiou's notion of the event as a revolutionary disturbance attractive – it provides some hope that an 'emerging singularity' (Badiou, in Engelmann, 2009: 33) will bring an end to the seamless, yet strangely complementary, promotion of two conditions that would appear on the surface to be diametrically opposed: security and war. The missing element in this discussion, which explains how these two features of bourgeois modernity coalesce in a single enterprise, is the defence of one overriding principle – that of capital accumulation.

Privatised interventions

In 2005, London First, a 'business membership group', was assigned the copyright of a 48-page booklet titled *Secure in the Knowledge: Building a Secure Business*. Another organisation, the National Counter Terrorism Security Office (NaCTSO, a 'specialist police organisation' set up in 2002[5]), claimed responsibility for its actual production. The cover of the document displays three symbols. The first is the emblem of the Association of Chief Police Officers, which describes itself as 'a private company limited by guarantee' (ACPO, 2005/2007). The second is the seal of the Security Service (MI5),[6] the declared purpose of which is to '[protect] the country against covertly organised threats to national security' (London First, 2005: i). The third is the rather more informal logo of the London First group itself.

Aimed at 'small and medium-sized businesses' (London First, 2005: 4), *Secure in the Knowledge* carries a foreword by Hazel Blears, who was at the time the UK's minister of state for policing, security and community safety. In this preamble, Blears set out the purpose of the initiative, explaining that it was devoted to 'the protection and prevention measures that you can put in place' in order to meet a number of hazards, including 'crime, the consequences of a natural disaster, electronic attack, acts of terrorism' and 'other events that would have an impact on your business' (1). Later in the text, a table appears, apparently intended to 'illustrate a range of scenarios' that could have a deleterious effect on commercial operations.

Before this template is analysed (see below), it is important to note the almost routine appearance of the term 'scenario', not only in everyday use, but more specifically in those documents that promote the concepts of security, 'resilience', economic continuity, and public safety. The US State Department, for instance, referred in one publication to 'the scenario' played out during an exercise run for senior officials, which 'simulated casualties and widespread contamination' caused by the detonation of a 'dirty bomb' (Top Officials, www.state. gov, 2007: 1). The existence of this kind of precaution, in a country that suffered the '9/11' attacks, may seem unsurprising. Yet references to the possible manifestation, or practical development of a particular 'scenario', also occur in circumstances that might appear rather less urgent or significant.

Why, for example, would Teignbridge District Council in the UK expect its leading officers to 'take part in preparatory measures' consisting of staff training and 'role play exercise scenarios' (Teignbridge District Council, 2008: 1). Similarly, why would an identical local body in Uttlesford ask the business community to 'think for a minute' – in itself a fairly stringent demand – before considering how best to cope if any one of a number of 'scenarios' became a reality, from severe weather to pandemic influenza (Uttlesford District Council, 2010)?

There are a number of reasons for the appearance of this phenomenon, which is composed of an activity (the practical coordination of effort) and the manner in which it is described (its designation as a certain type of event). In the first place, of course, organised groups have always tried to marshal resources and, where sophisticated enough to anticipate the recurrence of particular challenges, have tried to make provision for the future. This explanation must be considered together with the fact that the human subject shows a definite predisposition to seize upon useful strategic phrases, providing a linguistic short cut through the perils that any extended explanation may present.[7]

The *institutional* popularity of the term 'scenario' can be traced to its use by those who have an active economic or political interest in the consolidation of the specific sphere of activity to which it is applied: in this instance, the promotion of, and engagement in, emergency planning, national security, threat management and crime prevention. Taken together, these activities represent a profitable expansion in the state/corporate project of (semi-privatised) social control, organised under the guise of 'risk prevention'. Cast into a future that is always described as uncertain, the notion of an unpredictable threat is central to the manufacture of the 'scenario' as a practice.

The determination, however, to concentrate on the obviously rather indefinite character of the future helps to obscure another point of view. This is the conviction that the greatest threat to the human species is the inability of those in positions of political leadership to alter behaviours that presage the near *certainty* of disaster. The long-term monitoring of a deteriorating natural environment, for example, seems in retrospect (i) to lend substance to the perception that it is possible to make accurate predictions of the kind of catastrophe that may actually face the world and its inhabitants, and (ii) to indicate that human activity has contributed to this condition.

As the effects of this degradation are already being felt, one conclusion is difficult to escape: that certain types of forecast are more reliable than others. In the specific case of global warming, the basis of the projection is all-important. The belief that the planet's temperature will continue to increase is drawn from the study of detailed, scientific data, which suggests that an upward trend is already in evidence, and that the problem will continue to get worse.

Even if it is treated as a parallel example (an undesirable condition created by human agency) the same procedure cannot be applied to terrorism. While there is universal agreement about the meaning of 'temperature', and about the standard ways in which it should be measured, no such consensus exists about what constitutes an act of terror, or the extent to which terrorism is the sole preserve of the brutal, 'non-state' actor. It is only when rigid, and ultimately unsustainable, divisions are made between types of violence that the relative strength of terrorist activity can be discussed. This kind of comparison can be found in the peculiar arguments presented by military officials, when they argue that terrorist activity is reduced by the armed intervention of the state. If, however, both forms of combat tend to have similar results, then a decrease in one and an increase in the other may not mean that any kind of 'progress' is being made.

A number of factors militate against the successful promotion of 'terror' as the paradigmatic example of risk. The first is the absence of a viable definition of terrorism (see Price, 2010). The second is the fact that it is very difficult to use a particular terrorist event (such as '9/11', discussed in Chapter 6) to predict that a similar outrage will occur in the future. The third problem arises from the standard procedures adopted within the security apparatus. The state may well succeed in suppressing certain plots that, had they come to fruition, might have provided clear evidence of terrorist intent. If, however, such incidents are not given much publicity, on the grounds that the protocols followed within the secret services could be revealed, then they cannot be used to support a larger thesis about the dangers of terrorism.

Equally, some acts of subversion may exist largely because they have been manufactured by agents provocateurs, or because they have been fed to the media. Whatever the reason, such lack of clarity can reinforce the suspicion that the ruling elite wants to have the best of both worlds: drawing attention to a 'terror threat' because it can be used to reinforce its own practices, while refusing to come clean with the public on the grounds that this could compromise operations. At the same time, issues like climate change are downgraded: it is not, of course, the responsibility of the security services to deal with this issue, but it does seem odd that existential threats are sometimes regarded as less urgent than those posed by the would-be insurgent. This does not mean that the deterioration of the planet is entirely ignored, but rather that its effects on the future of the current system are regarded as the most important element of the problem. This approach is reflected in Cavelty and Mauer's list of transnational threats, which include 'organised crime, narcotics-trafficking, illicit sales of weapons, the spread of disease, radicalisation and the *geopolitical implications of climate change*' (Cavelty and Mauer, 2009: 125; my emphasis). Notice, in addition, that these authors draw attention to the 'illicit' sale of weapons, not their legitimate promotion by states. Finally, arguments about the 'catastrophic imaginary', which attempt to equate scientific concern about climate change and the excessive emission of carbon dioxide with the production of fears by the security regime, can lead to the dangerous assumption that both are based on an equally unfounded set of convictions.

Command and obligation

Ultimately, the existence of a command structure, through which the state sets out its expectations of subordinate powers, provides one of the most compelling reasons for the rise of 'scenario planning', whatever topic is given precedence. The senior officers who direct the work of local authorities, for example, are legally obliged to undertake certain activities. In Britain, under the Civil Contingencies Act of 2004,[8] a number of 'first and second responders' are required to make plans for unforeseen eventualities. In meeting this demand, it is clear that they have to take the central thesis of the exercise seriously, regarding the nature of the generic risks that are supposed to face them. In this case, the state's entreaty is based on the proposition that the occurrence of any one of a number of *categories of event* is a distinct possibility.

There are a number of advantages in pursuing such a broad approach, in comparison to the emphasis placed on one particular danger, as the discussion of terrorism (see above) tried to suggest. If threats are placed in a particular order of importance, then governments and ministers may be held responsible for having neglected one type of risk (that may well prove negligible), while in the event another hazard (that has been given a lower priority) may make a considerable impact. When a more nuanced assessment is produced – in other words, when a serious attempt is made to set out a rational assessment of future risks – some interesting conclusions can be reached. Of course, certain types of harmful activity never appear in these exercises. However, bodies that are supposed to achieve a more general, cross-departmental overview of events tend to assess the relative likelihood and impact of occurences in a more measured (and less hysterical) fashion. The difficulty which may then occur is that the type of problem that really interests the entity sometimes known as the 'deep state'[9] – terrorism, and political or 'anti-capitalist' activity that can be presented as potentially terroristic – can suddenly appear to be considerably less dangerous than disease or natural disaster.

This is precisely what happened when the National Risk Register estimated that pandemic influenza would have a greater impact on the UK than terrorist attacks (Cabinet Office, 2008: 5). The accuracy of this prediction was perhaps undermined by the failure of 'swine flu', a much-vaunted hazard, to reach the level of calamity imagined, but the point is that the Register did raise questions about the degree to which other threats, relentlessly promoted by government ministers, had actual substance.

Practical necessity, attitude and 'alignment'

Despite the arguments concerning the relative severity of various risks – a form of controversy which demonstrates the inevitable existence of divisions between the different branches and functions of the state and, perhaps, some dissension from the agenda pursued by the security lobby – there is a distinct advantage to be gained from presenting subordinate groups with a variety of possible scenarios. It forces an entire class of senior managers and functionaries to overhaul their systems in the interests of enhanced security, while at the same time using their participation in such activity as a means of drawing them more closely into the ideological assumptions that lie behind the whole exercise.

The challenge for the authorities in general, and for certain specialist divisions of the security apparatus in particular, is to 'materialise' the process of intellectual and emotional alignment, so that an essentially political conception of risk is placed in the domain of *practical necessity*. Attitudes, in other words, are embedded in procedures. Eventually, 'emergency planning' and the exercises it engenders will come to be regarded as the norm, and the range of paternalistic and authoritarian currents of thought associated with the exercise of oversight (by which I mean a combination of surveillance and regulation) may continue to thrive within the larger and ostensibly more liberal structures of capitalist patriarchy.

The task of the local elite is therefore to familiarise themselves with the terminology associated with the national project, in order to convey the essence of the scheme to the ranks below them. It is important, therefore, that they reuse the 'descriptive' categories employed within official documents, which constitutes an essential first step in the process of attitudinal/ideological alignment mentioned above. This, though, is only the beginning, because the material force of the dominant proposition *cannot be substantiated in words alone*. In effect, the scenario will remain a chimera (or, to use a more positive term, a potentiality) unless it is somehow brought into the realm of practical reality.

The process is similar to the way in which teachers, for example, are trained to appreciate the significance of a set curriculum, before they turn what they have learned into lesson plans, which are then used to guide pupils in the composition of appropriate assignments. There is a clear hierarchical demarcation at work, a 'command structure' (see below) that brings with it the usual side effects that both paternalistic and authoritarian systems entail. As a result of the horizontal divisions between groups, there is a tendency for some of those at the bottom of the pyramid to regard the tasks they are set by their superiors with, at best, a kind of amused tolerance, and at worst contempt. This, however, does not matter to those who direct the charade, since it is *functional alignment* rather than genuine conviction that matters (although under present conditions it might be more accurate to say that belief should be interpreted as little more than faith in the practical reproduction of systemic reality).

If the scenario is to be made convincing, in an attempt to reinforce the 'reality' of the unhappy proposition upon which it is based, then it must be dramatised and *enacted* by those who are meant to lead any 'real-world' response. There is a catch, however, because the exercise must maintain its distance from the real, since the point of the training is to present the participants with a limited perspective – they are there to carry out relatively simple tasks, not to think about the morality of what they are doing. The actual manifestation of an undesirable incident (a terrorist strike, for example) does not therefore, from the point of view of executive authority, provide the most suitable object lesson. It is not just that an attack is unpredictable, since this aspect of its constitution is, if anything, played up by the political class. It is rather that its occurrence suggests incompetence on the part of the security apparatus (giving rise to the question, 'with all this forward planning, why didn't they see it coming?').

This is why it is vital that the imaginary event (unlike, for instance, the more intrusive security event discussed in Chapter 5) is sealed off from any form of disruptive externality. The participants have to *concentrate* at this preparatory stage, so that their actions will become a reflex later. Senior participants are supposed to think 'I must perform my role well in order to prepare for the real thing.' It is the initial 'enaction' of the fantasy and its subsequent rehearsal that makes the whole exercise seem substantial, while in fact individuals are being trained to respond in a way that precludes or downgrades any rational analysis of present reality, made up of the larger context in which they operate. The real and immediate dangers – government cuts, military adventurism, corporate exploitation, a dying environment, and so on, do not feature in these narratives.

In other words, attention is meant to be focused on the practical challenges that may be faced (how to evacuate a workforce from a site, how to communicate with the emergency services, etc.), rather than the absurdity of the bigger situation, in which 'terror' is actually the product of the structural complicity between forces that stand in formal opposition, but that actually collude in the reciprocal futility of this form of violence. Ultimately, no rehearsal could match the sheer horror and social dislocation caused by an actual terrorist assault, as the events of '9/11' (see Chapter 6) and other incidents seem to confirm.

The process of functional/ideological alignment outlined above must be placed in its wider theoretical context, before any further analysis of the political character of the scenario, and its 'worst-case' variant (see below), is pursued. There must be no presumption that those who participate in the exercise, let alone those who witness it, find it particularly convincing. This does not mean that the whole procedure is futile. One of the central contentions of this book is that, while the attempt to manufacture 'belief' in a general political condition has foundered

– partly because the citizen has been (deliberately) detached from the political realm until such time as an electoral mandate is required – the ruling elite seeks to overcome the organisational problems this entails by providing certain groups of people with 'purposeful' training. There is a considerable difference between the types of instruction offered to a local leadership (which is passed on to those who occupy the lower ranks of an institution) and that form of propaganda generated for general consumption.

It is this, the practical application of all those supposedly profound insights about the nature of terrorism, that requires the creation of an *attitude* about the world – not, notice, a burning conviction (though that can be useful if not overdone), but a general perspective or *posture* grounded in physical activity and the *occupation of institutional space*. Little wonder, then, that when the US Joint Chiefs of Staff drew attention to the importance of doctrine and organisation, as opposed to simple 'material superiority', they placed an equally high value on education and training (*Joint 20/20 Vision*, 2000: 3).

Emergency planning and the security entrepreneur

The advantage – from the perspective of an executive authority – of providing a scenario is that it can be fleshed out by the participants, who are then encouraged to 'own' the process. The concept of ownership is, after all, an essential weapon in the 'post-ideological' constitution of the subjective mindset: the individual is always encouraged to *own insubstantial things*, while the truly powerful hoard more valuable re-sources. An important, though perhaps sometimes neglected, aspect of scenario and emergency planning is exactly the solid economic benefits it can offer the security entrepreneur. Since an increasing number of civic and private bodies, including educational institutions, hospitals and small businesses, come under government pressure to participate in the 'security exercise', resources that cannot be mustered at a local level are offered by specialised firms. These include the kind of ready-made materials that can be presented to managers and selected staff, which sometimes form part of those practical but often vacuous bonding activities designed to improve the political cohesion of an organisation's upper echelon.

One company, for example, provides 'a highly dynamic software system' that can be used for 'both planning and the interactive management of spontaneous or planned incidents' (www.armedforces-int.com, 2009: 1). This software, known as 'Atlas OPS', works by generating 'template' plans that can create 'any new scenario ... saving time and effort' (1). A brief examination of those bodies attempting to profit from the legal requirement to maintain emergency plans shows that not all attain the same degree of intellectual or presentational sophistication, which might be considered appropriate from companies that expect their customers to pay real money for their services. Despite using the same Atlas OPS software, the impression created by the Emergency Response Planning Group (ERG) is a case in point.

If the key to gaining new business is to ensure that the organisation's publicity material reinforces the desired aura of professional capability, then ERP might need to reconsider its approach. Although it offers 'Communication, Command Post, Table Top and Live Exercise Facilitation' (ERPG, 2008: 1), it is not, for example, clear why the company has chosen to illustrate the 'Event Planning' section of its website with a photograph of an adhesive whiteboard labelled 'Smalltown', which is covered with little figures representing the availability of emergency medical personnel. An unkind observer might remark that this rather confused diagram resembles the cheerful but uncoordinated efforts of young schoolchildren, anxious to complete a set task before it begins to eat into their playtime. In the group's final appeal to prospective customers, it declares that its 'fees are very competitive', but perhaps wisely adds the codicil that it is always 'happy to negotiate a rate to suit you' (1).

FIVE

The security event:
exercise, emergency and 'real world' crises

Diverted from training exercises, the troops and several Scimitar armoured vehicles swept on to the site before dawn yesterday, helping police patrol Heathrow's sprawling perimeter fence and nearby open spaces, including Windsor Great Park, from where missiles might be launched.

> N. Hopkins, R. Norton-Taylor and M. White
> (guardian.co.uk, 12 February 2003, 12.42 GMT)

More than 400 soldiers were drafted in to provide extra security at Heathrow airport today to combat terrorist threats to London, Scotland Yard said today.

Troops took up positions at one of the world's busiest airports at 6 am as part of a 'precautionary measure' linked to fears that al-Qaida could use the end of the Muslim festival of Eid al-Adha, which runs from tomorrow until Saturday, as a trigger for attacks.

> *Guardian* Agencies and Staff
> (guardian.co.uk, Tuesday 11 February 2003)

At one point on Wednesday, the Labour Party Chairman, John Reid, said the threat was of the same nature as the attacks on New York on September 11th.

He angrily denied the deployment of troops may have been political spin, saying 'this is not a game, this is about a threat of the nature that massacred thousands of people in New York'.

> BBC News online (14 February 2003)

The rehearsal of security: from exercise to event

The suspicion that the practical organisation of the security exercise is actually a standard recourse for 'the political administration of contemporary capitalist states' (Neocleous, 2008: 72) is reinforced by the role assigned to the public. So, for instance, the 'Urban Warrior' counter-insurgency exercise, played out on America's West Coast in 1999, envisaged 'an incident involving chemical or biological weapons', followed by 'a mid-intensity combat operation in an urban environment, against a backdrop of civil unrest' (www.defenselink.mil).

The operation was supposed to include 'humanitarian and disaster relief' yet was ultimately designed to 'restore order' (www.defenselink. mil). The real opponent appeared to be the civilian protestor, rather than a terrorist enemy. The ideological character of these highly theatrical mobilisations is therefore evident not only from their overblown and sometimes fanciful assessment of risk, and the depth of malevolence attributed to the 'terrorist', but from the attitude to citizens who may engage in protest.

This development, in which internal civic resistance is placed in the same categorical space as that occupied by the armed insurgent, is not confined to the USA. The UK's national security strategy, for example, presented the case that the 'lines between terrorism, subversion and legitimate dissent ... may become increasingly blurred' (Cabinet Office, *National Security Strategy* 6.36, 2009: 78). The 'legitimate' opponents of neoliberal securitisation are therefore placed among 'a growing number of hostile and predatory actors' who are aligned against bourgeois interests, ranging from 'anti-business activists and terrorists to foreign intelligence agents', all of whom are supposed to have 'a profound impact on the conduct of business and on our [*sic*] daily lives' (Martin, 2002: 4).

This principle extends to the belief that US armed forces will have to counter the threat of 'insurgents, serial killers, drug dealers' and even computer hackers (Turse, 2008: 245–6). Developments in technical capability are therefore linked to plans for the aggressive suppression of a variety of enemies. One scenario describes 'a team of hi-tech robots ... hunting down enemy snipers, lookouts, criminal gangs and road-side bombs' (Savage, 20 August 2008).

The refusal to acknowledge political and moral distinctions between the various opponents of Western capital is, however, already being replicated within the technological practices of war, so that procedures used at the periphery are returned to the centre in order to strengthen the paramilitary functions of the security state. This is demonstrated by, for instance, the use of aerial drones, employed to attack or identify targets in war zones like Afghanistan and the Palestinian territories (Evans et al., 25 November 2008; Pallister, 9 January 2009), then subsequently deployed in the skies above Western cities to monitor public gatherings (Sengupta, 6 August 2008).

Knowledge and foreknowledge

'Nothing', according to one security specialist, 'is more important in the world of intelligence than preventing surprise' (Hulnick, cited in Cavelty and Mauer, 2009: 124). According to this source, the rationale for the existence of the intelligence agency is the anticipation of various forms of threat – hence the appearance of 'civil contingencies' experts in the heart of government (Andrew, 2010: 678). The Central Intelligence Agency would seem to agree with this perspective, because it once defined intelligence as 'knowledge and *foreknowledge* of the world around us' (Warner, cited in Andrew et al., 2009: 4; my emphasis).

Considered as a guiding principle, there are two problems associated with this approach, one moral and the other practical: both emerge from the institutional position occupied by the security agency. Formally subservient to the head of state and the governing alliance, these organisations are nonetheless placed beyond the usual bounds of legal restraint, and possess sufficient autonomy to be able to determine what kind of event should be classified as dangerous: only a certain type of risk seems to lie within their operational responsibility. The proposition that an agency might work to prevent the most hazardous development of the age – the threat to life on earth, created by the industrial system – would be regarded as absurd, since this is the form of social organisation it is sworn, through its commitment to the maintenance of economic security, to uphold.

As a consequence, the 'prevention of surprise' is no more than the contemporary reproduction of established assumptions about risk. The 'worst-case scenario', disguised as genuine concern about the dangers of the future, reproduces a version of the present based on the structural iniquities of the past. There is, therefore, no guarantee that an agency will act on information in a way that benefits the social order as a whole: at the point at which the protection of the public and the defence of the state come into conflict, the interests of the system will prevail.

Another problem associated with the syndrome of prevention is that, by its very nature, 'surprise' is a condition that defies planning: a genuinely unexpected incident will demonstrate the weakness of established protocol. One such case occurred when protestors surrounded a car carrying two members of the British royal family during a student fees demonstration in London (Wintour and Watt, 10 December 2010: 1). The occupants, Charles and Camilla, escaped relatively unscathed, but the failure of security caused a furore. Not only were calls made for more effective communication between the various arms of the police service, but the incident encouraged some high-ranking officers to call for the use of more severe measures against demonstrators (Fresco, 11 December 2010: 1). The suggestions put forward included the use of water cannon, but this proposal had already been formulated over a year before, after the G20 demonstrations in London (Brady, 5 July 2009). Meanwhile, if those who inhabit the formal apparatus of government are ill prepared for immediate, specific emergencies, then the rehearsal of well-worn scenarios will have been a waste of time.

These arguments seem to be confirmed by a remarkable comment made by Ian Blair (the UK's Metropolitan Police Commissioner from 2004 to 2008). Referring to the failed London bombings of 21 July 2005, he noted that 'no-one had ever thought about, or practised contingencies for, a set of failed suicide bombers who were on the run and might attack anywhere in London' (Blair, 2009: 150). If nothing is really more essential than the prevention of surprise (Hulnick, cited in Cavelty and Mauer, 2009: 124), then it is precisely the endless reuse of *existing models and training regimes* that will guarantee the failure of the security apparatus. Blair went on to point out that, although the Metropolitan Police 'had developed plans for dealing with suicide bombers', all these schemes 'were predicated on prior intelligence' (Blair, 2009: 150). In the absence of solid information, the authorities depended on the identification of patterns of behaviour, the supposed ethnicity of the suspects, and a deeply flawed command structure, all of which helped to seal the fate of Jean Charles de Menezes (see Chapter 7).

The core of the state?

When Ian Blair and his subordinate Andy Hayman attended a meeting of the UK government's emergency committee COBRA on 21 July, to discuss what appeared to be a wave of failed suicide attacks, the officials present were very much in the dark. Blair, writing an account of the day a few years after the event, noted that the prevailing question was 'how many more attacks were being planned?' (Blair, 2009: 145). He also made a remarkable admission: 'in that room [containing the COBRA committee], *at the very centre of the British state*, the simple answer from the security services and everyone else was that we had no idea' (145; my emphasis).

If Blair's recollection is correct, then certain questions should be posed. First, if the operative core of the state found itself at a loss, could this situation be regarded as an indication that *no part* of the entire security structure, which is clearly much bigger than the COBRA committee itself, had knowledge of any part of the conspiracy? If the answer to this question is yes, then it must be the case either that the current methods used to provide an early warning of an attack are inadequate, or that no agency could ever be capable of preventing such an incident. If the answer is no, then it may be that the whole idea of placing faith in the competence of a clearly delineated 'central command' is a mistake.

The only other conclusion that might be reached is that the COBRA committee was not – nor was, perhaps, ever intended to be – 'the very centre of the British state'. Instead, it could be regarded as a coordinating rather than an executive body. This implies that the effective core of the system is to be found elsewhere, or that it does not exist because power is dispersed, or alternatively that it changes in its exact composition (though not its fundamental principles) according to the situation.

While COBRA may bring together the various components of the government, police and security apparatus, its weakness lies in the fact that some of the 'key players' may be reluctant to divulge everything they know. This is a common drawback within all authoritarian, hierarchical systems, since there are always a number of turf wars raging within and between the various departments that constitute the modern state ensemble. It is obvious, however, that this kind of conflict has serious implications for the construction of any response designed to meet an emergency.

'Muslim plot to kill the Pope'

As already noted, an obsessive preoccupation with the future can distort the ability of the security operative to concentrate on more immediate tasks. Equally, the intelligence analyst or surveillance officer may be too ready to imagine that minor discoveries are part of a 'bigger picture' that cannot yet be discerned in its entirety, requiring pre-emptive action just in case the signs point to the manifestation of a major incident. Just such an example was reported on 18 September 2010, when the *Daily Express* carried a headline that announced 'MUSLIM PLOT TO KILL THE POPE', followed by the subheading 'Bogus street cleaners held' (Twomey et al., 18 September 2010: 1). The first paragraph of this piece declared that 'Islamic terrorists disguised as street cleaners allegedly hatched an audacious plot to blow up the Pope' (1).

It seems unlikely that this incident could be attributed to an evil scheme initiated on behalf of an entire religion. The use of the word 'allegedly' in the report raised a question mark over the existence of the scheme itself, but did not interfere with the basic notion that there were indeed a number of 'Islamic terrorists' disguised as street cleaners. A less hysterical approach was offered by the *Guardian*, which noted that there was little real alarm in Whitehall. Its journalists noted that 'there was no meeting of the government's emergency committee, COBRA, and the terrorism threat level remained unchanged', all of which indicated that 'there was no credible evidence pointing to an imminent attack' (Dodd et al., 18 September 2010: 1). The men arrested were, in fact, what they appeared to be – street cleaners – and were later released without charge.

Cases of this type, though faintly absurd, offer an important insight into the ways in which suspected malefactors are pursued, and why it is apparently so easy to make an error when trying to identify malicious plots. Whether or not one accepts the idea that this particular operation had to be carried out, the use of certain tactics like the dawn raid, employed in this instance, depend on the mechanical initiation of procedures that are almost impossible to rescind once they are set in motion – this, indeed, is part of the reason they are used. The hierarchical 'chain of command' that assigns different tasks to specific sub-groups and then, at the crucial moment, allows paramilitary units to take discretionary action is one of the main reasons for the occurrence of the Stockwell incident described in Chapter 7.

The security event

The security event can be distinguished from the exercise or rehearsal by the serious 'real world' mobilisation of material and human resource, concentrated at a particular location, and used to occupy, reinforce, surround or seize an actual site or public space. It is not the routine provision of protection, evident when bodyguards are assigned to leading political figures, or when armed police guard public buildings. It is instead a pre-emptive gesture and, where public, is designed to occupy centre stage, creating an impression of productive activity.

It might be accompanied by an announcement of purpose (which need not be truthful), or may rely on the affective timeliness of its own appearance. Any occasion that is represented as an attempt to take control of a situation before it 'develops into a crisis' – a raid on a building, the seizure of goods, a show of force in a public place, and the *armed demonstration* described below – qualifies as a security event. The danger it is supposedly mobilised to meet may never materialise, either because the presence of security personnel has kept it at bay, or because it never existed in the first place.

The security event is therefore a deliberately engineered phenomenon, represented as a necessary rejoinder to some situation or condition that is implied by the organisation of the event itself. No visible threat is usually discerned, because it is always absent from the protected area: though physically immaterial, it seems nonetheless to loom large in the discursive realm, as though the existence of the 'worst case' is confirmed by its cunning invisibility. The security event is not, therefore, a genuine reaction to an immediate material risk: it is the adoption of a posture designed to exemplify the preparedness of the state apparatus to meet a serious threat (usually inflated into something approaching the 'worst case').

An actual response to an unexpected event, or the calculated deployment of force that prevents a major incident, can, on the other hand, be recognised by the fact that unexpected circumstances are much less easy to 'showcase' and control, as described above. In such cases, there is a greater sense of urgency and a tendency to act on an ad hoc basis. The security event is therefore ideally conducted in a secure, manageable space, where real hazards are kept to a minimum. Yet, just as it is important that this type of procedure should not take on the messy appearance of unpredictable reality, so it must also dispense with the trappings of the dummy run or live exercise. No one involved could take it seriously if it included any hint of simulation or role play. The event might eventually be described as a false alarm, or a regrettable mistake, but at the time the operational leadership will maintain a straight face.

Towards a police state?

The imposition of a command structure on the civilian population during the security event may be described as a response to a credible threat, but, since this is often invisible, the question is, against whom or what exactly is the repressive potential of the state displayed? In the absence of the terrorist enemy, the security operative must have a subject upon which to act. This is none other than the citizen, who can be ordered to carry out any number of actions: to vacate the streets, to remain indoors, to stay outside the security cordon, and so on.

Intended as a way of giving weight to the reality and gravity of a particular situation, this kind of performance is never quite sufficient to convince every observer. Without tangible evidence of the presence of a real opponent, the display of repressive capacity may resemble a pantomime in which the villain has declined to appear. Of course, the higher echelons of the security regime may know full well that there is only a limited possibility of the designated risk actually occurring, or even, in some cases, that there is no chance at all of a threat becoming real. The temporary containment of the civilian population provides, nonetheless, an object-lesson that sends a clear signal to opponents and subordinates alike.

The evidence of a gradual increase in the use of authoritarian tactics like 'kettling', ubiquitous surveillance, armed response and pre-emptive arrest has given rise to the proposition that some countries within the Western social order have begun to move towards the creation of the 'police state'. The traditional definition of this concept is a totalitarian entity controlled by an overtly political form of policing that penetrates into the heart of civil society, and that is dedicated to the covert monitoring and overt direction of the populace. There are of course a number of other theories about the development of policing – these include the growth of managerialism, models of collaborative governance, the rise of the private security sector, and the establishment of international agencies (see McLaughlin, 2007) – but these developments could conceivably coexist alongside the authoritarian practices described above.

In the British case, the question has been confused by the conflation of the police with the public interest, to the extent that the police are meant to be the public in uniform. This, according to one writer, is 'related to a further key feature of liberal mythology', which is that only totalitarian systems integrate police and state functions (Neocleous, 2000: 115). The reproduction of the police state is often said to be unlikely to succeed because the overall direction of police activity is subject to the law.

While the legal process will at least mean that the word of the (anonymous) security operative can be tested in court, this condition is not enough to prove that the secret services and the police are truly subjected to its edicts at the time at which some intervention takes place. This is not the rule of law over illicit state activity, so much as a post-event review of particular 'excesses'. The perception is that the state's mandate to govern (to impose order) is based ultimately on the threat of violence and the close supervision of the population, but the contemporary technologies of rule are far in advance of those associated with the cruder regimes of terror that flourished in the 1930s. This should suggest not that the prospect of a police state has receded, but rather that a more sophisticated, less visible and more naturalised form of oppression has replaced it. Based on a less overtly political proposition, the close monitoring of identity and public conduct allows the authorities to catalogue those illicit activities, from shoplifting to 'violent' protest, which are supposed to define the behaviour of a deviant minority.

Missiles in Athens, tanks at Heathrow

In a situation where the 'paramilitary' capability of the state does not match the progressive, inclusive discourses promoted by some of its own senior commanders – such as Ian Blair's insistence on promoting the Metropolitan Police as an institution that was interested in 'Working Together for a Safer London' – it is important to understand the role of both the physical intervention like the security event and the rhetorical utterances that accompany it. In order to demonstrate this point, two events will be used to illustrate the comparative strength of sovereign power.

The two occasions are the appearance of Scimitar armoured vehicles at Heathrow Airport in February 2003 (described by the BBC on 14 March 2003 as 'a public relations disaster'), and the installation of US Patriot missiles around Athens in July 2004, when Greece was the host for the Olympics Games. The argument advanced here is that the behaviour of the authorities (i) relied, in both cases, on the use of the armed *demonstration*, a type of dramatised response produced by states which, though presented as a measure designed to counter a 'global' terrorist threat, may actually represent a calculated reaction to internal political dissent, and (ii) was aligned with the policy interests of the United States government.

The mobilisation of the Household Cavalry's armoured units took place four days before the UK's largest peace demonstration (called on 15 February 2003 to protest against the threat of a US-led attack on Iraq), while a series of minor explosions in the Athenian suburb of Kallithea on 4 May 2004 provided an important point of reference for those who argued for increased security during the Athens Olympics. The context of this analysis is the fact that displays of military power in the UK and Greece were made in the name of security and were thus presented within the wider discursive context of the 'war on terror', depending for their political impact upon the attempt to create symbolic resonance through media forms.

Such displays represented not only the political determination of two sovereign states, but also the intentions of powerful external actors, most particularly NATO and the US government, which in the case of Greece provided the missiles on the basis of 'invitation' (Agence France Presse,

10 May 2004). These acts therefore constituted an intervention in the globalised *representation* of terrorism, imposing temporarily 'militarised' zones within the cities concerned, revealing an uncomfortable tension between the pursuit of state and human security (Thomas, 2002).

The 'spectacle', power and rhetoric

If armed demonstrations are organised as material interventions in the spatial and temporal structures of 'everyday' life, they must also – because the actual incursions would only be witnessed by a fraction of the intended audience – be constituted as a form of mediated public spectacle.[1] Debord's original depiction of the 'society of the spectacle' in 1967 was not, as some suppose, limited to a critique of mass mediated culture. It was rather an attack on the appropriation of 'the entirety of social activity' by institutional power (Jappe, 1999: 7). In Debord's view, everyday life had been subsumed within the 'autocratic reign of the market economy', a condition accompanied through 'the totality of new techniques of government' (Debord, 1998: 2).

If the spectacle is mediated, it will always be accompanied by some form of explanation, dependent in many cases on the use of a simple rhetorical technique. The appearance of the 'inclusive *we*' (Atkinson, 1984) is understood here as one important indication of the ways in which political discourse prepares, accompanies and justifies actions taken in the name of public security. Extensively deployed throughout political speech (and evident to a lesser extent within academic discourse), *we* depends for its effect on suggesting the existence of shared purposes, without necessarily providing evidence of any real commonality of interest.

In response to questions in Parliament, concerning the deployment of 450 troops at Heathrow airport (in February 2003), David Blunkett, then home secretary, used this formulation, declaring that 'the terrorist must not be able to assess what we know or how we know it' (BBC News online, 14 February 2003). This utterance, made 'after bowing to pressure from opposition parties to deliver a statement', contains a hint of the absurd: if the enemies of the state are prevented from learning its intelligence secrets, then they will of course be unable to guess how something of which they have never heard was assembled.

Insisting that 'we do nothing to undermine the work of the police and the security services', Blunkett justified his reluctance to provide a detailed explanation for the military deployment by invoking the spectre of terrorism.

The formal political utterances made by ruling groups, while expressed within a broad, apparently inclusive apparatus of civil rule (characterised as the appearance of networks of 'governance'[2]), remain examples of *allocution* – that is, a type of address that is made by a leader to a group of followers. It is the production of this type of speech event that, however intimately the actual address might be phrased, attempts to reinforce a strict distinction between an elite and the bulk of the social order. Formal speeches are thus structured interventions designed to initiate, accompany and reinforce multidimensional events that are, in turn, purposely organised as manifestations of power. As Gill argues, the primary energies of the state are devoted to 'the continuing *projection* of public power in the pursuit of its aims' (Gill, 2003: 7; my emphasis).

Conventional depictions of democratic rule offer little sense that a gulf exists between those allowed to exercise power through rhetorical utterance and those whose efforts to communicate are regarded as politically irrelevant; nor is there much sense that the effect of government is to establish anything approaching a despotic 'totality'. Governance, for example, is often presented as the development of innovative, more equitable, sources of power (Bevir and Rhodes, 2003). Yet the integration of state and economy characteristic of the 'total' system described by Debord depends on the ability to dominate the material environment.

References to a *public* rationale for state action may therefore provide the 'legitimate power source external to the orator' which Graham and his co-authors identify as a long-standing requirement of political discourse (Graham et al., 2004: 199). In other words, speakers habitually appeal to external sources of moral authority rather than argue a case on its merits alone. Sharman, in a study of the rhetorical strategies used by Martin Luther King, makes a similar point, noting that the civil rights activist referred to 'accepted ideals and homilies within American society' in order to advance his programme of reform (1999: 85). Attempts to mobilise broader values may, however, encounter problems, especially when *state actors* pretend to use the public as their moral compass, since the public interest is often used as a cover for the exercise of executive power.

Announcements are (within formal democracies at least) timed to take advantage of the publicity which news media can provide. Irrespective of content, each time official pronouncements are staged, the hierarchical relationship between powerful social actors and their chosen audience is reinforced. Karl, for example, argues that 'statecraft may have become the hostage ... of stagecraft' (in Ammon, 2001: 7). In his statement (see above), Blunkett used the rhetorical advantages offered by the *indeterminate* character of the pronoun *we* in an attempt to mobilise a sense of commonality and obligation.

The production of 'we' also meets a number of official requirements. It presents individuals as legitimate sources, authorised to speak on behalf of the British government, and thus able to define security, terrorism and democracy. In addition, the range of reference encompassed by *we* can easily be expanded to include wider entities, such as the nation-state, which by implication must include all those who live within its borders. The listener is then, at least in theory, obliged to align him- or herself with the speaker, in order to remain within the broader category which one model of national belonging dictates. Refusals of a seamless identification with normative authority may suggest a reluctance to express 'patriotic' allegiance or even to acknowledge national subjectivity.[3]

The shift from one linguistic reference to another offers an apparently natural transition, in the sense that politicians and state functionaries habitually attempt to incorporate a wider set of constituencies within an original proposition, conflating (at least within speech) quite disparate interests. The appearance of the concept *we* enables this mutation to occur and, often through an appeal to the requirements of national security, obscures distinctions between social actors. No wonder then that 'we' has been defined as the 'collective name for [the] speaker and all others of the class that context shows him [*sic*] to be representing *for the moment*' (*Concise Oxford Dictionary*, 1964; my emphasis). In other words, the alignment of speaker with his/her audience is temporary (see Price, 2010: 63). The existence of a forced affinity between two ostensibly antagonistic practices (exclusive 'governance' and inclusive language) may also imply that they share other characteristics.

Another example of the problematic character of the term 'we' can be found in an academic context. In an analysis of the war on terror, Charles Townshend wrote that, 'after September 11th, we found ourselves in an apparently open-ended and permanent state of emergency, a "war against terror", whose ramifications are as inscrutable as terrorism itself' (Townshend, 2002: 1). Townshend suggests that mysterious effects are produced by hidden processes, and makes a direct comparison between this situation and the obscure character of terrorist activity: in this case, 'we' represents a group that is threatened by terrorist activity. The introduction of the *rhetorically* inclusive sign 'we' reveals Townshend's attitude to the role of the educated observer. The 'implied audience' for his remarks shares his position as an intelligent subject, forced by an obscure threat to confront an 'open-ended' crisis.

Military exercises

One writer noted at the time of the Heathrow event that, despite thirteen arrests under terror legislation and the visible build-up of security, the prime minister of the day had not cancelled his holiday abroad to return to the UK. This author also noted that none of those packed into the drinking dens of the City of London seemed in the least frightened by the prospect of a terror attack (Knightley, 8 August 2004: 25). Another commentator wondered if the 'government's sudden deployment of the troops' could have been connected with the later admission of a terror suspect called Khalid Sheikh Mohammed that he had once planned to attack the airport (Hewitt, 2008: 43). According to a third expert, this plot had involved a British citizen of Kashmiri descent called Rashid Rauf, who was a member of the jihadist group Jaish-e-Mohammed, or JEM (Curtis, 2010: 287). Eventually, news emerged of an official US report, which argued that al-Qaeda had planned to hijack flights from Heathrow in order to use them as missiles against a variety of targets. This, however, did not relate to the mobilisation in 2003, but to another rather vague contention that Canary Wharf was to have been attacked in 2004 (Corea, 22 June 2006: 1).

The 2003 mobilisation was not, moreover, the first time that soldiers had been deployed at Heathrow. In 1974, during the miners' strike of that year, military exercises were held at the airport, which involved a contingent of the Special Air Service (Head and Mann, 2009: 27). The whole event had been presented as a precaution against terrorist hijacking, but the chief of the defence staff at the time, Lord Carver, eventually admitted that 'fairly senior' officers had talked about the possibility of a military takeover (27). A series of articles in *The Times* had reported similar discussions, which were supposed to have described the possible response of the armed forces if 'the extreme left' had continued to make progress in Britain (27).

In all such cases, there is always a psychological dimension at work, but this is not, as sometimes imagined, the work of rhetoric alone. In fact, the creation of ambiguity and uncertainty is a useful tactic because it creates an *impression* of siege or emergency. The material arrangement of resources provides the undeniable 'reality' associated with the security event, while the authenticity of the mobilisation is then publicly demonstrated through the media. In other words, mediation is supposed to act as the underwriter for the whole deal between the authorities and the public, despite the fact that this also helps to publicise aspects of an event – the absence of a threat – that might ultimately reduce its credibility.

In his studies of simulation, Baudrillard deals with the inversion of the real, and notes the supposed difference between Debord's original description of the *spectacle* (in which there is still space for a critique of power) and a new condition where the onlooker becomes an actor 'in the performance' (Baudrillard, 1996: 27). Debord did, in fact, acknowledge the development of such tendencies, noting that 'the empty debate on the spectacle' is 'organised by the spectacle itself' (Debord, 1998: 6). Yet, at least in the cases of military mobilisation studied here, there seems to be a return to a cruder procedure. Although a display of power is ostensibly produced on behalf of a public, its value as an integrative strategy is reduced by the public's exclusion both from the background intelligence or rationale for the display and from active participation against the 'terrorist' threat.

The individual is repeatedly told to 'report anything suspicious' and then, in effect, to 'leave it to the authorities'. When formal power fails to protect the citizenry, their anger is often directed at a political leadership that seems to have encouraged the growth of a general passivity. In the UK, the revelation that jihadist militants living in

London had been known to the security services (Curtis, 2010: xi), and that two of the 7 July bombers had been under surveillance but were not thought to represent an immediate threat (Hewitt, 2008: 101), has increased suspicion that the protection of the public is not always at the top of the security agenda.[4]

Politics, utterance and representation

Formal political utterance might seem to represent a performative act[5] (Austin, 1975), able to bring circumstances into being through forms of *directive* address (Price, 2007). It is clear, however, that effective examples of public discourse are based on more than the power of their propositional content. Although it is true that the substance of any political executive's work is inextricably bound up with presentation (Seymour-Ure, 2000: 157), events can only be 'ordered' by language and appearances where there is some parallel material force which can reinforce the intention of the speaker. So, for example, a policy initiative is 'put into effect' at the moment of expression, but requires some established command structure or resource to make the desired outcome felt.

From a governing politician's point of view, an oration forms part of the repertoire of social control. In other words, its attempt to be 'persuasive' represents a necessary formality within a system that *expects* dominant positions to be justified. The problem with 'authoritative' political speech is that it attempts to achieve two sometimes incompatible ends, one immediate or contingent and the other normative.

In the first case, especially when it is produced at short notice or attempts to persuade the listener to accept a declaration on trust, a speech or reply is devoted to the *timely* generation of a response. In such cases, hasty or circular arguments are often produced, creating positions which fail to generate productive meaning. Two brief examples may illustrate this point. Responding to the November 2003 attack in Turkey, Prime Minister Blair refuted the accusation that the 'war on terror' was counterproductive and encouraged terrorist activity: 'what has caused the terrorist attack today in Turkey is not the President of the United States, is not the alliance between America and Britain' (*Guardian*, 21 November 2003). He went on to insist that 'what is responsible for that terrorist attack is terrorism, are the terrorists.'

In this case, Blair reverts to the *literal* meaning of responsibility, rather than addressing the deeper political implications of the question. Whenever politicians maintain oversimplified views in the face of a logical critique, it is likely that they will produce explanations which produce a linguistic short-circuit. Paul Wolfowitz generated the following example, speaking after an attack on the al-Rashid hotel in Iraq, an event he witnessed (he was inside the building during the incident). Here, the need to categorise American intent as benevolent is undermined by the fact that the attack would not have occurred without the presence of the 'coalition' itself: 'these terrorist attacks will not deter us from completing our mission, which is to help the Iraqi people free themselves from the types of criminals who did this' (Wolfowitz, *Independent*, 27 October 2003).

Where the overriding aim of a speech event is long term and more carefully prepared (often intended to express and execute policy), the discourse produced has a better chance of creating the conditions under which the action described will be understood and ultimately assessed.[6] This second condition tries in advance to categorise an act or event or purpose, although the constant development of events will usually require an adjustment in the descriptions used.[7] Yet it is the expectation that *all* political utterances are matters of record (providing a point of comparison between utterances made at different junctures, and an opportunity to compare what has been said with what has been done) which continues to provide the overriding rationale for serious journalistic enquiry.

Journalists and analysts recognise an authority's 'right' to describe and categorise public events, knowing that the corollary to this privilege is that politicians can be held to account for their statements. Journalistic awareness of the disparity between description and truth means, however, that they may well regard political discourse as a guide to the *intentions* of those in power, rather than a completely accurate account of any individual situation.

States, authority and status

The successful materialisation of power rests in the first instance on the governing authority's ability to mobilise various resources and to generate plausible accounts of social reality. This means that government ministers and their aides must produce credible references to individuals, situations and events. When official perspectives do not seem to match an audience's experience, this often indicates an attempt to disguise some uncomfortable truth. There is always a tension, therefore, between the disciplinary character of language produced by authority and the need to produce believable depictions of reality.

It is, however, the more incremental processes inherent in language use which may provide a more successful resource for the orator than the grander claims of extended rhetorical passages. Once a listener regards a statement as a reasonable description of an actual condition (the existence of terrorism), new concepts may be built upon the notions already established. However, the limitations of a practice that concentrates upon timely but sometimes hardly convincing utterance can be seen from the types of hurried and inadequate response already described above.

No form of public representation (including the armed demonstration) is therefore guaranteed success. The more polished rhetorical propositions that achieve coherence within party conferences do not necessarily attain the same impact when they are filtered through the news media.[8] News conventions, meanwhile, demand a sense of immediacy and 'liveness', which state agencies can provide. As Lichtenberg argues, the policies and actions of governments have more 'exemplary significance' than those initiated by citizens, owing to 'their inescapably public nature' (Lichtenberg, 2003: 1). The other obvious element that helps to reinforce the position of an executive is the existence of functional and utilitarian modes of rule. The actual exercise of power relies less on a consistent 'world-view' (or notions of a 'dominant' ideology[9]) than on the production of orders that can meet contingencies.

In other words, the persuasive effort contained in linguistic references is always augmented by efforts to *bring into being* some palpable aspect of the condition described, irrespective of the parallel invocation of moral values or appeals to a sense of emergency. The use of armoured vehicles at Heathrow in 2003 was presented as a necessity, yet the timing and character of the response struck some commentators as a 'counter-demonstration' to the London anti-war protest organised for 15 February 2003.[10] The event was in essence part of a phenomenon of public 'appearances', the deliberate materialisation of a threat intended to send signals to a variety of constituencies and 'issue proponents' (Dearing and Rogers, 1996). The sense that this material act was in some sense a riposte to those who thought that the terror threat was less substantial than had previously been stated was confirmed by an extraordinary intervention made by the director general of MI5 during this period, Eliza Manningham-Buller, who declared that 'comments to the effect that the troops at Heathrow were a cynical government manoeuvre to prepare the UK for war in Iraq were quite wrong' (Manningham-Buller, 16 October 2003). This seemed to underline the wide currency and perhaps even the truthfulness of the proposition it attempted to dismiss.

Olympic gold?

Formal authority, however powerful in terms of its ability to command public appearances (and to create bureaucratic structures),[11] is exercised within a contested discursive environment; that is to say, opposing perspectives will circulate and provide a counterpoint to the positions espoused by governments and their spokespersons. The London bombings of 7 July 2005, for example, demonstrated not only the reality of 'home-grown' terrorist activity, but a discursive tension between common perception (the notion of a link to the invasion of Iraq) and the disciplined, consistent denials from government spokespersons of a real connection between domestic circumstances and overseas adventures (Price, 2010). As Manningham-Buller's statement attests, it is possible to trace the existence of currents of opposition *within* the formal utterances and documents produced by officials and authoritative organisations. The official website of the Athens Olympics, for instance, insisted that 'Athens 2004 is working in close partnership with the Hellenic police, the Greek Government and international security experts to host a safe and secure Olympic Games' (www.athens2004.com). This was in part a reply to the criticism that Greece was not able to exercise the proper degree of sovereignty over its own event.

Questions about the cost, purpose and safety of the Olympics assumed at times a general air of negativity, producing a litany of complaints that were, in turn, held up as counterproductive by those who preferred to support the occasion on the basis of its supposed value to the whole Greek nation. Nonetheless, the point here is the existence of opposing viewpoints and the production of a counter-discourse to officially preferred narratives and themes. The outcome is the appearance of 'repressed' ideas in those statements designed to maintain the composure of official positions; the authorised line is in effect an 'answer' to a perspective which is not permitted to appear in its original form.[12]

Another challenge emerges from the need to accommodate power-ful external actors, who may produce demands that make a national leadership appear no more than the local clients of a foreign power. In the Greek election of March 2004, the loss of power by the 'social-ist' party Pasok to the right-wing New Democracy was followed by intense diplomatic activity, cast always as the meeting of equals who shared identical concerns about the problem of security. After minister of public order Georgios Voulgarakis met Condoleezza Rice in May 2004, he produced a description of the meeting that maintains this perspective:

> we had the opportunity to review many issues which are important for the two countries. We discussed in detail issues of security, especially for the Olympic Games. Mrs Rice shares the view that many important steps have been taken to ensure that the Olympic Games in Greece will be safe, and their assistance is something that we can count on. (Press Release, www.athens2004.com, 7 May 2004)

The concept of 'partnership' was certainly stretched to breaking point by the dispute over whether foreign security agents would be allowed to carry weapons when guarding athletes (*Independent*, 22 November 2004). In an attempt to reassure the Greek public that their country's sovereignty was not compromised by the appearance of Patriot missiles, the authorities maintained that 'any decision to use Patriot missiles to shoot down planes ... rests with Greece's premier and will be made within two minutes of detecting a problem' (www.livingroom.org. au/olympics/archives/greek_premier, 31 July 2004). At the beginning of the Olympics the author George Kassimeris declared that the whole process had been 'a public relations disaster'[13] (an identical accusation to that directed by the BBC at the Blair government's troop deployment at Heathrow a year before). Kassimeris went on to produce a counter-narrative to the 'megalomania' he perceived in his homeland, describing Greece itself as 'a small, historically significant, European country of peripheral status' (Kassimeris, 3 August 2004).

Democracy and the rhetoric of security

Faced by challenges from the right, with a US administration that regarded 'third-way' reformism as irrelevant, and a domestic population which 'increasingly distrusts institutions ... or is simply not interested in them' (European Commission, 2001), Europe's 'centre-left parties' and their associated policy networks were faced with a dilemma in the early part of the twenty-first century. They had to satisfy their free-market partners, acknowledge American power, yet continue to promote a vision of modernity that can attract broad electoral support. The perceived disappearance of a class base for politics has become, however, a self-fulfilling prophecy, justifying an end to activism and the creation of *executive partnerships*.

Established political parties have forged alliances with private enter-prise, policy centres, transnational organisations and corporate think-tanks. The development of this 'managerial-technocratic elite' (Bewes and Gilbert, 2000: 9) has provided the organisational and rhetorical framework for 'the management of things and people' (Hansen and Salskov-Iversen, 2002: 5). The challenge for mainstream politicians has been to reinforce this managerial approach while repeating the discourses of democracy.

When Greece was elected as a non-permanent member of the United Nations Security Council, references to this form of liberal world-view were much in evidence. The then Greek foreign minister Molyviatis declared that his country was dedicated to 'peace, respect for inter-national law, democracy and human rights' (Molyviatis, 15 October 2004). Identifying the most urgent challenges facing the Council, he spoke of the necessity of 'confronting ... international terrorism, and ... strengthening ... stability and peace throughout the world'. In political announcements such as this, the difficulty of reconciling divergent aims is concealed by the simple cohesion of the sentence itself.

If, as Duffield argues, 'liberal peace requires a political *rationale*' (2001: 108), the act of manoeuvring a 'liberal democracy' into a warlike stance places great strain on any official declarations of higher moral purpose. The process of invading Iraq, initiated in 2003 by the armies of the United States and Britain, clearly produced an insoluble contradiction; acts of military aggression call into question precisely those values like justice, freedom and democracy which, ostensibly, wars are fought to defend. When George W. Bush (US president at the time of the invasion) welcomed then prime minister Blair to the White House on 31 January 2003, he began the press conference by declaring his appreciation for 'my friend's commitment to peace and security' (Bush and Blair, 31 January 2003).

Later in the same forum, a reporter asked Bush if it was not the case that 'you have always intended war on Iraq and that international diplomacy is a charade' (Bush and Blair, 31 January 2003). The president's response was to argue that he had moved from a 'policy of containment' to a new 'strategic vision' after the attacks of 11 September 2001 (Bush and Blair, 31 January 2003). From this and other examples it is possible to see that one of the key terms used by politicians to justify military action, and which later acts as an alibi for the movement from peace to war, is exactly the reference to security. Universal peace might appear as the logical precondition for genuine security, but is unlikely to be achieved during an endless 'war on terror'. Aggressive forms of counter-insurgency may in fact frustrate the 'liberal' state's declared intention to establish settled conditions within its own borders.

Perceived threats to 'national security' can, therefore, emerge from both internal and external sources, demonstrating the flexibility of the concept and its ability to limit or even close down debate. Indeed, phrases like 'national security' are particularly useful for those 'strategic actors' who need reliable 'forms of interpretation and analysis' in order to justify their intentions (Duffield, 2001: 108). The reproduction of a shared language helps to establish common perspectives between the individual members of policy elites. In Duffield's opinion, political speeches may appear to produce 'information', but their primary purpose is more regulatory, concerned with 'deepening governance networks' (108).

In February 2003, when Jack Straw (then British foreign secretary) spoke of *collective* security, the same kind of manoeuvre seemed to be in evidence: to reassure powerful partners of the seriousness of British intentions in the 'war on terror', while assigning a moral value to the process. He announced that 'the search for collective security has been the inspiration for some of diplomacy's most noble endeavours' (Straw, International Institute for Strategic Studies, 11 February 2003). The opening gambit of Straw's statement is significant because it establishes an ideological frame for the address that follows, altering the established theme of 'collective security'.

The success of meaning-creation depends upon the mobilisation of themes, substantial aggregations of subject matter (Price, 2007) that rely for their impact on the ways in which they are aligned and delivered. Such themes (crime, terrorism, justice, etc.) are inevitably recapitulated and recombined, but taken as individual signs retain permanent features that limit their ideological flexibility. The statement of Straw reproduced above constitutes a declarative, or formal assertion, which attaches a moral distinction ('noble endeavour…') to what is in essence a pragmatic activity. Collective security, in its earliest form, turned on the notion of 'collective action to prevent war' (Pick and Critchley, 1974: 25). This positive quality endures as a sedimented theme, and is exploited by a speaker who suppresses its implied character as code for an alliance of limited imperial interests.

The questionable attribution of positive values to an ideological attack on the Iraqi regime may not, however, have produced the desired effect in the expert audience that bore witness to the event. As Gordenker and Weiss argue, the concept of 'collective security … emerged from international political systems so different from the present one that questions may be posed about the contemporary relevance of the idea and the tenability of its assumptions' (in Weiss, 1993: 3). Yet the academic and professional audience that attended the event was not at liberty to challenge the speaker on the grounds of veracity. Rhetoric as a practice depends on speaking from a position of dominance and, as argued above, attempts only to generate plausible depictions of the social world; where it seeks accuracy of reference, this is a strategic option, and does not represent the principled or conscientious pursuit of truthful explanation.

Although the power of the rhetorical domain is often attributed to the repertoire of techniques available to professional speakers, such as juxtaposition, repetition, the rule of three, and so on (Atkinson, 1984), its fundamental strength is drawn from two dimensions: the formal conditions which public speech both anticipates and reproduces (mentioned above), and the character of the utterances, sentences or 'units of meaning' produced in these official settings.

Economic globalisation as threat

Threats are perceived and constituted in various ways. To argue that they are simply produced 'through discourse' (a common assertion) may suppress proper enquiry into the relationship between representation and public action. Much rests on how 'discourse' itself is understood. If one accepts that human beings inhabit a 'material-symbolic' environment, in which the characterisation of a thing can to some degree alter behaviour or perception (and in which an inadequately 'represented' action may be, as a consequence, ineffective), then it should also be apparent that there are limits to the power of description alone. The endless assertion of one condition will eventually require evidence of an extradiscursive nature, or at least the production of alternative sources; their absence ensures an erosion of belief in the stated perspective. This is true with regard to the 'terrorist threat', but it applies to other perceived challenges.

The concept of 'globalisation' presents a similar case. Cameron and Palan, for example, ask to what degree globalisation can be described as 'a "real" objective process as opposed to a form of communal storytelling driven by parochial interests' (Cameron and Palan, 2004: 1). The point is not to investigate such narratives as falsehood, but to gauge to what degree the depiction of the process compares with other forms of evidence which go beyond those rhetorical positions that attempt to 'naturalise' processes which are actually the product of the decisions of those in authority.

Tony Blair's description of globalisation, set out in 2005, provides a useful example of this tendency, in which it is presented as an external, unstoppable force, as inevitable as seasonal change (see Price, 2007: 111). 'I hear people say we have to stop and debate globalisation', he declared, using an Americanism that allows a noun ('debate') to assume the status of a verb, and deploying a form of attribution ('I hear people say') that cannot be verified because it is supposedly drawn from personal experience (Blair, Labour Party Conference, 27 September 2005). He continued by arguing that 'you might as well debate whether autumn should follow summer', addressing in this case the 'multiple you' (Price, 2010) that is meant to supplement the 'inclusive we' (Atkinson, 1984).

In Blair's opinion, the issue was not being discussed 'in China and India' because these countries were 'seizing its possibilities, in a way that will transform their lives and ours' (Blair, 27 September 2005). Blair had, of course, to recognise the economic differences between East and West, noting that 'both nations [China and India] still have millions living in poverty', but they were at least 'on the move'. Vietnam and Thailand were finally cited as 'nations have labour costs a fraction of ours'.

The illocutionary force of the final sentence is quite clear. It implies that British workers need to alter their expectations. It is not the prelude to a call for a campaign on behalf of underpaid individuals in the 'new' economies. The repressed element is seen in the sly acknowledgement of the 'millions living in poverty', brought into the discussion only in order for the whole concept to be negated by the idea that some forward motion has been established. Language can, therefore, be used to initiate processes that will bring British employees into line with the prevailing reality, which neoliberal economists have already partially established through other symbolic practices. As Clarke and Newman argue, modernisation of this sort 'is a practical project: producing a series of reforms of the economy, the state, public service organisation', yet they also understand it to be 'a narrative form that gives coherence to a profoundly uneven and often contradictory series of interventions and initiatives' (in Steinburg and Johnson, 2004: 54).

The economic condition of a society is actually an important component of a state's 'security agenda'. The use of thousands of extra police officers in Athens and the 'liaison' with NATO powers pushed the cost of security above £660 million, yet when the budget for the Olympic Games grew beyond a total of £4 billion, the government failed to honour agreements to pay Olympics-related bonuses to employees, causing protests by doctors, hotel workers, ambulance staff, service workers and taxi drivers (*Independent*, 5 August 2004). At this point, security was turned to its traditional use, the policing of working-class dissent.

Terrorism, language and appearances

If political interventions are recognised as meaningful (whether or not they are convincing as 'truth claims'), then this is because they depend on 'the recognisable unity or connectedness of stretches of language' (Stubbs, 1983: 9). These patterns of connection underpin all forms of written and spoken expression, including the use of comparison and the development of argument, and are created when 'formal markers' relate what is about to be said or written to what has already been expressed (Halliday and Hasan, cited in Brown and Yule, 1983: 191). Such references (known as internal or 'endophoric') create 'cohesive relationships' both within and between sentences. In other words, endophoric coherence is that form of meaning created by the *apparent unity* of grammatical and semantic elements.

Public rhetoric must do more, however, than achieve mechanical consistency; unlike the kind of self-referential management-speak which invites conspiratorial exchange (see Brighton, 2002), rhetoric simulates broad inclusivity and demands the use of terms which have the potential to achieve some form of public resonance. George Bush's presidential victory of 3 November 2004 was not simply based on the repetition of themes such as 'security', but was attributed to 'a better ear for the cultural tone of America', in an election where 21 per cent of those who voted cited 'moral issues' as their most important consideration (Webb, BBC Radio 4, 4 November 2004).

Inclusive forms of expression appear most obviously whenever the use of the plural subject 'we' tries to associate the listener with the speaker's declared position. In some cases, limits are set to the range of reference, yet in others it is potentially boundless, as in Straw's discussion of terrorism: 'we must never allow the carnage to breed fatalism' (Straw, 2003). The 'we' in this case is predictably the British government, perhaps the political 'class', and by extension the nation and all its sensible international associates.

Coherence in public discourse depends on the structural combination of disparate references. Security, patriotism, democracy and morality must, for instance, be presented as though 'naturally' aligned. Audiences must not only understand these references, but should if possible accept the implications of such combination; recognition must lead to the creation of positive associations between 'authoritative' expression and public values.

This position is accepted by most mainstream opposition parties, as evidenced by Simon Hughes's statement on behalf of the Liberal Democrats, when he said that 'nobody would expect ministers to reveal their information, sources and tactics' (BBC News online, 14 February 2003). This attitude persists, despite the inadequate character of explanation offered for the war in Iraq. The difference between the UK and Greece lies in the type of *authorisation* each nation was able to apply within their own borders. The Scimitar vehicles in Britain were mobilised by the executive of a sovereign state that usually manages to disguise its domestic dependence on US military power, though its subordination on the world stage is nonetheless clear. However, the arrival and installation of US missiles, and the provision of security around Athens, made the Greek state appear more clearly the client of external forces, despite public knowledge of very similar controversies within both Britain and Greece. American insistence on the use of its own security officials had already made the news in the UK during President Bush's visit in November 2003.

When this chapter described armed *demonstrations*, it first presented an unexceptional thesis, to the effect that they may serve to intimidate not just their apparent target, but in addition those who might have cast doubt on the reality of the terrorist threat. As an apparent response to a 'globalised' spread of terrorism, it may also be regarded as a calculated reaction, a way of pre-empting internal dissent or disturbance. In particular, such occurrences seemed designed to 'contextualise' the mass protest against the Iraq War. The actual existence of a specific threat was in this sense irrelevant. Although the *visibility* of armed authority within European democracies has come to be accepted, and over two hundred countries play host to US military bases, permanent military display offends liberal conceptions of 'progressive governance', notions of national sovereignty, and ideas about civic independence. This guaranteed the removal of the more obvious parts of the security apparatus. The security event had been organised and the timely materialisation of threat achieved.

SIX

The mediated event

The whole incident has stunned not just members of the emergency services but also members of the public and members of the media ... it's very difficult to keep up with the pace ... the sheer pace of these successive explosions and events ... it's going to take some time to establish ... what sequence these things happened in.

Greg Barrow (BBC News 24, 11 September 2001)

We had a trauma, but it's really not a national trauma. If you were not in New York on September 11th, what you saw was an event on CNN.

Morgan Freeman (cited in *New York Daily News*, 3 June, 2002)[1]

September 11: emergence and description

The excerpt from a news bulletin reproduced above was broadcast on 11 September 2001, approximately an hour and twenty minutes after American Airlines Flight 11 struck the North Tower of the World Trade Center (at 8.46 a.m. Eastern Standard Time). The South Tower, hit by a second aircraft just after nine in the morning, had collapsed only a few minutes before the BBC journalist went on air.[2] The remaining building was at this stage still on fire, but at 10.28 a.m., the entire structure gave way, and it too sank to the ground.[3]

Early reports suggested that the original crash had been an accident, caused perhaps by a light aircraft veering off course.[4] The second collision, however, dispelled any notion that the first had been a random event. Instead of a single, arbitrary occurrence, two separate but essentially similar acts suggested the existence of an organised plot. One eyewitness recalled a 'loud, high-pitched roar' as the second plane smashed into the South Tower, and noted that 'in just seconds, it became amazingly obvious that [this] was really an act of hostility' (Handschuh, 2002: 5). Another, who had seen the second impact, spoke to a television journalist as smoke continued to pour from the buildings: 'I don't think that would be accidental' he said (BBC News 24, 11 September 2001).[5]

Based on such evidence, it seems clear that the second strike, rather than the first, provided the 'vital information' or vantage point, from which an observer could read backwards and forwards in order to identify, or invent, patterns of cause and effect (Branigan, 1993). The second incident created a general awareness that an emergency had begun, but was also the chronological mark from which the previous impact could be understood as an (earlier) act of malevolence and, with hindsight, as the 'true' onset of the crisis.[6]

As the magnitude of the situation became clear, news organisations faced a difficult predicament: they were obliged to produce a coherent account of a complex incident, when the event itself was still in progress. This circumstance, together with the scale of the devastation and the concentration of activity within a brief period – the 'sheer pace' of 'successive explosions and events' described by the BBC journalist Greg Barrow – made it hard to establish a consistent perspective. The confusion was increased by the assault on the Pentagon and the destruction of a passenger jet in Pennsylvania, two spatially discrete and less visible episodes that seemed nonetheless to have a common origin.

Of particular significance, however, was the fact that no group had made a credible declaration of responsibility, while for their part the US authorities seemed unable to offer leadership or even reliable information.[7] Britain's ambassador, who was in Washington on the day, recalled that in the absence of hard facts 'wild rumours' began to circulate, and noted that 'no-one knew where the President was' (Meyer, 2006: 188). After making a four-paragraph statement to the media at 9.30 a.m. (Woodward, 2002: 15), George W. Bush has been whisked away in Airforce One, and would not appear again on television until 8.30 p.m.[8]

Since journalistic practice is based on the expectation that 'events must contain actors' as well as action (Bell, 1991: 169), the absence of political direction from an authorised centre, together with doubts about the exact identity of the perpetrators, increased the media's dependence on expert testimony, journalists' reports, and comments made by witnesses who had been at, or close to, the site itself. This, however, could not provide enough detail for those closest to the disaster. As a consequence, 'blogs, discussion boards [and] personal homepages' were 'transformed within hours into important resources for New Yorkers' (Matheson and Allan, 2009: 97). The invisibility of formal authority meant that narratives could be composed without the event being forced into a dominant perspective.

By the evening of 11 September, a consensus had begun to emerge: that a terrorist attack had occurred, the full consequences of which were as yet uncertain.[9] This realisation provided the narrative protocol needed to govern movement between individual incidents, so that they could be made into a *succession of episodes* within a larger story. The media had in effect identified the 'core' of the event, had separated it from both its (obscure) preparation and its ambiguous aftermath, and had selected a specific 'paradigm of description' to make sense of new evidence (Montgomery, 2005: 240). The fall of the North Tower, which came no more than an hour and three-quarters after the first impact, represented the completion of the 'dynamic' phase of a catalogue of incidents that came to be known by the numerical/temporal designation '9/11'.

The absence of authority

As an 'affective' phenomenon, '9/11' entered the consciousness of all those who had observed the process of mediation. Yet, for an occasion that was supposed to have attained worldwide notoriety, a great deal remained hidden from view. Politicians and officials seemed to be 'unavailable for comment' during the crisis (Montgomery, 2005: 246). Since journalists were only really able to refer to those actors playing an active part in the drama, the limited visibility of the country's executive elite meant that professional communicators were denied their usual opportunity to promote the hierarchical primacy of the political class. The absence of the nation's leaders also forced the media to concentrate on the role played by 'ordinary' people: firefighters, medics, rescue workers and police officers. Barrow's reference to 'members of the emergency services', 'members of the public' and 'members of the media' (Barrow, BBC News 24, 11 September 2001) is an example of this development, but also illustrates the conventional demarcation made between social roles, in which the 'public' is summoned to mind as an invariable and largely passive category.[10]

The inadequacy of official interventions may also have confirmed the suspicion that nothing could compete with the spectacle of the burning towers, in the sense that the electronic media had demonstrated the existence of a new strategic reality. The difficulty of explaining the event was based therefore on the realisation that 'America' (and by implication US state power) had suffered a massive affront. This conception proved exceptionally difficult to assimilate within the existing structures of the country's social, discursive and political order. Within mainstream US culture it was impossible to characterise the attack as a form of retaliation: it had to be an exceptional intrusion into the everyday, unexpected and undeserved. The US executive, subjected to the same existential insult as the rest of the population, went on to insist that '9/11' had 'changed everything' but was reluctant to acknowledge that the event called into question more than American invulnerability – that it might, for example, signify the revisitation of the violence upon which US power was founded. This meant that the principle that actually required change – imperial 'intervention' overseas – was reinforced while other alternatives were closed down.

Yet it was precisely the reluctance to carry out a forensic assessment of cause and effect which allowed the US executive to (over)compensate for the weakness of its initial response, and to promote the distorted narrative of Iraqi complicity.[11] Instead of placing '9/11' within an established taxonomy of criminal acts, so that those responsible could be pursued under the auspices of the legal system, the Republicans chose to pursue the rhetorically nebulous but materially deadly 'war on terror' (Graham et al., 2004), combined with enthusiastic investment in extralegal mechanisms like rendition and torture (Sands,

2005). The overall consequence of these acts, which only deepened the onset of an international crisis, was the validation of the political (terroristic) meaning of 9/11, and the rejection of an alternative view – that the incident was best handled by placing it in the more debased category of pure (though spectacular) criminality. It also contributed to the eventual rise of conspiracy theory, a form of conjecture that supplemented an official stance that at times seemed just as threadbare and irrational: the tortuous and highly suspect explanation offered for the president's absence from the centre of power on 11 September is a case in point.

Mediation, 'visibility' and the event

The assault on the World Trade Center, unaccompanied by any ideo-logical avowal, seemed to have altered the political and psychological landscape of the USA through pure activity or demonstration. The media were left to monitor the visual evidence of this material/symbolic transformation – the spectacle of the burning Towers. This sight became, according to some commentators, the paradigmatic example of a live 'global' event (Bennett, 2005), one of such importance that it was even said to have disrupted 'the whole play of history and power' (Baudrillard, 2003: 4).

The considerable moral shock produced by '9/11' is often explained as a function of its mediation.[12] Taking into account the enormity of the act – directed against a supposedly inviolable state – and the ability of broadcasters to reproduce powerful images, it is hardly surprising that the visual mediation of the day provided the starting point for discussions about its status as an event. Zelizer, for example, argued that 'the events of September 11th were shaped largely through their visual representation' (Zelizer, 2002: 50). Taken literally, this remark implies that every element of the occasion – phenomenal, practical and symbolic – had been ('largely') created by the production and circula-tion of images, suggesting that the physical collisions themselves had somehow been formed by an act of visual mediation. This claim, which emphasises the power of visual mimesis, is however less common than the near ubiquitous assertion that certain sequences (like the second impact and the final collapse) were given *unlimited* airtime.

Debrix, for example, referred to the 'endless replay of the initial visual shock', considering it to be an 'obscene visual rehash' of the original disturbance (Debrix, 2008: 3). Virilio claimed that 'the historic terrorist attack' was broadcast 'on a continuous loop on the television screens of the entire world' (Virilio, 2007: 4). Zelizer made an identical point, when she described the 'endless loop of reruns of the actual attack' (Zelizer, 2002: 50). Houen also believed that the media replayed 'endlessly the images of the planes smashing into the towers' (Houen, 2002: 1), while Gupta argued that the most potent element of the coverage was made up of the 'still and moving photographs' of the 'two aeroplanes crashing, in a sort of fatalistic silence, into the two towers' (Gupta, 2002: 13). These images, he believed, were 'replicated endlessly' in news media (13). Both Houen and Gupta were, however, mistaken on this point: only one impact featured in the initial coverage.[13]

While such an error might be excused, the substantive issue remains the pervasive interest in the pre-eminence of the image, and the hyperbolic insistence that certain pieces of footage were duplicated without end. How, then, to account for the popularity of these two phenomena (visuality and repetition), both as media techniques and as standard arguments within cultural theory? However attractive it might be to read these devices as proof of collective obsession and hysteria, the reappearance of key images was in essence an act of corroboration, an attempt to provide indisputable evidence of an event where other forms of (official) confirmation were unavailable. It was the simplest way of offsetting the *transitory* nature of the moving image. The duplication of entire reports was, of course, a technique that was much in evidence long before the evolution of this particular crisis, because it offered a cheap solution to the economic demands of 24-hour rolling news.

Ultimately, the belief that the most salient features of media systems are visuality and reiteration sets limits to the interrogation of the text. Deference to pure 'visuality' resists the standard requirement of media analysis: that reliable interpretation must consider the *development* of the (mediated) event over time. The fact that identical images or sequences were recycled does not mean that they always fulfilled the same function, or that they had the same effect, since they were embedded within larger elements, were accompanied by different forms of verbal interpretation and, crucially, appeared for (and at) different periods of time. It is important therefore to distinguish between the type of mediated impact created when the event was under way and the recorded material that would eventually form part of the historical record.

If the recorded evidence of '9/11' is considered, it provides an insight into the mundane reality of institutional practices, observed within (i) the sequential form taken by particular broadcasts, (ii) the internal transitions from one scene to another, and (iii) the actual duration of individual segments. Close study of this primary source also demonstrates, as argued above, that its presentation of visual phenomena was subject to commentary and forms of explanation. In the hands of some commentators, however, this seems to go no further than considering the 'linguistic context' of the image. Gupta, for instance, acknowledged only the weight of factors like the 'inflections of tone and delivery' used by newscasters, and the ways in which the material was given contextual meaning by 'different commentaries and reactions' (2002: 13). Debrix, though again somewhat limited, at least seems more aware of how meaning is configured, explaining the media's apparent obsession with the 'endless replay' of the visual as 'a desire to name and classify' the event (2008: 3).

On the day itself, the visual 'dominated' the surface of the electronic media, but once it had to be described and given form, a set of *provisional sentiments* and *conditional perspectives* were generated. It is not even necessary to follow the dictum that 'every description … is already a moment of some argumentative scheme' (Žižek, 1994: 11) to see that the attempt to order material and explain phenomena within a regime of mediation constitutes the news media's ideological management of various resources – linguistic, visual, auditory and so on. This procedure, built upon the practical necessities of 'presenting the facts', is certainly ideological, but not in the sense of misrepresenting a condition in order to exercise power over a bewildered class of observers: it is rather because it tries to convey the reality of existing relationships between, on the one hand, those groups able to exercise decisive authority and, on the other, those that are given just enough information to follow the terms of whatever 'debate' is played out in various media forms. It is worth repeating Poulantzas's argument (see Chapter 1) that ideology is less a 'system of ideas' than an 'ensemble of material practices' (Poulantzas, 1978b: 32/17). One of these practices is the process of *categorisation*.

Principles of analysis

Before the procedure known as categorisation can be explored, it is worth noting the importance of the different communicative forms that exist *within* a medium like television. The confluence of speech, image, caption, design, gesture and sound can be interpreted as a form of 'multi-modal' communication (Kress and van Leeuwen, 2001; Machin, 2007), an approach that examines how a 'variety of semiotic resources' are used 'to make signs in concrete social contexts' (Kress and van Leeuwen, 2001: vii). In other words, the multi-modal analyst assumes that an act of communication is an amalgam of different practices, forms and techniques, and that no mode of expression is necessarily dominant.

This insight can be applied to '9/11' and the problem of the visual. If the contention is that images of the Twin Towers became the primary instrument of representation – that is, that they were used in retrospect to express the essential significance of the event – rather than, for example, simply an attempt to reproduce its initial phenomenal impact or effect, then the question is what this 'core' meaning might include. The undoubted ubiquity of the images of the Towers as sense impressions must not obscure questions about their status as instruments of connotation. If a full and reliable interpretation of the source is desired, it must also address the distinction between phenomenal impression (the sensory experience of encountering an event or its representation), cognitive processes (the acquisition of knowledge), commentary and directive address (the attempt to organise 'attitude'), and that form of *para-emotive corporeal shock* or influence known as 'affect'.

Discursive frames

The electronic media, often accused of complicity in disseminating the essence of the terrorist 'message' (see below), were of course obeying one of their core functions: the transmission of data from an identifiable site during an emergency. Although the repeated display of the original footage may well have suggested a sense of expressive paralysis, to the extent that the entire day seemed suffused with the images recorded in New York, the point is that the visual material was actually embedded within *a gradually modified discursive frame*. In other words, it would be a mistake to characterise the reappearance of the pictures as the repetition of an *identical* form of content, because new forms of explanation were produced as the day progressed.

The root of this understandable but flawed tendency to give semantic precedence to the visual is sometimes accompanied by the closely related notion of 'instantaneous telecommunications' provided by Virilio (2007: 3). An emphasis on immediate and unfettered transmission, which concentrates on the velocity of dissemination, is allied to a belief in 'an accelerated temporality' (3). This, in turn, supposedly 'affects customs and moral standards and art every bit as much as the politics of nations' (3).

Although there is indeed a strong feeling that the apparent speed of progress alters everyday life (Scott, 2009: 80) as well as political exist-ence, the technological and generic practices of broadcasting institutions together reproduce the entrenched 'regularity' of mediated communica-tion. This means that, even under the most extreme circumstances, an effort is made to assimilate the unexpected, assigning it a place within an established constellation of significance (see categorisation, below). The theoretical model that emphasises the 'compression' of events under the discipline of a new order of time is therefore offset by the use of existing *interpretive* mechanisms, such as the hourly news review: this acts to reconfirm the stability of the social order, ensuring that events are eventually embedded within established semantic categories.[14]

The dominance of references to the visual mediation of '9/11' (de-scribed above) might be understandable, but may also have impeded the production of a more nuanced analysis. As argued above, an essential characteristic of the meanings generated within media reports is the linguistic and auditory material produced by news organisations. On 11 September, verbal commentary accompanied, and helped to shape, the 'transitory' character of the images shown. In other words, it acted as a form of interpretation, both describing what could be observed on screen and offering a rationale for the transitions that were made between different angles and scenes.

The witness, the viewer and the 'indivisible' event

The essential difference between the experience of the immediate witness and that of the distant observer is that the former will include personal, as well as mediated, determinants. The television viewer is, by comparison, presented with a series of spatial perspectives (and concomitant ideological 'angles') over which he or she has no control. In both cases, although the quality of the two types of report might differ, the referential intention of the speaker is to describe some aspect of reality. When people speak of '9/11', their allusions are based on a simple assumption: that a foundational, anterior event provided the material basis upon which any mediated narrative had to depend.

Besides the theory of 'dominant' visuality and the relative neglect of other factors in the manufacture of news, a second obstacle to understanding the character of the event is the idea that highly prominent occasions 'become more or less indivisible from their representations', especially within that form of display known as 'mass media spectacle' (Holloway, 2008: 5). Although Holloway does not claim an exact coincidence between an original phenomenon and its subsequent reproduction (qualifying his remarks with the phrase 'more or less'), he does suggest that, for all practical purposes, the actual difference between an 'original' event (where one exists) and the forms of public mediation that bring it into the discursive realm are almost indistinguishable.

At first sight, this statement appears reasonable enough. After all, the majority of those who gained a panoramic or 'objective' view of September 11th would have watched the scene on television, and would not have been present in New York on the day.[15] It is exactly this sense of distance and spectacle that was identified, albeit from a negative perspective, by Morgan Freeman, when he referred to the outsider's experience of witnessing 'an event on CNN' (see above). It would be fair to say that for most people it was a 'media phenomenon' that was actually observed.

A simple and rational distinction can, however, be made between the different types of experience involved. The first is a mode of knowledge that belongs to the direct eyewitness, the individual who sees, hears and even feels the sensation of the unmediated phenomenon itself. The second, where someone is physically present in the wider locale, but not in direct contact with the event, is sometimes conflated with the first. Freeman's statement, reprinted above, is an example of this tendency. It represents an attempt to make a distinction between the supposedly genuine perspective gained by those who were in New York on 11 September and the more remote impression created through the medium of television.

Of course, it is clear that not all of those who were actually present in the city would have been particularly close to the site itself, and that most of these individuals would have gained at least part of their experience from watching news bulletins. In some cases, proximity was irrelevant, like the young journalist who avoided going to the site and heard of the first collision on WFUV radio, and saw the second on the local television news channel New York One (Sapsford, 2002,: 332).

The third circumstance is that of the viewer who has no claim to the types of physical or moral proximity described above, and who follows a broadcast report in real time. This is not a 'pure' experience, in the sense that it often includes an unexpected encounter with recorded material. Footage of the first collapse, for example, was inserted *as a matter of urgency* by the broadcaster into the live stream, in order to update the viewer and to provide a context for the (apparently suspended) experience of the mediated present. The effect of this practice is that an 'immediate' past is briefly presented as more imperative or obdurate than the present, disturbing the linear rationale implicit in the act of on-screen narration.

The fourth condition may be described as that which prevails when the recently accomplished event is 'reviewed' on the same day, when an observer will be offered a summary based on a gradual process of rationalisation. The fifth is the experience of viewing news reports at any point following the day's occurrences. Though categorised in particular ways (see below), the significance of the episode is never settled absolutely, because new information and attitudes are brought to bear on the phenomenon concerned. In effect, some aspects of an event may remain more prominent than others.

Even those close to the event were not necessarily immune to the aura of media influence, since many of them were first alerted to the catastrophe because they saw it on television or heard it on the radio. Indeed, without the media as a resource, it would have been more difficult for individuals to coordinate their responses at the time of the attack. Many others went on to recount their stories on camera, which meant allowing their interlocutors to select and refine particular elements at the expense of others. It is even possible to argue that the visceral, subjective experience of eyewitnesses and survivors (though more immediate) will always produce a less comprehensive account than that obtained by television coverage. The *power* of mediation as 'a constitutive process in social life' (Mazzarella, 2004: 345) is therefore not in any doubt.

The *cultural primacy* of mediation in general, and of 'televisual' representation in particular, does not, however, prove that an *event* and its reformulation as a *media event* are somehow so close as to be (nearly) identical. In attempting to distinguish between the two, it is helpful to return to the definitions outlined in the Introduction. If, for the sake of argument, an event can be defined as the actualisation of a state of affairs, at a particular place and within a specific period, then it is quite natural to ask how and where an individual event (in this case, '9/11') is brought into being, and how it is possible to decide where it begins and ends. The question is therefore not only how to distinguish between different aspects of an event, but whether it is possible to think of unitary or integral events in the first place. 'September 11th' is a case in point. In common with many other news organisations, the BBC gave priority to the devastation in Lower Manhattan, which became the leading symbolic element.

The media event

For its part, the media event has been described as a kind of 'situated performance of mediated communication', which is focused on a 'specific thematic core', and which reaches 'a wide and diverse multiplicity of audiences and participants' (Hepp and Couldry, 2010: 12). This definition is also concerned with the site or place of an occurrence, and through the notion of performance seems to accommodate the notion of *dramatisation* and thus, once again, the concept of intentional behaviour.

Hepp and Couldry's characterisation of a media event could, apart from the qualification that it must include its own widespread dissemination, apply to an event in general. Dramatisation on its own simply means that there must be an original mode of expression or experience that can be presented in a striking or impressive way, or some first principle that might be exaggerated for effect. This could provide the basis for beginning to talk about the role of the media, but might equally refer to a more ordinary, small-scale process of bringing an occasion – like a party or wedding – to the attention of an intended audience. It is useful to remember that the *actualisation* of an event mentioned above depends on the social process of categorisation (see below). Categorisation is thought of as a primarily linguistic procedure (that is, it is both descriptive and inevitably ideological) that is associated with a behavioural outcome (the manifestation of a general social demeanour).

As a procedure, categorisation must now include the process of mediation, since many of the ways in which a public culture expresses its own significance emerge from the routine depictions popularised within media and 'new media' forms. The assignation of an occurrence to a particular class of phenomena suggests at the very least that some form of transformation is necessary, in order to make the original incident meaningful and to bring it into being as a fully fledged event in the realm of the social. In this sense, the role played in the contemporary world by mediation, as an institutional process with distinct procedures for making (limited) sense of the wider natural, social and virtual environments, must be recognised.

This should not, however, allow the analyst to assume that the only real – or at least more developed event – is the media event, or that the event and its mediated recomposition are the same. Many original features are lost, or smoothed out, in the transition between these two conditions. It might, on the other hand, be necessary to discriminate between the different stages through which an occurrence must pass if it is to become socially visible. For the purposes of this enquiry, these include the 'proto-event', the event and the media event (see below).

Where there is an original occurrence, mediation cannot convey the exact character of the original because complete descriptive fidelity is impossible, since there is always more to discover about a phenomenon, because the act of description is also one of recomposition, and because accurate representation is clearly not the purpose of mediation. In certain cases, of course, the media event is able to give a particular form to a phenomenon, to the extent that it can be made to appear more coherent than it might otherwise have seemed. Mediation can, therefore, create the impression that something has happened, or that something has happened in a particular way.

The advantage of maintaining a distinction between the two categories is the production of a more detailed account of how a public event is enacted and codified, first as the manifestation of an intent that anticipates its own mediation, and second as the *accomplished* product of institutional representation. There is continuity between the two stages, but they are not identical, for the following reason. Any deliberate effort that is designed to create a significant impact should first take account of the opportunities and constraints that are offered by the particular context within which the action is supposed to gain attention. What cannot be known for sure is the exact character of the *eventual* outcome.

The media institution as 'guilty party'

If it is true that intentional actions are acted out within, and are therefore shaped or configured by, established institutional structures, this must apply to those episodes, like the hijacking of aircraft, that appear to take place 'outside' the system, as much as to bureaucratic initiatives that occur within it. So, for example, the use of civil airliners to destroy the World Trade Center took advantage of a structure that had a script for dealing with a certain form of hijacking, but not a type that was not interested in using the aircraft to strike some kind of bargain.

There is no doubt that the hijackers intended their actions to be magnified and amplified through the media, and in that sense the original event was partially determined by the opportunity to exploit existing structures of communication, just as the al-Qaeda operatives took advantage of the existence of advanced technological conditions to fly the planes into the Twin Towers. The impact or significance of the attack certainly depended on the provision of a suitable vehicle and a convincing symbolic act. This means, in effect, that an event can indeed be identified with its representational form.

Clearly, there are some cases where the original event has a low degree of autonomy, or where it has been designed solely for a media environment. Yet the fusion of conditions apparent in Zelizer's perspective (see above) appears to assimilate two features of experience: the antecedent/material and the dependent/representational. The discussion of this problem should consider the notion of the *intentional* production of effects, observed in those occasions that are associated with human endeavour, rather than phenomena associated with the 'natural' world (itself partly composed by the intervention of the social). Combined with the idea of 'locale' and 'duration', the concept of intention may generate comparisons with the mediated affair into which the event is often thought to be subsumed.

A closely related conviction, stemming from the same belief in the power of rapid visual transmission and the way it is meant to overcome the senses or even judgement of the viewer, is the notion that television broadcasts have become the *practical* instrument of the insurgent. Referring to September 11th, Blondheim and Liebes make the unequivocal statement that it was 'the terrorists who set the agenda and shaped the event and, to a surprising extent, its coverage' (Blondheim and Liebes, 2003: 192). These authors go further, however, arguing that television, in 'bringing [the event] to the public, followed the terrorist's script' (192). The position of these writers is clear: that the act of *reporting* such an incident is in effect the reproduction of an opponent's agenda.

It is certainly the case that those responsible for the atrocity on the American mainland would have expected the world's media to relay and thus to amplify the event. There is also no doubt that they wished to promote their cause by setting the news agenda. They could not know, however, that the coverage would be so extensive; nor could they have anticipated the ways in which it was framed. It makes no sense to argue that the hijackers had a script in terms of a specific conception of particular effects: they had a goal, the attainment of which depended on their ability to control their immediate environment and to overcome practical obstacles. This perspective leads to the peculiar idea that television, and even the media in general, have become 'weaponised' (Hoskins and O'Loughlin, 2007: 15).

This position depends on a series of assumptions, first that 'there was little opportunity for Americans' to 'escape from the immediacy of the coverage, nor for television programming to deliver any alternative' (Hoskins and O'Loughlin, 2007: 15). This is followed by the audience's supposed 'compulsion for immediacy', and then by the penetration of the event into the human psyche, leading in turn to anxiety and then a form of 'compulsive viewing' (15). Although the impact of the occasion may indeed have produced such outcomes, their exact character would depend in large measure on the general attitude of the viewer and the nature of their exposure to the event (see above).

The mediation of emergency

While the process of mediation is to some degree a uniform practice, it is still possible, especially at times of crisis, to identify periods when a variety of standard journalistic procedures are brought into competition, contending for prominence within the same broadcast. In order to demonstrate this point, it is worth recalling that the initial *relay* or transmission of the 'proto-event' – when footage of the North Tower, shown before the second impact, made it possible to imagine that the crash had been an accident – was presented within an essentially linear, open-ended temporal frame. The disaster was the subject of contemplation, until the first sequence was superseded by the next and a more dynamic form of narrative began to emerge. As the live feed continued, it was at times intercut with recorded material, based on the need to provide updates for viewers who might have missed important episodes, like the collapse of the South Tower.

This meant that the sequential order of events was disturbed, as the competition between two conventions (the value of 'liveness' versus the urgency of review) was played out on screen in 'real' time.[16] Attempts to resolve this problem included the use of split-screen techniques, in which two separate scenes were presented to the viewer. When, for example, then prime minister Tony Blair was shown making a short statement to Britain's Trades Union Congress on the day of the attack, BBC News 24 showed him on the left of the screen, while on the right a sequence of images from New York was displayed. The Pentagon appeared once, but the depiction of the second plane hitting the South Tower was repeated no fewer than three times in a brief period.

BBC News 24 reports: orientation during the 'media event'

The potential for confusion arose from the apparent immediacy of the recorded images, which sometimes overwhelmed the ability of the journalist to keep track of their origin or status. In some cases, material that seemed at first to be live was rewound on screen, or else a particular fragment was repeated twice, revealing that it had been recorded earlier. In other examples, footage that had already been seen was broadcast with the caption 'LIVE' still superimposed. This kind of disorder was particularly noticeable when there were periods of transition between different episodes.

So the attempt by the BBC News 24 presenter to bring one of his New York correspondents into the discussion was brought to a sudden end when a 'third' explosion interrupted the exchange. This not only sabotaged the retrospective account that the news anchor was trying to elicit, but also caused doubt about the sequential order of events. The transcript that follows, chosen to demonstrate the forms of recapitulation and questioning that characterise the mainstream news report, contains a total of six sequences. It should be noted that speech is continuous throughout, and that transitions between shots are shown in square brackets with the sequential letter at the point at which each phase begins (transcript by the author):

[Sequence (a) of 1 minute, 41 seconds, showing firefighters at the Pentagon, including, at the bottom of the screen, the superimposed caption 'EXPLOSIONS IN AMERICA: Two passenger planes have crashed into the World Trade Centre in New York': the tag 'LIVE' was placed on the left of the caption. 1 minute, 22 seconds into the sequence, the studio anchor announced that he was going to speak to his New York correspondent]

(a) Presenter: In fact I can cross to Steve Evans eer (.) who was *in* the World Trade Center *in* New York when the first of the two planes hit the World Trade Center eerm… Steve (.) what was it like to be in the World Trade Center when it was hit.

Unidentified male voice in background: Oh my God

Stephen Evans: There's some (.) there's another explosion happening as we speak [voice is cut off]

[Cut to sequence (b) of nearly 12 seconds, a shot of the top of the North Tower, which appears to be a recorded piece with the caption 'BREAKING NEWS: Voice of STEPHEN EVANS New York', as the tag LIVE disappears from the screen]

(b) Presenter: We are seeing *another* explosion as we speak (1) we (1) we (1) [addressing viewers] the pictures that you're seeing now are of the World Trade Center in [cut to sequence (c), a long shot of the collapsing South Tower with the North Tower at right, with the caption 'BREAKING NEWS: Voice of STEPHEN EVANS New York' still carried at the base of the screen]

(c) Presenter: New York eerm these are *live* pictures however that we are now seeing [material from this point, 5 seconds into the sequence, is captioned LIVE, while at 9 seconds the caption 'Voice of STEPHEN EVANS New York' disappears from the screen] (.) we're now seeing *live* pictures of *another*

building exploding in New York (.)
Steve (.) I know you're at the World
Trade Center

[cut to sequence (d), a very long
distance shot of the North Tower and
skyline, correctly captioned LIVE,
lasting 7 seconds]

(d) Presenter: there have been two
explosions the:re (.) but a *third* explosion
has now taken place in New York (.)
Steve what can you see

[silence from Steve Evans as sequence
(e) of 21 seconds begins, using the same
angle as sequence (c), a long shot of the
collapsing South Tower with the North
Tower at right, and correctly captioned
LIVE]

(e) Presenter: Steve are you with us
(.) what can you see (.) in New York
[silence from Steve Evans] well we
seem to have lost erm Steve Evans in
New York we'll try and get him back
as soon as we possibly can but just to
update you (.) we now have two eer
explosions in the World Trade Center
New York we have an explosion in the
Pentagon in Washington

[cut to sequence (f), of 27 seconds,
showing the recorded collapse of the
South Tower, beginning with a close-
up of the building's fall, before drawing
back to show more of the scene, all of
which is incorrectly labelled LIVE and
is sourced from ABC News, which
has its logo at the bottom right of
the screen: after 16 seconds, an ABC
caption appears that reads 'MOMENTS

AGO: WORLD TRADE CENTER New York', followed 21 seconds into the material by the superimposition of a BBC caption that says 'EXPLOSIONS IN NEW YORK: There has been a third explosion in New York']

(f) Presenter: (.) the Pentagon has now been evacuated (.) and we're now getting pictures (.) these are live pictures that you're seeing of a *third* building in Manhattan (.) now collapsing (.) it appears after being hit (.) as well (.) that's a third (1) explosion in Manhattan (.) these are quite extraordinary scenes

Woman's voice in background: let's bring in our diplomatic editor Brian Hanrahan in your long career have you ever seen seen anything like this

Brian Hanrahan: I've I've never this is clearly a terrorist spectacular which is intended both to hurt and humiliate the United States

Unable to maintain contact with its journalist Stephen Evans (and even at one point ABC News, its primary US source), it is little wonder that the BBC anchor in London became confused by stories of a 'third explosion' in New York. This mistake was not entirely the fault of those in the studio – the misconception that a third detonation had occurred was, for instance, shared by firefighters in the North Tower. Some of these men, unable to gain access to south-facing windows, assumed as a consequence that the structural disturbance they felt, the noise they heard, and the debris they saw blown up the stairwells, were evidence of another explosion or bomb: it was, in fact, the collapse of the South Tower.

In the BBC bulletin, the Tower had fallen immediately after the studio presenter had asked 'what was it like to be in the World Trade

Center when it was hit?', and the unknown man in the background had uttered the words 'Oh my God'. The assertion that 'we're now getting pictures ... these are live pictures that you're seeing of a *third* building in Manhattan now collapsing' was made in error: the material had in fact been recorded, as ABC News stated, 'only moments ago'.

The difficulties experienced by the reporters on 11 September were not all caused by the fact that some news organisations were based in other countries, thousands of miles from the US mainland. Part of the problem lay in the ordinary expectations that they were supposed to fulfil. The standard requirement that media forms should create a chronological account of various events means that 'on-screen' time is always inevitably manipulated, even before a crisis is encountered.

During exceptional circumstances, where an emergency is declared or is still in progress, particular episodes are subject to forms of temporal distortion, suffering for example compression or extension. For instance, the worldwide recapitulation of the 9/11 attack on television news seemed in some cases to prolong its duration. One writer, for example, was convinced that the interval between the initial collision and the final collapse had actually been 'a few hours' in length (Debrix, 2008: 3).

In effect, the schedules of broadcast television seem to reinforce 'the socially accepted temporality of clock time' (Hutchings, 2008, 6), while the bulletins themselves have to obey the dictates of narrative composition. Nonetheless, the conventional view of time as 'unidirectional and irreversible' produces an account of causation in which 'cause must precede effect' (6), so that any success in establishing an intelligible *sequence* of events may then mean that simple models of cause and effect 'become a key to their explanation' (6).[17]

In a period of extreme uncertainty, the attempt to set out precise temporal and spatial boundaries, within which the incident could be analysed, offered one of the few opportunities to gauge its wider significance. In other respects, journalists were confronted with a number of challenges that made the exercise of rational judgement tremendously difficult.

The earliest coverage used relatively neutral, technical terms to describe what had happened: 'explosions' and 'attacks' exemplified the provisional character of journalistic commentary. As the day wore on, descriptions began to alter: the BBC changed its caption to 'TERROR-ISTS ATTACK AMERICA', while expert opinion began to be heard. The American politician James Rubin called it 'the biggest terrorist event in history', while the UK prime minister described it as 'a tragedy on a global scale (BBC News 24, 11 September 2001).

Text and event

If it is important to consider the textual reproduction of an event with regard to its linguistic references, as well as to its visual impact, then it is equally necessary to pay close attention to the semantic units that can be identified in the text itself (words, phrases, sentences and themes).[18] The study of such units of meaning, indeed the analysis of signs and utterance in general, is usually associated with efforts to interpret some underlying ideological position within the text: the standard assumption is that this particular form of critique looks for evidence that can undermine the apparent innocence or 'artlessness' of the textual surface. What is said or represented, and even what is elided or forgotten, is then to be compared to some – perhaps flawed – conception of an external reality.

Represented in this way, it is no wonder that the whole process has been vilified as a form of 'paranoid reading' (Grusin, 2010). More sophisticated perspectives on the purpose of ideological structures begin from rather different positions. First, and most crucially, the ideological is not regarded as a mode of general persuasion. Instead of an attempt to convince the observer that the false is real, in order to keep him or her in a state of bewilderment or ignorance about the true state of the world, ideology is seen as a mode of cohesion that helps to shape and *pronounce* the intentions of a disparate ruling elite.

Second, it is thought of as an inadequate mode of expression, not because it deliberately restricts the semantic range of utterance, thus refusing the working masses the tools of critique, but because no system can describe the fullness and extent of the real. Third, ideology is not confined to discourse, but is more firmly embedded in the organisation of the social, so that the triumph of the ideological is its reproduction, not only in the attitudes of all classes, but in the routine behaviours that confirm that each individual is indeed living in a viable reality.

Of course, these approaches to ideology still require the exercise of a certain moral decisiveness. As Porter so ably points out, the act of engaging in a critique of ideology 'presupposes an intuitive call to the real', together with a commitment to a rather difficult undertaking, the process he calls the 'evaluation of values' (Porter, 2006: 135).

Returning to the text under discussion, the first noteworthy aspect of the report is the journalist's use of the word 'incident' to describe the assault on the Twin Towers. This term might seem inadequate or inappropriate, considering the magnitude of the event and the thousands of fatalities it entailed.[19] As a technical expression, however, employed by law enforcement agencies and repeated in journalistic parlance, 'incident'[20] is often used to refer to a violent or illicit act, the exact nature of which has not yet become apparent or which, for some reason, defies classification.

Considering the scale, audacity and suddenness of the attacks,[21] the tentative character of the early phase of media representation is to be expected: the existence of uncertainty can be attributed to the universal awareness that the event had not yet reached a state of 'completion'. The reference to an 'incident' appears in this case as a provisional description of a nebulous state of affairs. In referring to 'the *whole* incident', however, it is clear that Barrow was prepared to identify a distinct episode, even as he acknowledged the difficulty of describing its exact configuration or significance.

When he noted that the attack had 'stunned' members of 'the emergency services', as well as the public and the media, he also drew attention to a fundamental characteristic of contemporary social life, one which explains a great deal about the ways in which meaning is established in the public realm. This is the distinction routinely made between organised groups of social actors, in this case between those which carry out specialist functions ('emergency workers'), those engaged in professional mediation, and all those others who, by default, must assume the largely passive role of public witness – the general population. This demonstrates the recognition by the BBC journalist of the existence of *structural demarcation*, or the actual separation of functions within the social order.[22]

Of course, there are two qualifications to make if Barrow's description is taken seriously: first, that the traumatic character of the event had confounded everyone, irrespective of status, so that a form of shock or inertia is attributed to all; and second, that a number of designated roles do not appear in this list – of most significance is the absence of any reference to the political authorities. Here, therefore, we seem to have found an interesting example of the elision referred to above in the discussion of ideology – until it is made clear that this was not the consequence of some decision taken by the news media, but a simple reflection of the fact that many members of the ruling class had gone to ground!

Barrow's declaration that it was hard to follow the 'sheer pace' of the 'successive explosions and events' not only confirms his understanding of these roles, but also acknowledges his own place in the production of meaning, by offering an explanation for his inability to present a comprehensive overview of the occasion. The failure to provide any coherent synopsis is not, quite reasonably, attributed to professional incompetence, but to the apparent velocity of the phenomena being observed, both those that were visible and audible on screen, and those that were received as verbal or written reports from other sources. As Barrow was based in Manhattan, his interlocutor in the London studio had to try to draw out more detail about the event, in order to fulfil the standard expectations held by the overhearing audience.

At this stage, although the destruction of the Twin Towers could be presented as an accomplished fact, its effects were still in evidence, and in this sense no one could be sure that the full consequences of the episode had emerged. As the reporter argued, 'it's going to take some time to establish ... what sequence these things happened in' (Barrow, BBC News 24, 11 September 2001). This demonstrates that the speaker, in depicting the temporal/spatial environment for the benefit of the studio and his wider audience, had tried to distinguish cause and effect over time, but that the sequential development to which he alluded was nonetheless uncertain.

A full appreciation of causation was therefore impossible and, by implication, entailed a major difficulty in making judgements about where distinctions should be drawn between *types* of event (see categorisation, below), though it is clear that Barrow thought that the main attack could be distinguished from its aftermath. The sequential confusion which attached to the details, however, combined with the rapid movement between live and recorded material (illustrating the sudden collapse of the South Tower), meant that the material shown could not, at times, provide a clear distinction between the 'now' of the live report and the 'then' of the very recent past.

The substantive point, however, concerns the early phase of the occasion, and how the crisis affected the media's presentation of temporal/spatial norms. It must be used to illustrate a more specific point about linguistic performance, the act of mediation and the management of crisis. This concerns the difficulty in providing the usual attributions of *cause and effect* (and the narrative sequences upon which this activity depends), when the established conception of the *social* order is called into question by an interruption in the perception of spatial and temporal reality.

Although unforeseen circumstances (whatever their origin) are bound to interrupt the routine production of meaning within hierarchical institutions, the existence of established mechanisms, practices and interpretative formulas mean that sudden developments are eventually interpreted within existing frames of meaning. In effect, therefore, events are *received* by a structure that uses technical and narrative solutions to reproduce social parables. An event may be presented, for example, within the paradigm of 'breaking news', while 24-hour rolling programmes are able to regulate stories (and reduce costs) through the convention of 'updating' information: where no obvious crisis is in evidence, this means the repetition of self-contained segments.

In the case of 9/11, the diffusion and propagation of ideas – the extent to which particular discourses or perspectives could be circulated within the public realm – depended on finding a plausible explanation for the event, which seemed at first to defy explanation. Although the attack came quite literally from 'a clear blue sky' (Parsons, 20 September 2001), it also emerged from 'nowhere' in the sense that it revealed a massive hinterland of political ignorance. The expansion of the event was guaranteed by its distinctiveness, scale, malevolence, visual impact and mediated reproduction. While the whole affair was still 'in play', television news had to try to follow the only normative condition that offered a chance of composing a coherent narrative – the linear progress of the destruction itself.

In effect, a particularly significant occasion of malignant but uncertain origin, or that which appears to extend its development beyond the narrative capacity of an established structure – remaining, for instance, 'incomplete' or unexplained at the next scheduled point of analysis – proved that television organisations can do no more than monitor the evidence they have, until the occasion can be said to have ended, and/or until a convincing reason can be provided for its occurrence, at which time the process of classification can begin.

From duration to category

The analysis of sequential markers and estimates of duration is an important part of the analysis of events (see below), but it cannot supply a full account of meaning. There are other issues to consider when a highly visible public occurrence is studied. Whereas a full understanding of textual material must depend on the analysis of all those elements that act as co-determinants of meaning, which would include a study of source (or origin), content, form (or mode of expression), purpose (or intention), discourse, context and reception (or resonance), the interpretation of public events must also include reference to category, setting, participants, duration and effect.[23] The purpose of this form of enquiry is therefore to understand the deliberate production of *social* impact through the mechanisms of representation as a form of governance. The next step is to attend to the attribution of specific qualities to an occasion, and the existence of contextual features that help to determine its assignation to a particular category (or, perhaps, the imposition of a category on the occasion).

The basis of mediation: categories

In the meantime, it is clear that, even with the best will in the world, the classification of any event is bound to entail problems. This is because the process of categorisation is essentially one in which an object or event is 'placed in a network of hypothetical inference' based on its 'observable properties [and] effects' (Bruner, 1957: 126, cited in Oakes et al., 1994: 108). The point here is that the observer can use a variety of hypotheses, depending on a host of subjective factors, to decide how to characterise the stimulus under consideration.

The decision that an event like 9/11 was an act of terrorism may seem self-evident, but only because other possibilities (that it was primarily an act of criminality or an act of war that used 'terroristic' methods) were excluded. Although the process of classification must depend to some extent on the use of normative inferences (suggesting an almost unconscious procedure), the act of placing an event or practice within a particular class of phenomena can sometimes be more deliberate.

Take, for example, the politician's habit of distinguishing between 'front line' services and 'back room' support. This may well be an established distinction, but its significance alters considerably when it is used to justify spending cuts: at that point, the dividing line between the two categories can be shifted. The external manifestation of a particular quality is not, therefore, always used to meet the *inflexible* categorical expectations of human collectives. Certain attributes can be selected in order to fulfil the timely or dynamic requirements of powerful social actors.[24]

This does not mean that an observer can 'perceive similarities and differences that do not exist' (Oakes et al., 2004: 112), but it does suggest that a certain emphasis can be placed on those who do. This leads, in turn, to an important question: how, by whom and for what purposes is this form of *discretion* exercised? The creation of categories of 'belonging' by authoritative groups suggests that events are not merely described and then placed in an appropriate class, but that they are also 'authenticated' or *sanctioned* as they are brought into established linguistic frames and social practices. In effect, influential actors establish a hierarchy of value, so that enhanced meanings, whether negative or positive, are easier to assign to any other manifestations that can be said to belong to the subject concerned.

Linguistic concepts are thus subjected to a type of procedural standardisation, which helps to disseminate meaning and ensures their subsequent use in the reproduction of the broad social themes that circulate in the public realm. A major feature of this process – the selection and representation of symbolic or *emblematic* events – is therefore their deliberate association with particular values.

This is of course a normative procedure, and represents a form of ideological[25] integration: the linguistic division between acts of war and acts of terror carries with it a host of conventional assumptions. This reference to ideology should not suggest that events, or their representational signs, must necessarily become the explicit instruments of a specific cabal or world-view, but rather that the application of major descriptive categories (war, terror, democracy) to specific incidents or conditions can be traced to the utterances and activities of powerful social actors (Montgomery, 2005; Price, 2010).

'9/11', Abu Ghraib and 'affect'

Language, as argued above, is not the only element that requires analysis. Some explanations for the reuse of the most familiar *visual* tropes suggest that it attests to the institutional existence of a disorder, in which the media are so concerned to capture the sensational nature of epoch-changing events that they became complicit with the agenda set by the insurgent. Although the hijackers certainly intended to take advantage of the power of mediation to relay their activity to a world audience, the notion that this proves media collusion is oversimplified. Rather than assume that the media fell into the trap of reproducing a terrorist 'script' (which makes news organisations into scapegoats), or argue that the hijackers took advantage of the West's 'openness' (which takes neoliberal propaganda at face value), it would be more accurate to state that al-Qaeda played into the West's obsessive narrativisation of its own democratic grandeur, which depends on the media to reproduce at least the main precepts of the notion.

This process of representation must be 'open' in the sense that the mainstream or traditional media must be ready to receive and then relay any of those standard narratives that celebrate the normal operation of the (patriarchal) class system. The attack in New York took advantage of a principle of communication, while refusing to distinguish between the division of 'civilian' and 'military' functions so essential to the maintenance of the proposition that the Western social order is an armed democracy rather than an integrated imperial system.

There is little doubt that the recapitulation of the original visual transmissions of the disaster continue to ensure that 'the historical event of 9/11' makes itself 'felt in the present' (Grusin, 2010: 8). It would, however, be impossible to know how the mediated event was actually configured during its exposition without some reference to its concrete, momentary development. One way of answering this question is to ask what kind of *impression* these excerpts might have created when they first appeared in the course of a linear narrative exposition. This approach, pursued in detail below, takes into account what Grusin, in a discussion of the Abu Ghraib photographs of 2004, calls the 'non-discursive or pre-discursive affective intensity' of certain types of image (71). This formulation draws attention to one of the most significant aspects of mediated communication: the reproduction of an impact that cannot be measured in simple cognitive or representational terms.

There are significant differences between the televised, sequential depiction of '9/11' as an event and the digital reproduction of scenes of torture from the US facility in Iraq, which offered a number of separate visual positions from which a sense of the overall story could be extruded. The sense of chronological development and reappraisal that belongs to the televised spectacle of '9/11' is absent from the Abu Ghraib pictures, which resemble objects of private contemplation set in a public context. The major difference, according to Grusin, is found therefore in the *form* of their mediation.

Grusin contends that the Abu Ghraib pictures were regarded as shocking because they were first encountered '*affectively* within our everyday media practices' (2010: 83; my emphasis). That is to say, they were integrated and circulated within 'our everyday unconscious use of technology' (72), so that they ran parallel with standard, near automatic practices that allow someone to take a picture of family or friends and post that material on a file-sharing website. The question as to whether such activity is really unconscious, or whether this condition is nominated because it sits more easily with the concept of 'affect', is a matter for debate, but the consequence of this form of circulation, Grusin believes, is that routine media behaviour becomes continuous with 'the violence of empire, or of torture' (72).

Although Grusin describes the television coverage of September 11th as a combination of mediation (the use of what he calls the CNN 'collage' to contextualise the image) and the erasure of mediation (the use of extreme close-ups of the burning Towers), it is also possible that the experience of watching the events of '9/11' unfold may have resembled the shock attributed to the Abu Ghraib images, at least in one respect. This is its relationship to the expectation that the observer will engage in a *routine* affiliation with media forms.

Although the media event known as '9/11', at least at the time of its first appearance, represented an *intrusion* into the 'everyday unconscious use of technology' (Grusin, 2010: 72) – rather than the 'perversion' of ordinary practices associated with the torture photographs – it nonetheless compelled its audience to pay attention to an uncomfortable use of a medium that was usually employed to monitor (and at times to exemplify) the moral norms of the capitalist social order. The point is that the (visual) coverage of the '9/11' attacks was not truly *informative* because it was unable to reproduce the usual cautionary tales, such as the undesirability of crime, the benefits of consumerism, and so on. Instead, it was used as a mode of authentication – what was 'beyond belief' had to be shown repeatedly (and thus felt or experienced) before it could be categorised.

SEVEN

'Real world' security: neglect, incompetence and the overproduction of force

> Migrants, caught up in and driven by the globalized sweep of late capitalism, seek to become members of risk society ... but ... pay the price of such risk with the currency most available to them ... that of their bodies and even their lives.
>
> Parvati Nair (2006: 67)

> Three hundred of the Arkansas National Guard have landed in the city of New Orleans. These troops are fresh back from Iraq, well-trained, experienced, battle tested and under my orders to restore order on the streets ... they are locked and loaded [and] know how to shoot and kill and they are more than willing to do so if necessary and I expect that they will.
>
> Kathleen Babineaux Blanco, 2 September 2005
> (cited in Flaherty, 2007)

> Is this 'real world' or an exercise?
>
> Military officer in *United 93* (dir. Paul Greengrass, 2006)

An assessment of the role played by 'scenario planning' in the creation of auxiliary security institutions cannot be achieved unless some comparison is made between, on the one hand, the protocols and public announcements generated by official institutions and, on the other, the actual responses that are produced during a state of emergency. The various manifestations of planned security activity – the *scenario*, the *exercise* and the *security event* – can be contrasted with phenomena initiated or monopolised by entities that are not primarily controlled by the state. One example is the *media event*, used here to indicate an occasion that is not simply 'mediated' but engineered by the media, in contrast to the definition offered by Dayan and Katz, which identifies the existence of some form of national festivity or celebration, relayed to an audience by electronic means.

The reason that '9/11' has assumed such notoriety in the minds of politicians is not just because of its magnitude, nor because it represents the failure of intelligence agencies, but because two non-state institutional forces – al-Qaeda and the media – took the initiative. Thrown into shock by September 11th, the security apparatus has tried to achieve two aims: to reconstruct its standing with its various publics, and to vent its frustration at being unable to strike at its most dangerous enemies. The first of the two case studies presented in this chapter reveals the difference between the rhetoric of security and its practical application – the disaster that struck New Orleans in 2004. The second is an extended account of the Stockwell shooting, which took place in London in 2005.

The US state and Hurricane Katrina

Three members of an organisation called Common Ground Relief – which, in the wake of Hurricane Katrina, provided material support to the beleaguered residents of New Orleans – described the post-disaster condition of the city as the 'collapse of government structure at all levels, save for the military' (Hildebrand et al., 2007: 87). They also claimed that 'there were few plans for a catastrophe of this magnitude, *even though this scenario was predicted years ago*' (87; my emphasis). If this is true, then it brings into focus the question posed above – the extent to which the scenario is really intended to assist civil resilience and recovery, rather than to reinforce the growth of a parallel power structure. Examples of these 'new' security structures have, in fact, been described in some detail in relation to earlier events.

In Los Angeles in 1996, for instance, a Terrorism Early Warning Group (TEW) was founded, based on the creation of 'a networked approach to intelligence fusion' (Sullivan and Wirtz, 2008: 14). Its purpose in providing this facility was to identify the 'globally distributed threats', based on both local police intelligence and information drawn from national sources (15). The security operative's abiding interest in approaches that are meant to be creative and decentred explains the familiar animation of the 'network', but the TEW also claimed to have adopted a cell structure. 'The Los Angeles TEW was organised in six cells', Sullivan and Wirtz revealed, with an officer in charge leading or serving as the 'Command' cell (15).

There was in addition a 'Consequence Management' cell devoted to the assessment of the various consequences that might arise from 'an actual or predicted event'; an 'Analysis/Synthesis' cell that dealt with 'net assessments of known threats' and 'security precautions'; an 'Investigative Liaison' cell that acted as the link to the external 'counter-terrorist network'; an 'Epidemiological Intelligence' cell, responsible for monitoring any possible outbreaks of disease; and, finally, a 'Forensic Intelligence Support' cell that exploited 'a range of technical capabilities' (Sullivan and Wirtz, 2008: 15).

The expertise required to maintain these kinds of services can exist within the ranks of private enterprises, but the mobilisation of this provision is usually only effective when used in partnership with public facilities, and is always motivated by the desire to secure and develop the potentially profitable parts of the existing infrastructure. It is this acquisitiveness that leads to the perception that some elements of the patriarchal-capitalist system actually welcome not only the 'scorched-earth' form of accumulation described by Klein in 2007, but also any opportunity to maximise their position provided by 'natural disasters' like Katrina.

So, for example, it is particularly instructive to find that some analysts regard the destruction of the levees as anything but a natural occurrence, and even more interesting to discover that they focus on exactly the *predictive* ability of 'state and corporate' interests – the power to make forecasts that are routinely represented as generally *beneficial* – as the means of ensuring that the welfare of the majority is ignored (Sexton, 2007: 125).

Sexton draws attention to this aspect of capitalist 'futurology' when he accuses the authorities and their private partners of 'looking forward' to 'capitalising on a moment of predatory opportunity'; of greater significance, however, is his assertion that they depended on the clear '*foreknowledge* of impending destruction' of New Orleans (Sexton, 2007: 125–6; my emphasis). While it might seem odd to assert the existence of a genuinely predictive capacity (apart from the uncertain prescience created by the spatial oversight of weather systems), the virtue of Sexton's position is that it led him to argue that 'it is entirely unreasonable' to accuse the authorities of 'failure, an unduly delayed response, official negligence, or even government malfeasance' (126).

This was not because local and national state organisations were free from guilt, but because they were caught up in the throes of their own 'expectancy', defined by Sexton as 'waiting for the execution of a disaster that was not only predicted, but whose probability was also actively produced' by the racist segregation and the production of ghettoes (Sexton, 2007: 126). This provides support for the belief, pointed out above, that the types of forward-planning espoused by corporate power and the security state should be treated as attempts to create conditions favourable to their own long-term plans.

In the case of Katrina and the New Orleans disaster, the intervention of bodies like Common Ground Relief provided an example of an initiative that acted without official sanction. Common Ground was also notable for having turned the precepts of emergency planning upside down. Whereas the head of the government's FEMA operation declared that 'it's important that volunteer response is co-ordinated by the professionals' (Brown, cited by Hilderbrand, 2007: 91), one relief worker explained why he took an opposing view. He had, he said, attended 'emergency response trainings', in which he had been taught 'never to self-deploy' to the site of a disaster, or to act on his own initiative, 'without orders from the established chain of command' (Benham, 2007: 76). This lesson was emphasised on the basis that 'self-deployed first responders' were meant to 'endanger survivors and hinder relief' (76). The actual experience of this individual seemed, in fact, to illustrate the opposite case – that it was the official response that was inadequate, and the improvised contributions that were more worthwhile.

Some elements of the New Orleans population were, moreover, under direct threat not only from the Hurricane, but from the forces of 'law and order' that were mobilised to deal with its aftermath. This was a complaint expressed by the author Michael Dyson in 2006, when he described 'the repetition of scenes of black "looting"' that were 'endlessly looped' on television, essentially because there was not enough film of these offences to provide a variety of images (Dyson, 2006: 166). A similar point was made by Rebecca Solnit two years later, in an article on the legacy of the storm. She accused the mainstream media of promoting the idea that 'marauding hordes' of looters and other malefactors were running wild in the city (Solnit, 26 August 2008: 28). She also repeated the experiences of two stranded paramedics who, with other displaced people, approached the Crescent City Connection bridge and found that, 'before we were close enough to speak', sheriffs from the Gretna district discharged their firearms above the heads of the crowd (28).

The incident that received most publicity, however, was the occasion when New Orleans police opened fire on six civilians who were attempting to cross the Danziger Bridge to contact relatives and buy food. Two individuals were killed and four others wounded. The officers involved were eventually brought to trial in July 2010, after an earlier case against them had collapsed (Usborne, 15 July 2010: 4–5). The community had spent five years trying to get the case investigated, but under the Republican government no progress had been made: it was not until the change in the US administration that the investigation of these 'premeditated, murderous acts' (*Washington*, 15 July 2010: 5) was brought to fruition.

The mediation of 'terror': Stockwell, Operation 'Kratos' and public security

If, as argued above, the real question is not how authoritarian intervention is explained by the authorities, accompanied by the standard improvisations associated with the emergency exercise, but (i) how the security apparatus behaves in a 'real world' situation, and (ii) how this conduct is mediated for audiences, then some point of comparison must be chosen. The bulk of this chapter is therefore devoted to a study of the material generated by the British press in the immediate aftermath of the Stockwell shooting (22 July 2005), in which the Brazilian electrician Jean Charles de Menezes was killed by armed assailants officially identified as Metropolitan Police officers.[1]

The Stockwell incident provides an insight into a number of themes, or categories of meaning, which can be applied to the general activity of the security regime, and to its mediated appearance in public life, including: the perennial question of the 'balance' between security and civil liberty; the subjective positioning of readers/spectators as moral participants in the 'dilemma' faced by security operatives (in this case armed officers, rather than civilian witnesses or victims[2]); the production of mediated conceptions of identity and citizenship; the conflation of terrorism, immigration and asylum in some sections of the press; and finally the characterisation of an individual death as either a tragedy[3] or a regrettable necessity, within a more extended discourse of guilt and innocence (Price, 2010: 107).[4]

Armed police intervention can be examined within the context of other authoritarian measures, all of which are ostensibly designed to reinforce public security. The position outlined in this chapter is that current state policy in the West does not emerge solely from the conviction that new tactics are required to meet an enhanced threat from, for example, terrorism. Contemporary procedures like the UK's Operation Kratos[5] (which includes the authorisation to shoot 'suspected suicide bombers'[6]) have clear historical precedents in counter-insurgency operations, and also provide evidence of a more ambitious agenda. This is the determination, among some elements of the 'security state', to secure a much greater paramilitary capability than currently exists.

This power may then be deployed in circumstances that might well fall short of the 'crisis paradigm' disseminated by official sources, but, in an attempt to justify the extension of coercive force, the narrative of public emergency can nonetheless be repeated by politicians and security officials, and then replicated further within media forms. In propagating a 'worst case' scenario, Britain's political executive has refined (through trial and error) a number of techniques that represent not so much an open 'war' against its own citizens (Bull, 2006), but rather the secretive *overproduction* of repressive capacity. When this power is applied to real situations, the result is the kind of outcome characteristic of the Stockwell shooting of July 2005, and also evident to some degree in the apprehension of the fugitive Raoul Moat who died, apparently by his own hand, five years later, in July 2010.

A particular concern of this chapter is the behaviour of the mainstream media – specifically the British press – in covering the events that led up to the death of Jean Charles de Menezes. The first point to note is the appearance of a number of largely 'defensive' themes in the pages of various newspapers. A theme is understood as a substantial aggregation of subject matter (Price, 2007), while the defensiveness lies in the tendency to produce articles based on an attempt to reduce the damage done to the reputation of the authorities by, for example, questioning the innocence of the victim or emphasising the predicament in which the firearms officers were placed.

Much of the mediated narrative material generated in the press served only to obscure the essential question that the killing of Jean Charles de Menezes should have raised: the degree to which it represented both a dangerous concentration of lethal force and the *strategic* diffusion of responsibility (Price, 2010: 183). In its first acknowledged appearance, the procedures mobilised under the aegis of 'Kratos' (the policy that governed the shooting of suspects at this time) were characterised by breakdowns in communication; yet this very confusion may have allowed senior commanders, surveillance personnel and firearms officers to act with impunity. They were in effect protected by the 'catalogue of errors' referred to in the Independent Police Complaints Commission report, so that no single individual could be charged with a crime.[7] The operatives on the ground were further protected by anonymity, a condition that remained in place during the inquest held in 2008. Such protection, which has since been used to conceal the identity of officers in subsequent cases, has produced vocal opposition in sections of the press otherwise known for their support of the police (see, for instance, the *Mail* newspaper group reports produced by Leake et al., 26 September 2010: 24–5; and Graef, 23 September 2010: 14).

Press confusion and docility during the initial period of the Stockwell crisis may be attributed to the existence of a number of structural factors. These include media reliance on authoritative sources, the use of pre-existing frames of reference in an attempt to categorise unfolding events, and the nature of crisis communications during a period of *mediated* vigilance. The difficulty faced by senior journalists and editors was how to modify their initial perspectives, which expressed no substantial reservations about the shooting, while maintaining their broad support for both the police and a 'shoot to kill' policy.[8] This challenge, I would argue, was met (at least in discursive terms) by drawing attention to the 'exceptional' nature of the event. The reports that emerged in the days following the death represented an uncomfortable reformulation of the earliest media responses.

Framing the event: authority and utterance

Just after 3.45 p.m. on the day of the Stockwell shooting, Sir Ian Blair, the Metropolitan Police commissioner, announced that the death of a suspect had been directly linked to the 'ongoing and expanding anti-terrorist operation', and provided a brief rationale for the use of firearms. The incident was indeed related to the hunt for the failed bombers of 21 July, in the sense that it was one by-product of the investigation, but the suggestion seemed to be that the dead man was implicated in the attempt to detonate explosive devices. Press reports, however, did not examine this issue; instead, they carried excerpts from the official announcement, and gave a reasonably faithful account of the terms used.

If, however, journalists had examined the police version of the original source, they would have discovered a discrepancy between the account given by the commissioner and their own stories. So, for example, the *Financial Times* online of 22 July 2005, BBC News online of 22 July, the *Sun* of 23 July and *The Sunday Times* of 24 July all reproduced Blair's explanation for the killing. According to these sources, the commissioner had declared that the suspect had 'refused to obey police', 'refused to obey instructions', or more fully 'refused to obey police instructions'. Yet, according to the police website (www. police.uk/content), Blair had said no more than the victim had been 'challenged and refused to obey'.[9]

This seemingly trivial difference between the terms used raises an important question: had police excised the last one or two words because they wished to play down their own responsibility, and had they done so in order to obscure the fact that no 'police instructions' had been issued before the shots were fired? Even in the case of the truncated version, it seemed clear that an individual had been shot dead because he had failed to comply with an order, not necessarily because he was about to carry out a violent act.[10] This interpretation was not suggested within the newspaper reports that followed.[11]

The answer to this puzzle may lie in material that was not initially accessible. The minutes of the Metropolitan Police Authority of 21 March 2002[12] reveal that officers had two options for stopping suspected suicide bombers, described as follows: 'if 100% sure head Shot', and 'if not sure, challenge from a position of safety'. There is the possibility here that the first option does not require the officer to issue any challenge. It is this kind of information that suggests that the use of the Kratos 'technique' should not be regarded as an unfortunate mistake.

In 2002, the police had argued that a resort to extreme measures was unlikely, while describing the 'very positive action' that might be needed to stop a suicide bomber (Metropolitan Police Authority minutes, 21 March 2002). They also noted that 'any officer involved in the implementation of these tactics will be subject to full and proper scrutiny and investigation' and finished the paragraph by stating that 'we [the police] are not above the law' (Metropolitan Police Authority minutes, 21 March 2002). Evidence from Tube passengers who witnessed the Stockwell shooting three years later – provided during the 2008 inquest – ran counter to official claims that a challenge had been issued: they had heard no shout of 'armed police' before officers opened fire.[13] Such an utterance, it is worth noting, does not actually represent an order, the neglect of which could justify firing a weapon. In fact, one officer claimed that he had only shouted 'armed police' once he had decided to shoot de Menezes.[14]

During the initial phase of media coverage, the dependence on available police sources was hardly surprising, since the credibility of any public remark is not based simply on content, but depends to a large extent on its source,[15] the status of the speakers, and the setting in which it appears.[16] The inability of journalists to contest Blair's utterance lay partly in their predetermined role as subordinate elements in a hierarchical structure, so that the overall relationship between news media and authoritative sources can be characterised as one of press dependence.

In other words, the role of journalists was to act as conduits for information. It is also clear that, in ordinary circumstances, journalists already rely on the police as 'primary definers' for many of the 'crime news stories' they receive (Franklin et al., 2005: 248, after Harcup, 2004).[17] In addition, media workers are forced to recognise the dual character of the authority invested in the police, where authority is both the place of origin for a particular policy or enterprise and the 'right' of an established power to expect or enforce compliance (Watt, 1982: 11).

The Metropolitan Police may be acknowledged not only as a repository of certain forms of legal knowledge, but also as an essential element of the state's 'preponderance of force' (Gill, 2003: 5). Its personnel make up one part of the state's 'administrative staff', which is trained to uphold 'the claims to the *monopoly* of the legitimate use of physical force in the enforcement of its order' (Weber, 1978a, cited in Pierson, 1996: 7). The police appear therefore as both administrators and enforcers of the social order.[18] It is this concentration of powers that helps to explain, for example, the existence of the Independent Police Complaints Commission, and that reflects the anxiety of the IPCC to 'increase confidence in the police complaints system'.[19] The authoritative institutional position of the police also calls for other forms of accountability, meaning that the Metropolitan Police Authority is designed to provide a bureaucratic overview of police work, though it is clear from the Authority's minutes that the members were kept in the dark about certain developments.[20]

From an official perspective, *public* statements like the one issued by Blair are not meant to be definitive or even entirely truthful. They are conceived instead as holding operations, intended to fulfil formal requirements, offering no more than is strictly necessary. The 'safest' declaration, considering its inevitable reproduction within larger mediated narratives, is one that avoids complexity. The earliest police announcement, following the principle of simplicity, was indeed relatively straightforward,[21] but the tendency to produce forms of explanation was already in evidence, providing the first indication that official sources were attempting to justify the actions of armed police and their commanders.

In many of the early reports, critical perspectives were subsumed in the rush to produce formulaic observations, based on the reanimation of *established* themes.[22] Harris, in the *Daily Mail*, is a good example; he reproduced the misleading perspective that the *victim* was 'linked to last Thursday's London bombings' (Harris, 23 July 2005). Even in the simplest of processes, it is therefore possible to observe the use of 'framing' devices in the presentation of experience, where framing is the process of selecting 'some aspects of a perceived reality', which are then made 'more salient in a communicative text' in order to promote a particular point of view or perspective (Simons, 2006: 2, after Entman, 1993, 52). The *Daily Mail* journalist had not of course invented the rather subtle distinction suggested in Blair's remarks, but had simply made it explicit.

The initial statement had encouraged the assumption that the link between the shooting and the investigation was substantial and legitimate. Ian Blair had achieved this outcome through the power of *implicature*, the practice of creating meanings through suggestion or implication rather than literal forms of description (Grice, 1989). His statement may be seen as the generation of an appropriate *alibi* for timely purposes.[23] This cover story addressed the general conception of 'terrorist'[24] activity, and played on assumptions about the conduct expected from a police officer. Reinforcing these notions was not, however, ultimately helpful to the authorities, because they include the expectation that a suspect is supposed to be made aware that he or she is facing *armed* officers. The claims made by the commissioner were only plausible because his listeners remained in ignorance of two essential factors: (i) a change in police tactics, which had already moved to a 'shoot to kill' policy under Operation Kratos (see below) and (ii), the actual circumstances of the shooting, in which no challenge was given and no disobedience offered.[25]

Surveillance and 'shoot to kill'

When Mann expressed the conviction that the executive leaderships of the 'capitalist democracies' may suffer from dishonesty and corruption, but do not 'brazenly expropriate or kill [their] enemies' or 'dare to overturn legal traditions' (Mann, cited in Brenner et al., 2003: 55), it was probably difficult to anticipate the exact extent of current practice, which includes 'extraordinary rendition' (Rejali, 2007: 504) and the growth of the philosophy of military 'pre-emption'. In the wake of the attacks carried out on 11 September 2001, the demand for a tougher attitude to terrorist conspiracy was not entirely new, but did revive a number of dormant or hidden practices.

Although '9/11' is cited as the origin of much 'anti-terror' activity, precedents may be found in the growth of 'low intensity' conflicts fought by colonial powers after World War II.[26] The nascence of post-Second World War coercive authority, together with the increasing predominance of the secret state, may be traced back to British and American plans to control the development of European nations after the defeat of Nazism (Ganser, 2005). The CIA and MI6 were the 'executive agents' behind the creation of clandestine networks of armed groups that eventually 'fought a secret war against the forces of the left' (Ganser, 2005: 2). In some cases, the construction of a 'national security state' would lead to the imprisonment and maltreatment of a generation of radicals, socialists and trade-union cadres, in which the existence of armed conflict and 'terrorism' was used as an excuse for outright repression of all internal opposition.[27]

In Britain, increasing preference for a 'shoot to kill' policy was supposedly based on the simple perception that 'significant gaps' existed in the state's mobilisation against 'suicide bombing delivered by a person' (*Panorama*, 'Stockwell: countdown to killing', 8 March 2006). In examining this rationale, my point is not that such a conviction was completely unfounded but that, in common with all forms of structural change, a particular aspect of existing circumstance is selected as the justification for a more general transformation in policy.[28] The adoption of the 'suicide' rationale, we are told, led to the creation of Operation Kratos. In his book *Shoot to Kill*, a study of the police use of firearms, Punch notes that Kratos existed in parallel with another protocol called Clydesdale, which was based on a scenario where advance intelligence of an imminent bombing had been received; he also argues that, with Kratos, in particular, a 'fundamental shift' in police firearms policy had taken place. If a sea change had occurred it is still the case that, as with other responses to specific threats, precedents had long been established.[29]

The reality of such encounters does not, however, correspond to the conditions set out by security chiefs and military planners. So, when evidence has emerged at inquiries and inquests that particular killings have been unorthodox (such as the execution of wounded suspects), then the narratives composed *after the fact* by operatives are adjusted to match the range of activity which might be deemed reasonable in the circumstances. This often includes descriptions of suspects making movements that led the operatives to believe that the insurgents were about to fire guns or detonate bombs (Urban, 1992: 183). A similar example of this tendency was revealed during the 2008 inquest, when one of the officers said he had been convinced that de Menezes was a suicide bomber because the suspect had walked towards him.[30]

In the case of Operation Kratos, Barbara Wilding, currently chief constable of the South Wales police, was chosen to lead the 'Suicide Bomber Working Party', and was part of a group which travelled to Israel to learn how the Israeli Defence Force and police dealt with individuals engaged in 'spontaneous suicide attacks' (*Panorama*, 8 March 2006). The application of Israeli methods to the British context may appear surprising, but was presented as a necessary adjustment made in order to meet a special and extraordinary circumstance. The point, however, is that the British security state was in the process of refining techniques already established in armed confrontation with nationalist opponents in 'colonial' territories. Yet, in adopting the behaviours of a client power which is 'internally' *mobilised for war* and which is prepared to make aggressive incursions into the territory of deliberately subordinated enemies, the possibility of occasional episodes of armed 'response' being directed against certain ethnic minorities within the British population cannot be entirely discounted.

A sense of unease with this extraordinary condition emerges in even the right-wing press. The *Mail* journalist Paul Harris began his story by noting that 'it [Stockwell Tube Station] might seem an unlikely front line in Britain's war against terror', with people caught up in 'the kind of drama more normally seen in the Middle East' (Harris, 23 July 2005). Here, the 'drama' of terrorism, supposedly belonging to a distant sphere of conflict, is brought into the realm of current realities 'in full view of terrified passengers'. The emphasis placed on the visual corroboration of the shooting through the testimony of eyewitnesses confirms the relocation of the event within an urban and *British* setting. The vague invocation of the 'appropriate' location for terrorism (a generalised 'Middle East') may remind the reader, though perhaps it does so un-intentionally, that the root causes of violent dissent lie in unresolved social, political and religious conditions, exacerbated by the inability of 'the West' to mediate in an unequal struggle between opposing powers. Harris's remarks represent the shadowy existence of important historical issues – issues that should be made more explicit if they are to produce an understanding of 'anti-terrorist' actions undertaken by the state.

Although the actual confrontation with suicide bombers in the UK and Israel may appear identical, the different political conditions that exist within the two nations suggest that the implementation of Kratos may entail the growth of paramilitary capability.[31] The immediate consequence of the new policy was that pre-emptive killing became a *general principle*; and, once this was established, the *interpretation* of circumstances could itself produce the emergency leading to the application of 'shoot to kill'.[32] In this sense, the Stockwell incident represented the inevitable execution of policy in a real-life scenario, a 'dry run' which could be interpreted as a demonstration of its power. The situation envisaged in planning exercises, the instant incapacitation of a bomber by delivering shots to the head, set up the possibility of an application of force in similar conditions. Once the rules of engagement had been set, the initiation of the action proved difficult to control. Officers were given operational autonomy, and were protected by the diffusion of responsibility (see above) that meant neither those directing the operation nor those firing the shots could be held accountable.

Suicide bombing had, therefore, provided the rationale for the creation of a structure that favoured a *pre-emptive* act: based on the discretion of an individual acting in an 'emergency', this created the opportunity to execute suspects if enough of the necessary conditions could be argued *in retrospect* to have existed at the time of the incident, just as alibis were assembled in Northern Ireland (Urban, 1992). The fact that the Stockwell killing was shown subsequently not to have fulfilled the required criteria could not have compelled the security state to reconsider the use of a 'shoot to kill' policy. In fact, calling the incident 'a mistake' was in effect to argue that the procedure itself was justified, and simply needed a more suitable target to fulfil its true potential.

Surveillance and mediation

The genesis of the whole process was the *identification* by police of four men thought responsible for a series of attempts to detonate explosive devices on the London transport system on 21 July 2005. This helped establish the immediate circumstances in which Jean Charles de Menezes was killed.[33] The circulation of suspects' images within print and electronic media, accompanied by the production of official posters appealing for information, was based on CCTV pictures[34] released by the Metropolitan Police on 22 July 2005. The perception that their targets could be assigned to a particular ethnic group was one of the reasons why some, though not all, officers classified de Menezes as a possible terrorist.[35]

The provision of the CCTV images allowed newspapers to carry their own reproductions, which in some cases included additional captions giving details of suspects' clothing and subsequent movements. This represents a clear move from the use of image as mere illustration to a form of generic representation; this, in turn, suggested a general consensus that the press should help apprehend the individuals concerned. The *Guardian* of 23 July, for example, printed such information on its front page, under the headline 'Faces of the suspects', while the *Independent* of the same date devoted its cover to a declaration that identified 'THE FOUR MOST WANTED'.[36]

Such forms of publicity conform to the precepts held by state agencies, in which all channels of public communication are expected to help disseminate appeals in times of crisis. Yet the compliance of media organisations in obeying authoritarian norms is bound to focus attention on their ability to maintain a broader *discursive* autonomy.[37] The fabrication of front pages resembling 'wanted' posters does not necessarily suggest complete submission to a state agenda (since alternative perspectives may appear in other reports within the same publication[38]), but it is nonetheless evidence of an alignment with a disciplinary edict.[39]

Any discussion of editorial procedures in this case should ask (i) why CCTV material was presented in the format described above, (ii) if the reproduction of photographs and information in this way was a serious attempt to help identify the individuals concerned, and (iii) whether or not the strategic prominence assigned to this representation was decided in consultation with the police.[40] The front page of the *Daily Mirror* on 22 July provides an instructive contrast in this respect, posing a question ('IS THIS HOW WE MUST NOW LIVE?'), which, unlike the dominant practice followed in the other papers, is at least open to multiple interpretations.

Although it might seem absurd for a newspaper to depart entirely from convention and use the CCTV evidence of these particular activities to illustrate a discussion of civil liberties, it is *exactly* the circulation of closed-circuit images under 'incontestable' circumstances which reinforces the wider and largely unreflective reproduction of public surveillance *as a principle*. Lyon describes this trend as one that moves towards 'pre-emptive surveillance and "categorical suspicion"' (in Misa et al., 2003: 168). McGrath, examining these forms of electronic scrutiny, depicts the predominant frame of debate (engineered through discourses of *privacy* and *crime*) as ideological because they hide as much as they reveal about surveillance society (2004: 2).

Surveillance alone is not much use in the general reproduction of a culture, unless it can become an accepted *generic* form through which people can recognise their own activities. In other words, it cannot remain a private condition, viewed only by police, secret agents and private security firms. Surveillance comes to exemplify the trajectory of a public culture only when it is publicised. Television, for example, reproduces CCTV footage and hidden camera work in news reports, undercover investigations and entertainment. The cinema, in addition, has only to mimic on-screen the appearance of surveillance to demonstrate the relationship between the public and authority.

Where terrorism is concerned, CCTV and other forms of recorded observation provide an important part of the 'validation' of the state's role as overseer. This makes the original failure to produce CCTV footage of Jean Charles's movements, when a good half-dozen cameras may have tracked his progress, into an expression of the coercive state's inconsistency and untrustworthiness. It also gives rise to the plethora of conspiracy theories that allow for an easy dismissal of current policies as a cover for illegal activity.

The creation of a *convincing* sense of heightened national security ultimately depends not on the state's rhetoric about terrorism, but on the ability of media forms to present the 'terrorist threat' as an autonomous sphere of activity. In other words, violent conspiracy must be presented first and foremost as a genuine *discovery*, rather than the partial or fanciful creation of informants, intelligence agencies, politicians or indeed the media. Media institutions, for their part, present their own activities as a response to, rather than an enlargement of, existing material conditions; in plain terms, they retain the notion of objectivity as an important component of their claim to even-handedness. Notions which threaten to destabilise our supposed faith in the authenticity of representation, such as Boorstin's theory of 'pseudo-events' (in Leiss et al., 1990: 27), which argues that manufactured phenomena like news conferences replace democratic exchange, are not accepted by journalists *as a critique of their own practices*; rather, media organisations retain allegiance to 'objective' standards, and assign the exercise of dubious strategies to a separate political arena of spin and manipulation.

The animation of such issues can be interpreted as part of a general reflection on the effects of hierarchy and *structure*, in which a social order or formation composed of established, durable institutions produces standardised practices, forms of exchange and behaviour. Any analysis of media coverage is bound to animate discussions about news values, agenda-setting, journalistic practices and ultimately the exercise of power in a neoliberal democracy.

Where news media follow the ideal of objective reporting, they can generate highly principled journalism; where objectivity is designed to reinforce formal oppositions between 'the truth claims of the antagonists in conflicting situations' (Altschull, 1995: 64), it becomes no more than 'a strategic ritual' (Tuchman, 1972). In the early days of the de Menezes case, *corroboration* of one set of claims actually delayed the revelation of the truth. The use of eyewitness accounts was used as the basis for a 'factual' insight into events, but the persistent reproduction of errors proved difficult to escape once these reports had been circulated.

The *Independent*, for example, based part of its 22 July report on the testimony of the eyewitness Mark Whitby. It noted that 'he had been sitting on the train reading his paper as it was stationary with its doors open in Stockwell station ... he said that an Asian man ran on to the train pursued by three plainclothes police officers' (Brown et al., 23 July 2005: 4–5). In this case, the journalist is careful to attribute statements to the witness; the misidentification of de Menezes as Asian revealed the assumptions made by Whitby, but these are not the responsibility of the newspaper. The notion that the suspect was 'Asian' forms part of a recently disseminated conception, the threat of 'home grown' terrorism in which 'alienated' British citizens (described in the press nonetheless by ethnicity rather than simply nationality) turn against their 'own country'. The eventual appearance of a debate over the dead man's innocence turned on the fact that he was not a disaffected national but the citizen of another state motivated by the apparently laudable project of self-improvement.

Many reports at this stage, despite some attempts at qualification, helped to circulate a series of entirely bogus details, dramatic touches that took on a life of their own, directing the story's development.

The *Guardian* of 23 July described 'bewildered eyewitnesses' who 'told how they had witnessed the moment ... when the suspect was repeatedly shot'. This, which may be regarded as uncontroversial, is followed with the assertion that 'all described the man as wearing a bulky, winter coat, despite the warm weather, and at least one said he thought he spotted a belt with wires running from it'. The 'bulky coat' and the phrase 'despite the warm weather' appeared in numerous stories, while the reference to the belt and wires was attributed to one Anthony Larkin, who in fact claimed that 'I saw this guy who appeared to have a bomb belt and wires coming out' (Cobain et al., 23 July 2005).

A day later, the *Daily Express* had turned these assumptions into a coherent narrative: 'The Asian man, who was wearing a heavy padded jacket despite the warm temperature, was originally thought to have been wearing a bomb belt' (Willey and Flanagan, 23 July, 2005).[41] Perhaps the most remarkable replication of the 'bomb belt' myth appeared in a drawing made by Philip Argent and Paul McCallum on page 5 of the *Daily Mail*'s 23 July edition, which carried a large cartoon drawing of plainclothes police, about to shoot a man wearing a belt with wires protruding (see Harris, 23 July 2005: 4–5). No belt with wires attached and no bulky jacket had ever existed beyond the imagination of eyewitnesses, newspaper cartoonists and 'graphic artists'. The police did not intervene to correct these impressions. No retraction of, or apology for, a series of misleading reports was ever produced; the 'state of emergency'[42] and the 'disposable' nature of print seemed to provide its own justification.

It is worth observing that the material character of the press has been shaped, at least until the advent of online journalism[43] by its appearance as an 'ephemeral' physical product. Free from certain temporal constraints, to the extent that it can be consumed at any point within and beyond the day of publication, print is nonetheless limited by its apparent transformation into 'stale news' the day after publication. Unlike television reportage, which is able to 'clear the space' for more open-ended coverage of the unexpected (especially in the case of 'rolling news'), the press is unable to *simulate co-presence* with its audience, or provide the spatial/temporal anchorage which audiences are offered during 'live' broadcasts.[44]

In the case of Stockwell, the fact that no news organisation had direct access to the immediate site ensured dependence on official statements and first-hand accounts; these consisted of police conferences and press releases, together with eyewitness reports. Crucially, the symbolic production of meaning was limited by the inability of the public to 'view' the scene through electronic media[45] (unlike, for example, the destruction of the Twin Towers on 11 September 2001). This circumstance generated alternative forms of visual narration.

Until photographs from the shooting were leaked to the press, a number of representational phenomena, based on verbal accounts, supplied the deficit and were used to dramatise the course of events. Diagrammatic 'narratives', cartoons and photographs all contributed to mistaken accounts of the shooting. Jean Charles de Menezes was portrayed refusing to stop, vaulting barriers, running down escalators, and finally being shot by his pursuers. Press coverage of the Stockwell shooting then evolved from its initial phase, which repeated official assertions about the death of a terrorist suspect linked to the events of 21 July, to a confused recognition that the victim was not connected with the police enquiry.

Entering the domain of risk: 'tragedy', guilt and innocence

If the news media 'partly function to disseminate appropriate values and reinforce moral boundaries' (Manning, 2001: 27), then this role is emphasised during those events which most clearly offer an aberration from the norm. In the case of 'terrorist' activity, journalists composing news stories may give prominence to malevolent acts from this *implicitly judgemental position*. Subeditors, columnists and leader-writers, however, take up certain details of the established narrative in order to emphasise those aspects that seem to confirm the *explicitly* 'political' perspectives they espouse. In sum, material is inflected in order to resonate with the perceived prejudices of the readership. So, for example, the *Daily Express* produced a front page that traded on an established theme: the supposed correlation between seeking asylum, reliance on benefit and antipathy towards the host nation ('BOMBERS ARE ALL SPONGEING ASYLUM SEEKERS', *Daily Express*, 27 July 2005). Here, a dominant agenda is pursued by fitting new material into an existing perspective. In a similar vein, the *Daily Mail* of the same date produced a front page that discussed the question of asylum. Alternative themes that might have been animated remained in embryonic form.[46]

While the tendency to pass on fashions of speech and arresting narrative episodes is a common feature of everyday conversation, in the context of journalistic practice the repetition of particular incidents and images can establish them as unassailable *points of reference*. It is this process, the circulation of clichés and sometimes quite prosaic forms of explanation, which provides the basic elements of a burgeoning *ideological folklore*.[47]

So, the discovery that the police had been operating a shoot-to-kill policy could be discussed in the press as a pragmatic response to an extraordinary threat, and may therefore be used to circumvent the issue of civil liberties. An instance of this may be found in Melanie Phillips's comments on the same development, which showed that she could mimic the propositional content[48] of an account that police and security sources had presented as a justification for their actions.[49] Once such a position had been established, it could be developed without needing further direction from source (in this case, the police and other authorities). A close identity in political outlook between social actors in the media and representatives of established authority is enough to guarantee the generation of particular themes.

A condition of 'emergency' provides the alibi for such collaboration, allowing many commentators to reproduce official explanations despite the clear and widely shared perception that provisional utterances should be treated with caution. Another related question is the commonsense expectation of a significant difference between editorial or personal opinion, on the one hand, and standard reportage, on the other. This belief disguises the fact that the latter is equally capable of reproducing not only *uncritical* versions of official briefings, but also politically conformist positions within news accounts.

In the *Guardian*'s 23 July report, written by a team of reporters led by Ian Cobain, the shooting was described in a simple manner ('a man was chased by officers and shot around five times in the head at point-blank range as he lay on the floor of a train'), but framed through an almost obsequious narrative introduction which read 'the urgency of the operation – and the determination of police to prevent any further suicide attacks – were demonstrated dramatically at an underground station in Stockwell, south London, yesterday'.[50] Factors which might explain the readiness of journalists to maintain such positions range from the assertion that the institutions they serve are 'agencies of social control' (Altschull, 1995: xix), through perspectives which emphasise simple market calculation, to the belief that both news and other established practices such as the law are 'disciplinary and normalizing discourses ... fundamentally concerned with *policing*' (Ericson et al., 1991: 7), where policing is defined as a mechanism for maintaining 'moral' perspectives.

Although journalists across media forms cooperate with authority in emphasising the 'performative significance' of an important event (Blondheim and Liebes, 2003: 186), newspaper stories rely on a variety of techniques to attract the interest of their readers. Acting through the power of *display*, newspapers, certainly at times of crisis, offer readers an emotional connection with the events they describe. They also present a form of continuity in which certain occurrences are aligned with the imagined horizons of their readers. The treatment of the Stockwell incident bore a close resemblance to mediation of the Forest Gate assault in 2006, in which Abul Koyair was shot and injured by police; both events were set, in their initial phases at least, within the framework of terrorist rather than purely criminal discourses,[51] and both had to accommodate the eventual intrusion of a 'counter-narrative' based on the (nonetheless contested) innocence of the victims.[52]

Yet the particular circumstances of the Stockwell shooting reveal *a crisis of the state's own making*, a rupture in the perceived character of democratic procedures; the attempted resolution was to attribute the ultimate cause of de Menezes's death to terrorist activity and to exculpate the police. The attempt to repair the disruption can be found in those forms of explanation that employ the concept of a 'tragedy'. Once again, the origins of this idea appear in the announcement made by the authorities on 23 July; 'Scotland Yard admitted Mr Menezes had been shot by mistake and apologised to his family for the "tragedy"' (BBC News online, 17 August 2005). The theme was then circulated by commentators like Tony Parsons, whose reaction appeared under the title 'A TRAGEDY — BUT POLICE STILL DESERVE OUR SUPPORT' and began with the rhetorical assertion that 'last thing in the world we needed right now was screaming front-page headlines with the words POLICE and BLUNDER in the same sentence' (*Daily Mirror*, 25 July 2005).

Parsons reveals his understanding of the mechanism of cohesive association between terms and the production of simple themes. The idea of police error is, however, a notion he is anxious to dismiss, even as his remark calls it into view. Where the discourse of tragedy and innocence failed to prevent critical attacks upon the police handling of the event, other themes were rapidly deployed, casting some doubt on the sincerity of journalistic accounts that appeared more liberal. For example, broadly sympathetic but vaguely patronising positions which turned on the notion of de Menezes's attempts at betterment ('The hard-working son who moved to London in search of a better life', Bird et al., *The Times*, 25 July 2005), and which might have animated discussion of 'multicultural citizenship' (Isin, 2000) and globalisation, were curtailed by a countervailing process in which the victim's entitlement to reside in Britain was questioned.

The *Daily Mirror* of 29 July 2005, for example, ran a headline that read 'BRAZILIAN'S VISA 2 YEARS OUT OF DATE' (Roberts, 29 July 2005: 10). The most questionable tactic used to discredit the dead man was finally dismissed when the *Independent* revealed on 26 April 2006 that police had dropped an allegation of rape against de Menezes after his DNA was found not to match a sample taken from the victim of an attack. The circulation of this allegation had, nonetheless, helped to throw de Menezes's innocence into doubt. In effect, calls for unity with police during this period could be understood as an attempt to reinforce social solidarity and demonstrate defiance against terrorism. Such claims may also have entailed an unquestioning support for the principle of pre-emptive execution. Other individuals, as blameless as de Menezes but identified as a threat, may quite unwittingly have entered the domain of risk.[53]

Representation and meaning

All academic studies of mediated incidents, whatever their particular theoretical provenance, recognise that the structure of any public occurrence is partly determined by the act of representation; most also admit that events have a separate existence from their 'dominant' mode of signification.[54] Media forms constitute the primary location for the production and *circulation* of meaning, basing their habitual narrative practices upon a potent amalgam of accurate information and mistaken assumptions. The generic conventions applied to the 'core' material gathered by the press (official statements, eye-witness accounts, visual material produced at the scene, etc.) are largely automatic, and often unreflective, practices. As Bruck observes, the media may well employ 'their own codes and conventions' (Bruck, 1992: 142) when composing narratives, but rely on perspectives generated elsewhere, so that 'the discursive material they work with' is not their own' (142).

My contention here is that established symbolic practices seen in newspaper reports may be understood as the mobilisation of pre-existing themes[55] which are then consolidated by columnists into explicit positions.[56] Reports of the shooting typify the *dramatisation* of public events produced during periods of crisis. Gerbner, following Knight and Dean (1982), makes a similar point when he argues that crime and punishment are transformed into a 'selectively choreographed' event (Gerbner, 1992: 96). There are important comparisons to be made between the example Gerbner mentions – the Iranian embassy siege in London, 1980 – and the Stockwell incident. Considered as responses to terrorist activity, both reveal the existence of violent practices that could be classified as executions.[57] An important difference, however, was the difficulty of turning the death of de Menezes into a 'morally coherent' scenario of 'violence and terror' (Gerbner, 1992).[58] The concurrence of reports in establishing the clear innocence of de Menezes, despite the uncertainty about his status as a 'legal' migrant, made it difficult to use the event to justify a 'shoot to kill' policy. Instead, one newspaper, the *Daily*

Mail, attempted to present de Menezes as a 'victim of the terrorists' (Comment, 25 July 2005).

This would seem to be an extremely precarious strategy. If de Menezes is to be portrayed as a victim of *terrorism*, it would be reasonable to assign direct guilt to the actual perpetrator of the assault; in other words, it would be necessary to identify the terrorist. This, in turn, might lead to the conclusion that the officer who fired the shots must assume this role. The writer of the *Mail*'s piece seemed aware of this interpretation, arguing that the family of the dead man might 'perhaps in time come to accept that, although he was killed by a police officer', he was 'as much a victim of terrorism as the 52 innocent people killed on July 7' (Comment, 25 July 2005). According to this line of thinking, the death can be attributed not to the specialist firearms officers of So19, but to the 7 July bombers who were supposed to have provoked the urgent implementation of Operation Kratos.

Arguments that the Stockwell killing represents a 'paradigmatic' shift towards armed repression within the British state have been opposed by the contention that the event was no more than a tragic accident, or the unique product of exceptional circumstances. Though unusual, the death of Jean Charles de Menezes can be understood more readily if its rhetorical composition within news media is set aside. The shooting can be analysed with reference to a number of other events and proce-dures; these include past counter-insurgency operations, contemporary developments in 'anti-terror' techniques, and armed interventions made by police against civilians.

Although a full analysis of all these factors is beyond the scope of this chapter, it would be useful at this point to turn briefly to the 'ordinary' shooting of civilians, precisely because they provide an example of individuals who were not placed in the category of 'terrorists', yet whose actions nonetheless provoked extreme measures. One feature seems to predominate: this is the fact that no police of-ficer has been convicted for the death of any member of the public. In 2005, the *Independent* ran a front-page article which analysed thirty fatal shootings caused by armed police; in none of these cases had any officer been convicted of an offence (Verkaik and Bennetto, 21 October 2005). This is not to say that police had not been faced with some kind of threat on at least half of these occasions, and, according to the *Independent*, weapons had been discharged by civilians during four of the incidents.[59]

Although details of the circumstances are not provided for eleven of the dead, four of those killed had been completely unarmed.[60] A later article in the *Daily Mail* pursued this question, with particular reference to the anonymity that had been accorded to all but two of the fifty-five officers involved in the fatal shootings of (by this time) thirty-three victims (Leake et al., 26 September 2010: 24–5). While the increase in the use of firearms officers (Waldren, 2007) can explain in part the general toll of casualties in recent years, the situation in which de Menezes was placed was nonetheless atypical; although he was a civilian, the circumstances of his death did not resemble the ways in which many ordinary individuals had been shot. These events usually occur when some public disturbance has been in progress or where police have intercepted, or lain in wait, for armed criminals. Jean Charles de Menezes, another civilian victim, exhibited no sign of carrying, or having access to, a weapon. All the negative attributes that supposedly justified or at least explained his death were assigned to him by eyewitnesses or police.

The possibility that certain members of the public had felt terrorised by the police[61] could not be translated into a viable form of public discourse because, at least within the mainstream political parties and press, the political and communicative resources were not available; these were monopolised by established forces. More critical perspectives appeared within new media forms, where speculation about the growth of paramilitary action was more common. Ultimately, no police officers were charged with an offence. Instead, the Metropolitan Police as an institution was found guilty of endangering the public under health-and-safety laws.

The apparent proliferation of armed activity cannot in itself explain the events of 22 July 2005. It is only in the context of the British state's long involvement in counter-insurgency and 'anti-terror' policy that de Menezes's death can be understood. Even then, the emphasis on *minimum force* that once characterised military policy[62] (whatever the reality 'on the ground') cannot provide a fully comprehensive account of the turn to 'pre-emption'. Kratos must be studied in conjunction with other developments, such as the application of anti-terror legislation to public dissent, in order to appreciate the full implications of the Stockwell debacle. Demonstrations, acts of civil disobedience and even everyday public activities (Hewitt, 2008: 113) seem to attract the use of surveillance and other measures designed to repress dissent.

If this is the case, then certain qualifications should be made. The first is that an approach that emphasises the appearance of a 'unitary' state should be questioned. As previously noted, the state is a *composite* structure, or 'an ensemble of power centres' (Jessop, 2008: 37). These centres offer *unequal* chances to 'different forces within and outside the state to act for different political purposes' (37). Jessop continues by arguing that 'it is not the state that acts; it is rather specific sets of politicians and state officials' located within various parts of the state system (37). This leads to the uneven development of bureaucracy, as various factions, embedded in particular functional environments or agencies (different strata of the law, armed forces, police and political executives), defend and attempt to enlarge their own interests and social vision.

Clearly, in the case of paramilitary developments, these are advanced by the combined powers of different elements within the security state, whose operatives are given relative autonomy by the political executive. As a consequence of divided responsibilities and devolved power, it is possible for organisations like the Association of Chief Police Officers to set an agenda which 'liberal' elements of the state may find difficult to contain, largely because they operate in a different field of activity. The political direction of coercive authority may therefore be dictated by hidden agreements between an executive and selected agencies, without close scrutiny from elected officialdom, informal civil networks or liberal elements within the law and judiciary. Kratos avoids careful dissection because it is both a policy and an amorphous set of procedures; the type of response it envisages is not made explicit in public documents like the Terrorism Act 2006, and in this sense at least it stands outside the law itself.

The second qualification that should be applied to the notion of a 'police' state is that only a small part of this repression is directly physical; just as 'the war on terror' is economic and rhetorical, so too is the internal organisation of the security project. In sum, therefore, the threat to the core of the British *state* is negligible. The security establishment has therefore *overproduced* the coercive capital needed to prosecute a 'counter-insurgency' against domestic opposition. As a consequence, it has attempted to justify its expansion by trying to erode the distinction between terrorist activity and legitimate public protest, using stop-and-search powers under terror legislation to disrupt the organisation of environmentalist and anti-war events; even so, this action has still not provided enough live bodies to repress. Although the security establishment does not have universal power to develop all its aims, because it is structurally constrained by other social forces, procedures like Kratos will not be reversed. Without effective public access to, or control over, police activity, a repetition of 'the Stockwell syndrome', even where no shots are fired, may increasingly become the norm.

The application of lethal force is described by those in authority as selective, to be used against only the most unpredictable or implacable of foes, but the truth of the matter is that such explanations are designed to encompass a much wider range of eventualities; the consequence is that the demonstrable power of armed intervention is increased. When this power is discharged it may, like an electric current, run in unexpected directions, but this does not affect the structure that produced it. The armed intervention will therefore remain a useful tactic within the extensive repertoire of coercive power that is refined in secret by the security regime.

EIGHT

Pre-emption and
perception management

If it turned out [de Menezes] wasn't linked [to the failed attack] we would face the marathon task of adjusting and realigning the public's view.

Hayman and Gilmore, 2009: 194

Convincing the public may not be easy (as the Police are finding over terrorist threats in [the] UK) but shaping expectations is important for many reasons.

General Staff Analysis, Operation TELIC (item 17, p. 7, February 2005, *Daily Telegraph* online)

The projection of disorder

The strategic apprehension of disorder – a practice that lies at the operational core of the Western security state[1] – is based on the projection of a threatening circumstance into the realm of contingency. Although a contingent phenomenon is usually defined as one that may appear in the fullness of time, this explanation can be misleading. In directing attention towards a state of affairs that might never exist, the volatile and dangerous character of contemporary life can be attributed to the existence of an 'insecure' future, rather than the uninhibited growth of material exploitation in the here and now. References to the prospect of disorder are used to disguise the fact that the order endorsed by the state is leading to disaster.

Those in positions of executive authority are thus able to renew the dominant assumptions of the present: in practice, the ruling elite attempts to 'secure' the future only in so far as it is can revitalise those circumstances that favour the survival of its own precepts and endeavours. In order to advance this project, the construction of a watertight argument is unnecessary. The authorities are able to call upon shared assumptions, not only about the character of the political system but, in imagining a hazardous future, about the orthodox supposition that time is 'neutral, constant and measurable' (Hutchings, 2008: 6). A shared sense of periodicity means that value judgements can be made about the relative merits of life in the past, present and future. In defending life in the current era against the 'worst' event or influence, the current form of civilisation, though wasteful and oppressive, is valorised. The past, in turn, is cited in support of the various positions that the political class decide to occupy, though such a strategy is not always productive. This was demonstrated when two Oxford-educated politicians, Tony Blair and David Cameron, employed allusions to a specific period during the Second World War.

In the wake of 9/11, just a few months into his second term as prime minster, Blair tried to underline the importance of solidarity with the United States. He did so by declaring that in 1940 America had stood 'shoulder to shoulder' with the UK (Fisk, 23 May 2010). Cameron, who had gained office in May 2010 at the head of a coalition government, used a visit to the USA in July of that year to announce that Britain had been America's 'junior partner' in 1940 (Hasan, 22 July 2010). The implication in both cases was that during America's hour of need a reciprocal gesture was both justified and required. In fact, the USA did not enter the war until 1941.

These statements could be read as a symptom of the woeful ignorance that is sometimes discovered in high places, despite the fact that the culprits had endured an expensive education. Equally, the two errors might be understood as the subconscious sacrifice of accuracy in the service of a more important goal – the need to emphasise the commonality of purpose that was meant to unite Britain and America. There is indeed a marked propensity to make public statements that conform, not necessarily to established historical conceptions, but to a dominant policy agenda. At times, this produces assertions that may seem absurd, such as the well-worn proposition that wars must be fought abroad in order to prevent confrontations with the same enemy at home. Unfortunately, in trying to flatter the Americans, Blair and Cameron chose an episode that resisted the kind of association they wished to create, causing offence to their domestic audiences.

Any reference to '1940' carries a powerful antecedent meaning, easily activated by any organisation that is able to represent itself as a custodian of Britain's popular, collective memory – the significance of the year is frequently renewed and celebrated in ceremonies, documentaries and news reports. 'Solitary' British resistance to the Nazi menace is therefore one of those tales that supports the notion of an independent (rather than a subservient) Britain, forming the bedrock of national identity. It was, therefore, unwise to tamper with this narrative – which still generates the occasional remark about America's 'late entry' into both the First and Second World Wars – though the two mistakes did seem to underline the reality of the UK's functional subservience to the US superpower.

The scenario, contingency and social control

Although the scenario – one among a number of techniques used in the management of 'advanced' societies – is presented as an attempt to imagine (and thus prepare for) an unwelcome event, the truly contingent occurrence depends on the coincidence of various conditions. The scenario, by comparison, is always engineered, and begins life as a proposition about a state of affairs. Despite the fact that it can be reinforced by forms of activity – appearing, for example, as an exercise played out in 'real time', or as a fully fledged security event – it lacks the kind of irrefutable material effect that only an unexpected and externally determined incident will produce. An actual 'terrorist' attack has a greater impact because it intrudes upon or interrupts everyday life, and has to be assimilated into the dominant conceptual order after the event.

Heavily conditioned by the dominant economic and political environment, the conception of the scenario is employed as a form of 'procedural' social control. As suggested above, its apparent orientation towards the future is actually a means of replicating established assumptions about the administration of the present. The danger, especially with the circulation of the 'worst case', is that the scenario can assume an ambiguous or doubtful character, encouraging the perception that most threats will never materialise or can be deferred. The governing elite tries to avoid this problem by creating narratives that, as we have seen in previous chapters, can be substantiated through some form of activity. The contingent event, by comparison, is neither safely located in the past nor certain to emerge in the future, but is instead confined to a parallel universe of the 'ever-present' crisis or emergency. It is this highly political use of the unknown which marks out authoritarian modes of address from the everyday references employed to describe the usual exigencies of communal life.

Pre-emption and the scenario

When formally constituted authority is described as 'public', it suggests that its operations are carried out within, and on behalf of, a civic collective of citizens that has a right to certain provisions and benefits. Yet the practical existence of a connection between people and government need not be founded on equality or genuine reciprocal exchange. For their part, the various subdivisions of the state and media expect to refine their goals without interference. So, for example, the concept of periodicity, outlined above, combined with the institutional power given to the executive officer, allows the exercise of discretion over the timing of an announcement.

In media forms, the standard practice of casting events in a linear, causal sequence can be used to lend importance to a particular event. Pre-recorded interviews, leaks and embargoes are used to defer or enhance arguments about the value of specific events (see the material on Prince Harry, below). The details of a political programme or intervention are, for example, held back or forced to the top of an agenda through the use of that form of conspiracy known as the 'sneak preview'.

When, for instance, the highlights of a speech are released to the media before the event itself takes place, this is not a matter of courtesy, but is instead a way of making an incursion into a space that the intended recipients of the message cannot inhabit – the 'future'. The usual expectation of the mainstream media, that only elite actors have the right to take the political initiative, is reinforced by the nomination of a future time when the latest edict will be divulged. If citizens tune in at the appointed hour, they are shown that their masters already occupy the high ground of what is meant to be a shared electronic-constitutional space.

This is why pre-emption, so often thought to be a particular feature of the 'war on terror', is in fact a standard practice within the repertoire of government. Indeed, according to one author 'pre-emption is not a theory of war, but rather a path to or scenario for war predicted by some theories' (Reiter, 1995). The goal of pre-emption is the constant renewal of the hierarchical principle, forcing the subject to wait for direction in all matters political. In proclaiming its intentions, formal authority reinforces the division between its own *spatial-temporal command* and the subservient role of those groups constituted as the public. This form of manipulation is only the public form of pre-emptive determination. Besides the construction of scare stories about the severity of an external threat, this form of advance notification is also used when an especially undesirable situation is purposely created by the state itself. The difference is that a catastrophe that has been deliberately contrived or invited by the authorities will not feature in the pantheon of disaster that is used to discipline the public.

Just such a case was outlined in a little-noticed article which described 'secret "doomsday" plans for 20% cuts' in the UK's public spending (Oliver et al., 5 July 2009: 1). Two particularly significant aspects of this development should be noted. The first is the fact that the strategy was prepared by senior civil servants, not elected representatives; the second is that it was composed a full ten months before the British general election of May 2010. The importance of this snippet of news was that the full extent of the attack upon the public sector was not even made evident during the election itself.

'Whitehall mandarins', according to the report, had begun creating 'detailed dossiers' because they were convinced that 'politicians [were] failing to confront the scale of the budget black hole' (Oliver et al., 5 July 2009: 1). The idea was that these documents would be 'handed to cabinet ministers the day after the next general election, whichever party wins' (1). The general effect of this form of projection is to force civil society into a condition of stasis, turning politicians into the figureheads for a decision executed by a permanent cabal of officials within the dark recesses of the 'deep state'.

Once again, the event that has helped to bring this circumstance to public attention was the Iraq War. One individual, Carne Ross, who had helped to prepare Joint Intelligence Committee assessments on Iraq, was called upon to give evidence to the Chilcot Inquiry. In a newspaper article, he recalled his dismay when a representative of the Foreign Office 'repeatedly sought' to persuade him to 'delete references to certain documents' from his testimony (Ross, 25 July 2010: 5). The Cabinet Office in particular wished him to remove any mention of the response made by one official to a paper presented to the Parliamentary Labour Party, which the bureaucrat had described as 'pure propaganda, filled with ludicrous statements' (5). Accusing government bureaucrats of forming 'Britain's own "deep state"' and of covering up the mistakes that led to the war, Ross noted that the same nonsense that was presented to political figures reappeared in the media as part of 'the campaign to create public hysteria' over the war (5).

There are, clearly, specific periods when the moral or political trajectory of an entire nation is placed under scrutiny, and the governing elite is placed under direct pressure to explain its conduct. When, for instance, politicians are forced to recognise that a particular issue has become controversial, they often respond by calling for a 'national debate'. Their intention at such times is not to initiate a root-and-branch transformation based on the wishes of the national community, but to control the pace of events and to set up a limited dialogue between professional advocates. Members of the public (or, more often, telegenic individuals drawn from a party's membership) are sometimes called upon to act as a backdrop to this charade, which – based on a narrow range of policy objectives and a highly restricted conception of the public good – is then dramatised for the media.[2]

Harry's Helmand adventure: a real 'non-event'

The secret manipulation and shaping of events are one way of ensuring that some control can be exercised over the reception of meaning. Since the 9/11 attacks it had become apparent that, when a clear line from a political executive could not be produced, news media would engage in a form of improvisation. The state's response to this situation was soon in evidence – the use of embedded reporters, the provision of special access to military facilities, and the staging of bogus events like the 'rescue' of Jessica Lynch (al-Rehaief, 2003). These techniques contribute to the larger project of news management.

Of particular significance is the presentation of stories where the outcome has already been established. Jon Williams, BBC World News editor, described how the British media had used an established protocol, 'the kidnap agreement', as a model for the composition of a story about the appearance of a royal prince in the Afghan War: Williams revealed that the 'MoD and the UK media reached an understanding', which meant that news journalists would not report the deployment during its course, provided that the media would 'get access to him before, during and after his time in Afghanistan' (Williams, BBC News online blog, 29 February 2008). The disclosure that the British media had agreed to observe a news blackout during the 'active service' of a royal prince brings a number of substantial issues into focus.

A theorist like Baudrillard, if his counter-intuitive theoretical perspective could be revived, might have argued that Harry was indeed the (willing) victim of a simulated abduction. There is, in fact, some evidence that this was not the first time that he had been subjected to a stage-managed ordeal. During his time as a pupil and military cadet at Eton, he volunteered to take part in an exercise in which he was to be captured by five regular soldiers who were dressed as 'Taliban extremists' (Jobson, 2008: 76). Harry was subjected to one of the techniques that had once been used against Republicans during the British Army's sojourn in Northern Ireland: he was 'forced to stand leaning on his finger tips' against a wall (76) and interrogated.

The Helmand deployment itself, however artificial – with its tame interviews and stage-managed display of military activity – should have animated wide-ranging discussion about the relevance of prominent social narratives concerning masculinity, class, warfare and celebrity. Such issues were for the most part subsumed in a much simpler proposition, based on the notion of media 'responsibility'. The debate turned on whether a US website had endangered the prince by revealing his whereabouts.

At first sight, the narrative of royal service provides a useful reminder of the existence of structures that operate beyond public scrutiny, and confirms the ability of dominant authorities to co-opt national instruments of publicity during an 'exceptional circumstance'. The use of established procedures and relationships to engineer social and political outcomes may not be unusual, but the public revelation of particular arrangements, in which formally independent organisations readily comply with authoritative requests, might provide an opportunity to discuss power and communication within 'neoliberal' democracies.

While undoubtedly valuable, these initial observations require more careful exposition, for a number of reasons. First, in attempting to establish the institutional character of this event, theories that emphasise indeterminacy of meaning, and endless intertextual transition or flow, seem to offer little assistance in understanding how the occasion was configured in a spatial and temporal environment: how, in other words, a particular configuration of meaning was established in its public context, and given its 'occasional' form. If this procedure is pursued, an argument might follow in which three further points could be established: first, that there is a finite scope of legitimate reference to incidents and objects, beyond which it will become clear that a falsehood has been perpetrated; second, that the *real* existence of theatrical behaviour in a practical environment must be recognised; and third, that the timely production of meaning in a 'mediated' space helps to determine the scope of public debates that follow the event.

Although this may suggest a move towards the argument that a 'media event' had taken place, the Harry narrative does not resemble the salient features of that model, encapsulating as it is supposed to do 'the live broadcasting of public ceremonies' (Dayan and Katz, 1992: 188), and the 'festive viewing of television' during 'historic occasions ... that are televised as they take place and transfix a nation or the world' (1). The first point is that the whole incident was arranged in detail and then recorded for later consumption, at a point when it was impossible for the public to make the only useful form of intervention, one that – though perhaps limited to commentary on social networking sites and letters to newspapers – would at least be conducted in something approaching 'real time'.

The entire deployment could, however, be represented as real at the level of practical experience. The prince called in air strikes, fired a heavy-calibre machine-gun, went on patrol, and so on. The limitations of this practice can be determined by a number of factors – first, and most crucially, the intervention of supervening powers. His activities were organised by the Ministry of Defence and overseen by his superior officers. Although one might argue that the lives of other soldiers in combat are also manipulated, the difference is that Harry's activities were divorced from the ordinary set of consequences that might follow on from such actions.

In addition, the event was unreal at the social or discursive level, in the sense that there was a deliberate attempt to misrepresent the context of his service. The danger, from the perspective of the myth-maker, is that the public, schooled in the appreciation of generic forms, will recognise the type of event they are called upon to witness. To demonstrate this point, it is useful to consider the difference between the narrative convention of being 'under fire' – seen in footage shot during Taliban attacks – with the staged character of the Helmand fantasy, in which the prince seemed to be engaged in activities that looked more akin to the typical photo opportunity.

Sending a member of the royal family to a 'theatre of war' seems to exemplify and crystallise a number of useful public myths, such as the benefits of a maintaining a benevolent class hierarchy at a time when national unity meant supporting 'our boys' in the frontline. The success of Princess Diana as a royal celebrity provided the monarchy with a considerable stock of goodwill, a form of social capital that Harry had seemed to squander when he had appeared at a fancy-dress party dressed as a Nazi. The allegiance of the military, media and the political class to this form of 'constitutional' monarchy meant that they were prepared to attempt the rehabilitation of this wayward individual.

'Perception management'

If it is assumed that the ruling elite and its allies are engaged in a drive to perpetuate their own interests, the question must be how they attempt to manage the perceptions of the subordinate. Where the 'deep state' is mired in a disruptive or controversial process of its own making, such as a financial meltdown or the prosecution of a war, the tendency is first to play down its own culpability. Where this cannot be achieved, the apparent risks must themselves be made to seem less than catastrophic. This produces a peculiar situation in which an active engagement in destructive behaviour is separated from its obvious consequences, which are then attributed to another cause. An appropriate emotional condition, meanwhile, must be assigned to the population – anger at the excesses of bankers, sorrow for the human costs of war, pride in the bravery of a royal soldier. The point of trading on these emotional qualities is that they remove the public from the realm of active, intelligent agency.

Above all, whenever current circumstances are called into question by any form of national disturbance, state functionaries will compose an alibi designed to exculpate the authorities. Two obvious examples can be found in the response to the traumatic events of '9/11' and '7/7', when questions were raised about the efficiency of the security services, and rumours began to circulate about possible collusion between some branches of the state and the terrorist enemy. Failures were assigned to particular branches of the security regime, but the system as a whole was protected by its dispersed location and specialist functions.

The myth of 'decentralisation' and the role of authority

This process of dispersal and dissemination should not be mistaken for the transfer of authority from the centre to the periphery. Where some form of devolution takes place, this is purely instrumental, emerging from an organisational culture that enables 'low-level personnel ... to make operational decisions that meet the approval of higher authorities' (Sagan, 1993: 23). Weick, for instance, notes that decentralisation depends upon the careful socialisation of individuals, so that they will follow 'a homogenous set of assumptions and decision premises', ensuring that the rules will be 'invoked on a local and decentralised basis' and yet will preserve 'coordination and centralisation' (Weick, cited in Sagan, 1993: 23).

Even the armed forces are open to this kind of initiative because, while they do not wish to disturb the structures within which they operate, they are interested in improving their capabilities. The notorious 'Garden Plot' Civil Disturbance Plan, drawn up by the US Department of the Army to provide 'guidance and direction' for military participation in 'operations in support of civil authorities', argued that 'special emphasis should be given to lessons learned' which could indicate 'a need for changes in doctrine, training, or planning' (Governmentattic.org, 2009). The document went on to note that 'any successful improvisation, innovation, expedient, or stratagem should be addressed', while 'coordination with local authorities' was regarded as essential.

As a form of normative habituation, the scenario exercise is flexible and innovative, at least within the confines of its own remit. It is also, as argued throughout this book, part of a larger attempt to reinforce an authoritarian social perspective. The ruling elite will always attempt to 'shape [public] expectations' (General Staff Analysis, February 2007) or, where individuals have assumed an independent position, to 'adjust ... and realign' the public's view (Hayman and Gilmore, 2009: 194). The free deliberation of the human collective, supposedly the aim of democratic politics, is replaced by an automatic response to an imagined emergency, one that offers only a restricted view of the range of possibilities that constitute the contemporary domain of risk.

The limitations of this approach are easily recognised once a simple question has been addressed: if the point of creating a scenario is merely to anticipate some aspect of the unknown, then one might expect it to include some references to positive outcomes, besides the usual list of extreme ('worst-case') hazards. These more optimistic perspectives seem to be the preserve of the corporate sector, which evokes the 'better tomorrow' that will emerge under its stewardship – they are also discovered in the utterances of the political class, whenever it attempts to secure an electoral mandate.

The close relationship between corporate, political and executive authority, however, suggests that any distinction between the communicative behaviour of these bodies is no more than a convenient division of labour. The fact that the typical security scenario is negative in character may well match the declared purpose of resisting 'terror', but the *positive* spin given to the alternative picture – a rosy future created by commercial or political interests – should also be treated with caution. This, too, is a symptom of the prevailing mode of rule

– the use of timely interventions to smother any nascent challenge to contemporary authority.

In the first of these two story-worlds, Western values (interests) are under threat from groups of radicalised 'non-state' actors, whose chief characteristic is supposed to be their inclination to use terror to achieve their aims. In the second, more affirmative, fairy tale the hazards to be faced include more general and less controversial challenges, like climate change, cultural misunderstandings and the absence of educational opportunities. In both cases, the common factor is the existence of a strong centre of influence that is able to set its agenda in advance.

Strategic communication: five sites of institutional agency

In estimating the relative strength of the structural influences that determine the form taken by any single act of strategic communication (in this case, the composition of the 'threat scenario'), the constitution and behaviour of five types of institutional agency should be considered. These are: (i), *the state* as an apparatus or an 'ensemble' of institutions (Jessop, 2008: 9), which together constitute the site upon which (contested) activities take place, including 'coercive defence, political governance, administrative management, and judicial regulation' (Therborn, 1978: 37); (ii), the *core executive*, 'those organisations and procedures' (Rhodes, 1995: 12) that coordinate policy according to the prevailing conception of the 'national interest', and that give the appearance of resolving disputes within the state apparatus; (iii), the *security regime*, those structures and practices that, formally devoted to the maintenance of an idealised polity (the realm, the nation, the state, and so on), operate in defence of the upper echelons of the political, military, patriarchal, bureaucratic and corporate elite; (iv) major centres of regulatory authority or expertise (private, state or 'hybrid' forms like the UK's ACPO) that are responsible for passing on (or even creating) policy decisions; and (v), strategic bodies, such as PR companies, that help to shape the semiotic and propositional form of any strategic message, in accordance with the dictates of their own professional ethos and the wishes of their clients.

These five sites of agency, considered as possible influences on the creation of that specialised material/symbolic undertaking known as the 'scenario', are clearly dedicated to the production of concrete outcomes. In this sense, the individual organisations or networks that create an event are 'goal-oriented' institutions. This is not to suggest that they act according to precepts that they can determine without interference: as Therborn notes, the various bodies (particularly those that constitute the state), are 'formally bounded system[s] of structured processes within a *global* system' (Therborn, 1978: 37; my emphasis).

The existence of a worldwide system should not lead to the conclusion that there is some kind of monolithic, unitary centre, able to make a univocal declaration that perfectly summarises the aims of what is in reality a ruling group made up of various interests. It is the manipulation of contingency as a technique of rule or governance that most clearly sheds light on the actual practices associated with abstract concepts like 'global domination'. It is the simple articulation of propositions about the nature of the real, and the use of procedures that give this 'ideological' process substance, which turn a political agenda into a viable programme.

Beyond ideology? Forecasts versus contingency

There is a stark difference between the circulation of general propositions and the creation of an actual forecast, accompanied by a specific warning. When the residents of New Orleans were advised to prepare for the approaching hurricane, the alarming news that Katrina might devastate the coast produced a calculation that was as near as it is possible to get to prophecy. Drawn from a wealth of information that was part of a widespread public discourse about a genuine, universal threat to all those who lived in the area, the event also revealed the wider institutional weaknesses within which it was set. It was, nonetheless, actively anticipated – its development was mapped by satellite, and its possible effects were described in advance. Therefore, to all intents and purposes, its landfall lay in that domain commonly known as the 'future'.

The contingent event, on the other hand – unlike the concrete programmatic intervention – is not a prediction of any kind, and is ideally suited to the dissemination of a general sense of uncertainty. It is conceived as a *distinct* possibility, which may come to fruition at some unspecified point. It is this lack of assurance that helps to make the public receptive to each feverish revelation about a new terror cell or a fresh terror plot. Contingency allows the renewal of the same propositions, while the suddenness of a story's appearance – and then disappearance – suggests the manipulation of a narrative template that is used to limit the possibilities of interpretation.

Unless it takes place, the terror plot (however 'far advanced') remains a useful tool within the overall logic of pre-emption. The conception of the scenario is imagined not as a simple 'potentiality', or as a hazard located in one of a number of possible futures, but as an *ongoing circumstance*: this should not be explained simply as the promotion of fear, which cannot be maintained at the same level throughout the postulated emergency. The actual technique employed by the authorities is more akin to *the structural reproduction of uncertainty*.

'Resilience' as a rationale

If the practical expression of the contingent event is the scenario exercise, this is based, in the British case at least, on the circulation of one particular rationale, summed up in the notion of 'resilience'. The senior security operative David Omand (mentioned in Chapter 1) described how an attempt was made to 'design the architecture for national resilience and public security against the threats and risks of the twenty-first century, not least from international terrorism' (Omand, in Hennessy, 2007: 143). Omand, who was at the time the UK's security and intelligence coordinator, revealed that 'what we [appointed officials] principally had in common was the need to envisage the unthinkable, however disturbing' (143). 'The term "resilience"', he explained, was 'a borrowing from the science of materials', which 'came into use to describe our vision of a society that would be able to absorb sudden shocks and yet bounce back quickly into its normal shape' (143).

This goal is reflected in much of the security advice promoted by UK bodies like London First, ACPO, NaCTSO, the National Policing Improvement Agency, and so on. For instance, the UK government's 'Strategy for Countering International Terrorism' speaks of increasing 'the resilience of communities to violent extremism' (NaCTSO, 2009a: 14), while the Cabinet Office argues that a focus 'on community and corporate resilience will aid local groups and organisations to respond to terrorist attacks as well as other common hazards' (Cabinet Office, *Security for the Next Generation*, 2009: 79).

The question is why *resilience* appears to have replaced security as the nodal point of discursive practice. Booth defined security as 'the condition of being and feeling safe' (Booth, 2007: 110), and argued that the concept could be divided into a subjective condition (feeling safe) and an objective one (being safe). The overall goal of security, according to Booth, was to achieve universal emancipation from such threats as poverty and war, as opposed to the traditional view that was concerned with the territorial integrity of states.

Since it would appear that neither the subjective nor the objective conceptions of security can be attained while institutional structures are placed before the well-being of the human race in general, a shift towards resilience – where, for example, people might be killed but the 'system' is able to recover – reveals the exercise of a rather unwholesome form of discretion. If the state has abandoned what some of its functionaries may believe to be an impossible task – the attainment of complete security – then, under the cover of a rational adjustment, the 'domain of risk' mentioned in Chapter 7 may now have increased in scope.

Resilience and 'leveraged hegemony'

Yet, in foregrounding resilience as the political rationale for the promotion of the security enterprise, it is presented as a *defensive* measure. In all the literature produced by government outlets, despite the apparent reservations of many who work within the world of intelligence, one particularly disruptive idea is kept at bay. This is the notion that the actions of the West, in fighting a variety of what used to be called 'low intensity' conflicts, are somehow unrelated to the growth of insurgency and 'terror'.

Instead of a defensive posture, certain ruling elites among the 'advanced' nations have engaged in a wide-ranging attempt to consolidate their hold on power through an *aggressive* strategy of military, financial and political pre-emption. What, then, is the purpose of the emergency or 'resilience' network within this context? It acts, I would contend, as an auxiliary formation that can be activated to support the social perspective and material functions of the security state. It exists to help manipulate a future conducive to the short-sighted demands of the present – an obsession that has been imported from the capitalist adventurism that creates wealth from resources that have not yet been secured.

According to two of the most clear-sighted authors writing in this field, the growth of the modern conception of futurity is inextricably linked with the 'spread of bourgeois accounting' and what they describe as the '*development of probability*' (Nitzan and Bichler, 2009: 158; my emphasis). The financial sector is certainly well known for its ability to manipulate an absent or theoretical quality by engineering a deal that will only be actualised at some point in the future. A useful example of this form of projection is described by Millo, who produced an analysis of index-based derivatives. These are contracts that state the future terms upon which a transaction will be made, and they are as a result commonly known as *futures* (Millo, 2007: 197). In contrast to 'physical and deliverable assets', market indices are 'the products of mathematical procedures applied to market data' (197). If these contracts or futures derive their value from the terms of a *yet to be completed* transaction (based on a 'price to be paid' at a time selected for 'the delivery of assets'), then they cannot actually be handed over in the *same way* as physical goods when the contract is due (197). Yet, despite their insubstantiality, Millo argues that these 'abstract mathematical entities became the basis for the most popular financial contract of our time' (197). In effect, the capital markets had, like the security state, created structures that can be used to manipulate – and profit from – the mechanism of contingency.

Capitalisation and power

According to Bichler and Nitzan, the connection between the state and private enterprise is not only the ability to transcend the constraints of the present described above, but the way in which this power is constituted as a systemic social force. Arguing that 'the power to generate earnings and limit risk' goes far beyond the 'narrow spheres' of production and markets, these authors believe that it includes '*the entire state structure of corporations and governments*' (Bichler and Nitzan,

2010: 8; original emphasis). In other words, there is only a functional separation between economic and political power. Martin makes these links between risk, security, armed force and imperial power even more explicit, describing the doctrine of the pre-emptive military strike as 'a new national security policy, one that explicitly links force and finance', before designating the whole military/economic system as a form of 'leveraged hegemony' (Martin, 2004: 352–3).

One particular mechanism, according to Bichler and Nitzan, offers the key to understanding how this concentration of power has been secured. Capitalisation, the process of estimating the financial worth of a corporation, is in their opinion the 'most supple power instrument ever known to humanity' (Bichler and Nitzan, 2010: 1). Based on the difference between a company's equity (the value of its shares) and its debt (the amount owed by the corporation to other groups), capitalisation depends on making an estimate of '*expected future profit* and interest payments, *adjusted for risk*' and then discounted to give the overall market value in the present (8).

This analysis is useful in three respects. First, it returns the power relation to the centre of the equation, as opposed to the various theories of 'diffusion' and networked autonomy, which seem to lose sight of the forceful and decisive qualities of executive influence. Second, it helps to concentrate attention on the synthesis of political and economic power, a perspective that corrects the tendency to mystify both conditions when they are kept apart. Finally, it focuses on the manipulation of the 'future' – in this case, the way in which a financial value that cannot be known is inflated in order to enhance the worth of assets in the present.

Less successful, however, is Bichler and Nitzan's attempt to ex-plain the manner in which this power operates. They argue that, in hierarchical societies, 'every mode of power' rests on 'confidence in obedience', which is the general conviction shown by the elite that 'their subjects' will, despite the occasional outbreak of dissent, comply with the 'dominant dogma or ideology' (Bichler and Nitzan, 2010: 2–3). The problem here is that, in a society where the prevailing hypothesis is that the citizen enjoys democratic freedoms, there is no particular sense that orders are being given. As a consequence, there is of course no feeling that obedience is a necessary form of behaviour. Instead, the notion of the individual doing his or her 'own thing' is embedded in the cultural and leisure-based mode of existence which entertainment capital works overtime to provide.

Although their portrait of the subordinate mindset is perfunctory and underdeveloped, the advantage of the position espoused by Bichler and Nitzan is that the power nexus is located at the top of the social order *as an integrated configuration of interests*, or, in the words of these authors, as the 'state of capital'. This might seem like a return to a rather monolithic conception of authority, but it helps to explain how apparently disparate interests agree on the same principles and how they use the same language in describing them. Rather than 'confidence in obedience', contemporary power works through the delivery of activities and procedures, the practice of which can reinforce all those otherwise intangible assets that together make up the *sign value* of the institution – including the brand and the public relations makeovers that attempt to maintain its public influence – and of the patriarchal capitalist social order itself.

The success of this tactic does not really depend on the actual manifestation of particular events, but upon the inception of a perspective that the public is asked to share. Technological development, capital accumulation, patriarchal oversight, military intervention and unbridled consumerism are presented as normative conditions. Any danger, risk or threat that is meant to impact on the public is actually the consequence of the seizure by the state and corporate authority of the right to determine what constitutes a desirable future. By pretending to anticipate the *particular form* of an event's occurrence during periods of tension or emergency, the singular event becomes a contingency – a phenomenon that can never appear in the way it is imagined. Only the revolutionary event, or the fascist coup, or the terrorist atrocity, seem capable of disturbing, even temporarily, the regular production of this myth.

'Corporate' address and futurity: truth claims in a story-world

The argument advanced so far is that the routine production of forecasts, rather than the particular generation of negative scenarios, is essential to the reproduction of the authoritarian core of the security system.

It also provides the starting point for an investigation of the ways in which a blend of positive *and* negative messages is conveyed to the public. These are based on the communicative techniques that have evolved in order to reach a 'fragmented' marketplace, and that have come to provide an important model for the composition of public address (see below).

A superficial reading might suggest that the two activities – the sounding of an existential alarm and the production of homely, reassuring narratives – might have very little in common. One seems devoted to the manufacture of cautionary tales, based on the assumption that the future is not only uncertain, but positively hazardous – offering, in some cases at least, a dystopian vision of the world and its inhabitants. The other concentrates on the production of optimistic, positive messages, imbued with a light-hearted, broadly utopian spirit. The first practice is meant to characterise the more serious and responsible functions overseen by the regulatory apparatus of the contemporary state – the provision of advice to selected audiences concerning a variety of potential risks. The second is usually associated with the corporate sector and a determinedly commercial agenda – the sale of products and services to a specific target market through the promotion of supposedly harmless fantasy.

In practice, however, no act of communication is likely to depend entirely on the exclusive use of one particular sentiment or psychological approach. A great deal of the advertising generated by commercial interests, for example, can be read as a general warning about the need to make preparations for particular eventualities. Similarly, formal state authority is not always duty-bound to deliver an address that is laden with gloom. There is, however, one variant of communication practice that allows both forms of organisation to develop their strategic capacities, while encouraging their penchant for self-congratulation – 'corporate' address.

Following the precepts of progressive governance and corporate social responsibility, a host of private companies, political parties, state agencies, educational institutions, and the public–private hybrids created by governments, have all tried to learn and apply the basic principles of corporate address, and have placed *brand management* at the heart of their operations. According to their promotional material, these bodies are dedicated to the pursuit of ethical objectives, and driven by the desire to exert a positive influence on the social, economic and natural environments they inhabit. Every aspect of their activity is supposed to contribute to some larger moral endeavour.

Although the various institutions involved in the business of regulation and management may simulate belief in an exalted principle – expressed through the dissemination of 'core values', mission statements, brand identity and so on – it would be naive to expect either the internal ethos of an organisation or its actual practices to match the posture adopted in external publicity. This does not mean that every act of public diplomacy is necessarily fatuous or superficial, but rather that it would be a mistake to imagine that this form of communication is essentially descriptive. In some cases, it attains a messianic quality, though for the most part it mimics the inoffensive, broadly liberal values that an audience is assumed to share.

Besides the overt publicity found in brochures, on websites, in magazines or within the personalised communiqués sent out to individual customers or citizens, the more polished forms of promotional material are most evident in those television or web-based commercials that mount public relations campaigns on behalf of an entire company. The product or service is often entirely absent, or if supplied appears only as the alibi for a narrative that promotes the virtues of individual organisations. While the deliberate use of misinformation may cause some advertisements to be removed from circulation – as indeed was the case when a BT television commercial was removed from circulation for misleading customers over broadband speed[3] – the more subtle offence grows from a practice that is approved by regulators and market advocates alike: the generation of 'truth-claims in a story-world' (Price, 2007). This is the apparently legitimate composition of assertions about the ethical qualities, productive strength or general eminence of influential organisations, set within a narrative context that allows these statements to appear to be sincere and candid expressions of a genuine belief.

All kinds of 'affirmative' propositions are allowed to circulate within the rarefied atmosphere of this parallel universe. So, for example, BP's 'beyond petroleum' campaign (initiated in 2000) declared that 'it's time to turn up the heat on global climate change', and described how 'energy efficiency projects' had saved 4 million tonnes in carbon emissions (BP, 2005).[4] A year later, two journalists argued that the decline in carbon output from 2004 to 2005 had been achieved by recording only the CO_2 that BP had produced directly, rather than that generated by the oil and gas it had bought and then sold on (Seager and Bowers, 21 April 2006).

It would seem as though certain types of declaration are not supposed to be removed from their setting, and are therefore only meant to be taken seriously within it.[5] When the truthfulness of such publicity is questioned, one defence is that these narratives are the honest expression of good intentions, and essentially a set of aspirations. Many advertisements depend on this tactic, and carry explicit references to the future within their text. In one example produced by Shell, which showed young Japanese children playing with balloons, the organisation claimed to 'deliver natural gas to more countries than any other energy company', not just 'for tonight's warming bowl of noodles, but for years to come' (Shell 'Let's Go' campaign, 2010).[6] Having demonstrated its cultural sensitivity, the giant transnational finished on an inclusive note: 'Let's build a better future. Let's go.'

Despite these appeals to join hands with the private sector in the creation of a pleasant but nebulous future, the point of composing any address of this type is to obtain some advantageous outcome in the more 'substantial' present. The ubiquitous myth of progressive authority depends in essence on an essentially illiberal tactic – the timely seizure of space and resource. It is the fact that these strategic messages, bought at astronomical cost, fill the semiotic environment with a 'pro-business' perspective (leaving little space for the organised expression of alternatives[7]) that is objectionable, quite besides the doubtful veracity of the content. Just as economic expropriation separates the labourer from his or her means of subsistence,[8] so the peremptory utterance of corporate ideals – 'soft capitalism' in textual form – tries to monopolise the means of expression.

This does *not* mean that private companies and the state apparatus want to stop the consumer or the citizen from engaging in any form of communication, but rather that they wish this to take place within particular limits. British Telecom (known simply as BT) was, for instance, prepared to engage directly with the public, when it ran a

Facebook campaign to get people to vote on the future direction of its long-running 'Adam and Jane' storyline. The winning plotline was that Jane would announce her pregnancy to Adam: 1.6 million votes were cast for this suggestion (*Campaign*, 20 August 2010: 3). This approach can be reinforced by the use of 'crowdsourcing', in which an enterprise calls for original ideas from the public, offering a prize for the best submission. Unilever followed this course of action, posting a creative brief for its Peperami brand on the web and calling for responses – it created a television commercial based on the winning idea (12).

The goal of the private company may be to stimulate certain types of useful response; it is not used to encourage expressive democracy. A company will, of course, engage with its consumer base, especially through new media, but does so in order to acquire 'a wealth of consumer insight' garnered through 'focus groups, online blogs, video diaries and online tracking studies' (Dutta, 20 August 2010: 13). The conversation is essentially about the virtues of the company, and the overall process is in effect intelligence-gathering, conducted on a grand scale and essentially very similar to the procedures employed by security agencies. In fact, data held by 'private sector operators' is sold to police and intelligence organisations 'on a contractual, for-profit basis' (Sheptycki, 2009: 374).

In addition, marketing companies organise major events with the specific intention of trying to gain an intimate understanding of human motivation. The echoes of those psychological operations run by the military can be heard in the title of the '15th Annual Youth Perspective Conference', held in London on 21 October 2010: 'Win the Hearts and Minds of Today's Digi-Savvy Youth' (*Marketing* conference flyer, 2010). Sessions included studies of social media, providing the chance to 'understand the *online order*' (my emphasis) and to 'learn how to be *trusted*, recommended and shared online' (my emphasis). Other seminars discussed the benefits of 'using language and tone that resonates rather than repels', with the aim of becoming 'a credible youth brand' (*Marketing* conference flyer, 2010). The point of these exercises is twofold: to persuade individuals to buy into a consumer lifestyle, while increasing the reputational capital of individual businesses, since status is also a resource that can be translated into market value (Davis, 2002: 171).

Pride before a fall

One particular organisation, which began its existence as a UK government facility and then became a public limited company, offers a prime example of the corporate approach, producing publicity material which typifies the popular synthesis of commercial address and public interest discourse. In 2007, it issued a 16-page brochure that described its 'commitment to establishing and delivering long-term goals for sustainable development' (AWE, 2007: 2). The group argued that it wished to create 'a sustainable future, particularly for our employees and local communities' and declared that 'when we perform well as a company, our neighbours recognise that we are a valuable addition to the community' (2–3).

Considerable emphasis was placed on the need to run '[the] business in a way that reduces our environmental impact, but that also provides social and economic progress in the communities in which we operate' (AWE, 2007: 3). As part of this undertaking, the company announced a 'targeted drive towards zero waste' (7). The name of this organisation is the Atomic Weapons Establishment, Aldermaston, which manufactures and maintains the UK's arsenal of nuclear weapons. The fact that a facility of this type had adopted the progressive discourses and enlightened practices (such as 'offsetting carbon emissions') favoured by a new breed of corporation that claims to be socially responsible may seem at first sight a puzzling development. It is difficult to see how an organisation involved in the construction of nuclear weapons and the 'dispersal of radioactive and explosives waste' (6) could achieve its moral and environmental goals by fretting about the size of its carbon footprint and issuing information printed on '100% recycled paper' (6n).

In 2010, AWE's safety record became headline news. In July of that year Aldermaston suffered a serious fire in its explosives division, which left one member of staff injured and led to the evacuation of local residents (Doward, 2010a, 22 August: 6). This event prompted the director of the Nuclear Information Service to make the comment that 'it seems that we came within a hair's breadth of everyone's nightmare scenario' (Burt, cited in Doward, 2010a: 6). Other incidents included two fires in 2006, and in 2008 a collision between two vehicles – one carrying high explosives – outside the plant's perimeter (6). Between 2008 and 2009 there were nearly eight thousand 'abnormal incidents' at AWE's various sites, prompting the Defence Environment and Safety Board to warn that budget cuts would make it difficult to manage 'the defence nuclear programmes … with due regard for the protection of the workforce, the public and the environment' (6). Later in 2010, a report emerged that firefighters had 'lost control' of a blaze at Aldermaston (Doward, 2010b, 26 September).

This case shows that socially liberal postures can be adopted by any organisation, irrespective of its core activity; it might also suggest that the extent to which it is possible to change or disguise corporate practices depends on the nature of the business itself. While there is some truth in this notion, promotional material cannot simply be divided into one type that is irredeemably hypocritical, and another variety that should be given the benefit of the doubt. A more advanced argument is that all the activities undertaken by public relations specialists on behalf of formal, authoritative centres are based on the *assumption* of a particular kind of privilege: namely, the (purchased) right to advance an essentially political proposition under the guise of *unexceptional* communication practices.

These forms of address, both civic and commercial, can be described as political not simply because they lobby central government, or because they attempt to influence a consumer base that is at other times constituted as an electorate. While such efforts are undoubtedly made, the more profound reason can be found in the composition of the 'political' as a distinct function. Mainstream bourgeois democracy represents the formal constitution of a deeper structural antagonism, and may be understood as the product of an accommodation between powerful social forces. The raw antipathy that is sometimes thought to characterise relations in those societies that lack proper democratic structures is in the 'advanced' countries of the West supposedly concentrated and exorcised in a separate realm of deliberation.

Under this mode of government, official political structures – councils, parliaments, mayoral offices, and so on – are supplemented by other forms of representation that are supposed to provide avenues for the exercise of free speech. These include those channels provided by media forms (mass, social or mobile), and through traditional collective activities, such as public assembly and demonstrations. The availability of such outlets is based on the principle that every member of a community has the right, within the law, to make a case for any position that reflects their genuine beliefs.

In the case of powerful centres of influence, this widely accepted norm is, however, enhanced by the opportunity, already described above, to use professional communicators to make representations on their behalf. Since this is a provision that lies beyond the reach of the population in general, one of two interpretations must be made: either that this is a democratic right that should be extended to any entity that can prove its egalitarian credentials; or, if it is not, that its use should be denied to those organisations that currently use it to promote their own economic and/or civic dominance. It is this division, the discrimination exercised between essentially unequal bodies, that confirms the inherently political character of paid-for advocacy.

In other words, the core of the problem (for the public and in another sense for formal power itself) is not the relative trustworthiness of particular institutions, but the general dispensation given to powerful interest groups to distribute propaganda. This remark should not be confused with the usual objection that is made to the appearance of misleading information – that it is used to persuade or 'brainwash' the recipient. The purpose of any form of 'dominant' address (which is rarely autocratic in tone) is not necessarily to produce belief, but to manage the expectations and conduct of its intended audience. This is achieved by setting the parameters of debate, and working towards some material outcome, like a small adjustment in attitude that allows an audience to accept a proposition, make a purchase or cast a vote.

The citizen at a disadvantage

Meanwhile, individual citizens or civil organisations that attempt to secure a public profile on any basis that resembles an overtly *political* approach may find that they are regarded with suspicion. A useful example can be found in the response to those non-commercial organisations that try to organise street collections. Although they might present themselves as serving a charitable cause, they are often assumed to harbour illicit motives. It seems as though any form of political consciousness can be regarded as the first step that leads to a successful career in 'domestic extremism' (a designation without legal status), depending on the nature of the activity and the discretion of individual police officers. Advice issued to British police by the National Extremism Tactical Coordination Unit (NETCU), for example, declares that 'funds from unlawful street collections can be used by extremist groups' to finance a variety of activities (www.policeoracle.com, 8 August 2008). These include payments for 'websites that incite criminal actions', and the hiring of 'lawyers to fight criminal prosecutions'. The latter is not, however, an illegal activity in itself: it is as though NETCU has simply transferred the negative connotations of the term 'criminal' from the previous sentence. Nonetheless, NETCU's statement goes on to remind officers to 'record the full details of the collectors and promoters for intelligence gathering purposes', and to 'record the nature of the literature being offered either freely or for sale'.

Corporate and government conduct, on the other hand, is not subjected to the same kind of scrutiny (though it does have to undergo regulation and inspection, as the Aldermaston example (see above) demonstrates). No attempt is made, however, to prevent the actual activity itself: the promotion of military hardware at arms fairs, for example, is sanctioned by the state and thus free from interference. Once again, reference to extreme examples of moral transgression should not distract attention from a more fundamental critique – that the root of the problem lies in the fact that a number of unaccountable agencies have been allowed to commandeer the communicative resources necessary to advance their own interests, just as the capitalist enterprise reproduces the conditions of its own existence by seizing the resources of the present and the potentialities of the future.

The circulation of the 'worst case'

Within those formal structures specifically devoted to the 'defence' of the existing political and economic system, dangerous events are regarded as potentially catastrophic, not when they represent a threat to the public as such, but when they pose a challenge to the hegemony of dominant institutions. This ideological predisposition grows from the forced association between 'national security and public safety'

(Townshend, 1999: 166), in which it is assumed that dominant organisations or principles epitomise the moral foundations of the social order. Such a perspective can be used to reinforce the supposition that, when an existential threat is identified, it endangers an otherwise harmonious and legitimate social order.

This tactic is also employed to promote the insidious argument that, faced with exceptional hazards, the capacity of patriarchal, state or corporate power to 'protect' the citizen-consumer must be reinforced. These types of authority draw upon the still undiminished reputation of formal democracy, what Hobsbawm calls 'the miraculous qualities assigned to governments elected by arithmetical majorities' (Hobsbawm, 2007: 5). It is a term that he thinks has 'lost all contact with reality' (5), while those 'humane' military interventions that are meant to meet extreme eventualities are no more than 'the imperialism of human rights' (7).

Use of the worst-case scenario is not, however, confined to the political or economic realm, since it circulates as a major theme within journalism, certain types of adventure fiction, and mainstream cinematic narrative. The last includes *Independence Day* (1996), *The Sum of All Fears* (2002), *The Day After Tomorrow* (2004), and *Cloverfield* (2008). One noticeable difference between these films lies in their type of address. Before 9/11, the tendency was to present the spectator with a view of the action that emphasised a form of panoramic objectivity, while the period after September 11th has been more inclined to copy the mobile subjectivity associated with the use of hand-held devices like mobile phones and camcorders. The fact that these tales of disaster are generically distinct from political expression does not reduce, and may perhaps augment, their capacity to question the proposition that security can only be provided by the military hierarchy of the neoliberal state, although the fictional storylines produced by institutions like the motion picture industry are sometimes employed by centres of authority to rehearse their 'real world' responses to unexpected events.[9]

Indeed, in many cases, the mediated treatment of political and social jeopardy arises from the close affiliation between, on the one hand, military structures and, on the other, industrial and entertainment capital (Turse, 2008; Der Derian, 2009). This alliance is cemented by the exchange of shared ideological perspectives, based on a 'war-like' model of business (Martin, 2002) and a businesslike attitude to war (Price, 2010). While an authorised narrative, fictional or otherwise, may provide an extended pretext for a particular course of action – attempting, for instance, to justify military adventurism[10] – an authoritarian strategy can also be dramatised through the *staging* of a 'security event' (see Chapter 4). The performance of a 'real world' scenario,[11] which often entails the temporary imposition of exclusion zones in public space (Der Derian, 2009: 123), is usually presented as an essential way of testing the state's ability to meet those extreme contingencies that provide the typical form in which the scenario is cast.

Threat and social discipline

101,000 stop and searches. No terror arrests.
R. Verkaik (29 October 2010)

The objective is to have communities, both at home and ... abroad, that are prepared to cooperate with the security services ... the security and intelligence capability that is needed is ... the ability to 'operate among the people', including when operating overseas.
Omand, paper on the National Security Strategy for the IPPR(February 2009)

We don't want to be seen as 'self-pity city', but it is worse than the worst-case scenario.
Paul Brant, deputy leader of Liverpool Council, discussing budget cuts (in Davies, 22 October 2010)

The concerted attempt to present governance as a progressive, decentralised alternative to traditional forms of state power has probably come to an end. Too many intelligent critics, like du Gay (2007), have examined this argument and discovered its flaws. Now that governance has been shorn of its pretensions, continued adherence to its precepts is fast becoming the preserve of the right-wing policy wonk, the senior military officer and the conservative academic. Among the latter must be counted one Professor of Public Communication, Barry Richards, who observed the breakdown in relations between forms of authority and the citizen and decided to recommend a solution.

Richards believes that, just as marketers 'need to know how to address the consuming public', politicians must discover the 'most effective and inclusive ways of speaking to their electorates' (Richards, 2007: 21). His suggestion is that governments and their allies should pursue the 'informed management' of the 'political public' (10), in order to establish a regime of 'emotional governance'. This is summarised as 'a deliberate and sophisticated attention, through mass-mediated communications' to the sentiments current among the people (5). The overall aim of the project is to produce a 'cohesive national culture', in which the authorities try to 'inspire identification and strengthen pro-social impulses' (6). In pursuing this goal, Richards insists that politicians must draw upon the knowledge accrued by 'advertising and public relations professionals' (7).

The urgent need to re-evaluate public diplomacy is then traced to the existence of one condition – the terrorist threat. The various 'scenarios of global strife and domestic fragmentation' that Richards identifies (2007: 191) are in his opinion composed with reference to this menace. This perception is not, however, followed by an in-depth analysis of the nature of the conflict between state and non-state actors. Instead, Richards is absorbed in two other questions. The first is how to tailor the public declarations made by a national leadership to the emotional needs of its audience, and the second is the extent to which the subordinate group can expect to grasp the substance of any such message. It is the treatment of this second issue that reveals just how little Richards cares about the value of an interactive or 'democratic' model of political exchange.

Gamely placing himself in the ranks of the people, Richards observes that, on many occasions, 'we may not be in a position to judge the soundness of particular statements', and that 'the only bit of reality of which we can be sure is our own feeling about the issue' (2007: 191). This means that the members of the public should decide whether the politician making the address 'seems to us to know of our feelings and to understand them' (191). The deficiencies of such a limited aspiration are apparent even before the reader recalls that the promotion of empathy as a political tool has already been tried and found wanting: during the Iraq War, for example, Tony Blair made a particular effort to appeal to the emotions of his audience, but those in receipt of such messages seemed to expect to be given a more logical account of his actions.

Richards goes on to argue that 'we do not have to feel agreed with, but we do need to be noticed and *contained*' (2007: 191; my emphasis). Containment is presumably the psycho-social equivalent of being 'kettled' by the police, but Richards contends that 'only when we are reasonably well contained by a responsible and trustworthy person' will we 'be able to extend ourselves collectively as citizens' and make 'compromises or sacrifices for the common good' (191). My own perspective is diametrically opposed to this highly compromised project, and is founded on the conviction that the role of the academic does not include the provision of bespoke services to the political elite or state functionaries, so that they are better able to manipulate their audiences. It is important to note that when Omand argued that the 'security and intelligence capability' required in the current period is 'the ability to operate among the people' – a position originally expressed by General Rupert Smith – his remark was primarily directed at the oversight of the domestic population (Omand, 2009). Having accepted to some degree the liberal insistence that the security agenda be widened to include the protection of human beings, the security regime has interpreted this goal as an opportunity to spy on the public, and has simply transferred the theoretical assumptions of counter-insurgency to the home population.

Trading on uncertainty

The political advantage of describing a nebulous and worrying future is that it cannot be contradicted by an observer because it is not yet known. The dissemination of indeterminate possibilities is a useful means of governing the present. It avoids having to provide some evidence that the present is the most desirable condition. Politicians chafe against the idea of concentrating on the present, where there is a wealth of material that can be used against them. The constant doom-mongering associated with the terror narrative seems to disappear whenever the state is confronted with a genuine disaster for which it may be held partly responsible. The White House, for instance, was reported to be 'overly optimistic' in its assessment of the BP oil spill

(Goldenberg, 6 August 2010: 19). Similarly, when an event like 9/11 takes place it is not allowed to become 'historical', but because it forms the basis of a lesson about the effects of terrorism is cited constantly as something that remains contemporary.

The institutional development of the scenario has an ideological character, not because it is always framed as the 'worst case' – which can be singled out as an unfortunate exaggeration – but because formal authority is incapable of making any value-free predictions, no matter what the scale or severity is imagined. Every single description of the future identified by formal authority is used to reinforce the social philosophy and practical arrangements of the present. Contingency plans are drafted because hierarchical organisations must provide their subordinates with a rationale for action. In other words, various activities are described because they substantiate the idea that a form of state or corporate authority must endure within even the most inauspicious circumstances. The act of prefiguring an event requires the ability to follow *an administrative template*, which contains the ideological 'preconditions' for an exercise that is *disguised as a practical necessity*.

Two models of the 'security regime'

The fact that much of the planning regime seems irrational has led some critics to propose that a more balanced or logical agreement should be brokered. Gardner, for example, asks if it is possible to 'establish new systems and norms of international governance' and even to create 'regional security communities' which can establish cooperation between competing interests, such as those represented by the USA, EU and Russia (2005: 183). This concept resembles the traditional model of the security regime, in which states collaborate in order to create a more effective and reciprocal model of international relations.

The notion of constructing such institutions, in an attempt to resolve inter-state rivalry, draws attention away from the fact that such bodies are already embroiled in less overt forms of collusion and competition, and that the various secret accords are actually inimical to the free association of peoples. Gardner suggests that rehearsals of cooperation, such as 'peacekeeping exercises [and] anti-terrorist training operations' (2005: 184), might prove useful in encouraging the growth of peace.

In reality, such a proposal represents a *settlement* devoted to the consolidation of each state's security apparatus, the type of organisation referred to in this book as the true purpose of the (internal) security regime. My argument is that an objection should be made, not to the *chaos* of inter-state relations, but to the entire existence of hierarchical power, in whatever form it manifests itself. To repeat the plea made above, the challenge should not be *how to help the dominant present a public rationale* for their repellent impulses, but how to resist the dysfunctional projects dreamed up by this 'alliance of rivals'.

When the economist Andrew Gamble described the possibility that a 'crisis of capitalism' would manifest itself in 'unpredictable and sometimes uncontrollable events', he was referring to the economic disaster popularly known as the credit crunch: among the most undesirable consequences of this situation was in his opinion 'depression, polarisation, political unrest, even war, affecting all parts of the global economy and the international state system' (Gamble, 2009: 4).

These comments are at one level entirely reasonable, but are also typical of a mode of analysis that considers the failure and breakdown of a system, rather than its success, as the source of social dislocation. The Iraq War, however, was fought under relatively auspicious economic circumstances. This alone should suggest that it may be the smooth functioning of the state/capital/patriarchy nexus that is problematic, and that the system itself is geared towards the creation of strife and inequality. Rather than argue that only certain types of production (represented by the arms trade or the derivatives market, for example) are responsible for a kind of 'moral failing' in the structure of patriarchal capitalism, the alternative position is that the whole process – the order of things rather than their interruption – guarantees social and environmental degradation.

The growth of 'securitisation' associated with the creation of a powerful command structure is therefore much more than a theory of intervention, and relies on the use of anti-terror and public order legislation to achieve the *pre-emptive* destruction of effective resistance (see Taylor, 3 April 2009, 14 April 2009). This development is paralleled by the increasingly armed suppression of radical and criminal disturbances and extends to forms of governance that are not only undemocratic but also actively repressive.[1] The direct application of coercive power requires a range of resources and activities, including a dedicated corps of gendarmerie to carry out paramilitary manoeuvres against the civilian population.[2] The goal is to transfer learned behaviours, mental attitudes and practised routines from the worst-case scenario to more routine events.[3] The rise of the 'business continuity plan' is a good example of this form of defensive strategy, where the goal is to see 'how quickly and painlessly' the managerial class can 'get back to "business as usual" in the event of a terrorist attack, fire, flood or other natural disaster' (London First, 2005: 2).

From contingency to eventuality

The tendency to see events in a different light as time progresses – to revise their categorical place and thus their status – may suggest that a thorough critique of the scenario must depend on the insights generated by the study of real, individual eventualities. *Eventuality* is defined here not as a potential outcome, but rather as something that actually comes to pass. In opposition to the state/corporate manipulation of possibility, actual events should be analysed, together with the presiding conditions that allow any particular phenomenon to appear, including (i) the inherent quality of the phenomenal, (ii) the intervention of particular human collectives, and (iii) the culturally determined expectations of the observer.

Instead of imposing a template on the conception of the future, the point of studying eventuality is to work towards an outcome that offers a genuinely progressive alternative to the particular type of delusion generated within the current social order, represented in this book by the institutional behaviour of the UK and the USA. The problem is not so much that individuals enter into social relations through the dominance of a unitary spectacle, but rather that they *are trained to know their place* in the 'free' society. It is not the promotion of the worst-case scenario in particular (see Sunstein, 2007), but the general attempt to keep the population in a condition of dependent stasis which helps to thwart the development of social equality and the onset of rational economic planning – simple goals that are rapidly assuming the appearance of revolutionary demands.

The purpose of this book is not, however, simply to make a contrast between an ideal condition and one that has become entirely debased, in the hope of substantiating the former while shaming the various schemers and patriarchs who coordinate the latter. It is, rather, based on the thesis that the contemporary Western social order is a system of mutually competitive hierarchies, founded on the reproduction of political quietism and social conformity.

This book's argument, in sum, is that plans which appear to describe external threats may actually testify to the authorities' fear of *internal* disaffection. Whatever the circumstance, the scenario is used to accomplish a number of closely related aims, which can be summarised as follows: (i) the evasion of democratic constraints on executive power, (ii) the strengthening of a parallel structure of semi-privatised hierarchical authority, (iii) the circulation of an authoritarian narrative based on a narrow reading of security, (iv) the prevention of democratic initiative through the manipulation of time and space, and (*v*) the subsequent repression of alternative political visions. The last of these goals is partly accomplished through the creation of the first four conditions, since the point of establishing a dominant structure is to allow the circulation of narratives, codes and practices that help to determine the practical expression of the prevailing world-view. This must be circulated within the dominant organisation itself and, upon contact with those designated as 'stakeholders', distributed throughout the relevant branches of the social order as a set of practical activities.

Meanwhile, the security regime continues to 'get ahead of itself', interrupting the temporal routines and spatial integrity of everyday life in order to demonstrate the principle of command. Its functionaries, however, are acutely aware of the ideological disadvantage that this can entail. It gives rise to the accusation that, within the heart of many liberal democracies, a police state is being developed. This, in turn, is countered by the argument that each exercise, each emergency and each confrontation with the terrorist enemy is born out of necessity, and represents no more than an 'extraordinary' and transient procedure, conducted within a larger and constitutionally robust democratic environment. This testifies not only to the expectation that circulates in a formal electoral democracy, to the effect that actions need some form of (often retrospective) explanation, but also to the desire of executive power to deny the comparison that it has itself inadvertently invited, between its own activity and that of the totalitarian states – past and present – that it still pretends to regard as the epitome of evil.

Notes

INTRODUCTION

1. See, for example, the British government's *Iraq's Weapons of Mass Destruction*, London, 2003; *Home-Grown Terrorism: What Does It Mean for Business?*, London: Lloyd's, 2007; *National Risk Register*, London: Cabinet Office, 2008. Some studies depend on a more considered assessment of 'actual' risk, including for instance the IPPR's *Secure Foundations: Key Issues in Crime Prevention, Crime Reduction and Community Safety*, London, 2000. This type of report bears a superficial resemblance to academic work, but departs from this paradigm because think-tanks are sometimes reluctant to allow anything to overturn their central thesis.

ONE

1. The UK's National Security Council was formed in May 2010, and held its first meeting on 12 May 2010 (see Prime Minister's Office, at www.number10.gov. uk/news/latest/news/2010/05/establishment-of-a-national-security-council-9953).
2. See, for example, Abercrombie et al., 1980; Therborn, 1980; Buxton, 1990; Billig, 1991; Larrain, 1994; Žižek, 1994; and van Dijk, 1998.
3. Or, to take a specific example, it is now perfectly acceptable for a company to advertise itself as an 'equal opportunities' employer, while exercising absolute discretion over who should be regarded as worthy of equality.
4. According to the study of armed police written by Punch, *Shoot to Kill* (2011), the 'Gold–Silver–Bronze' system did not function properly during the operation that ended in the death of Jean-Charles de Menezes.

TWO

1. In his analysis of 'the new managerialism', Stuart Hall described it as 'the vehicle by means of which neoliberal ideas actually inform institutional practices': see 'New Labour's double-shuffle', *Soundings* 24, Autumn 2003: 10-24.

2. Useful examples of the discourses mobilised to promote state governance can be found in *The Governance of Britain*, London: HMSO, 2007.

3. See, for example, bodies like the International Corporate Governance Network (ICGN) and its *Corporate Governance Principles* (London, 2009).

4. In the US State Department's *Afghanistan and Pakistan Regional Stabilization Strategy*, the goal of 'improving governance' is pursued in order to 'help develop more responsive, visible, and accountable institutions in Kabul' (February, 2010). The argument that imperial power has been reconfigured as an informal, non-territorial power is outlined in A. Ayers, 'Imperial Liberties: Democratisation and Governance in the "New" Imperial Order', *Political Studies* 57(1), 2009: 1-27.

5. The work of these 'partners' in government might include assistance with the coordination of policy, the delivery of services and the regulation of 'information flows' to the public.

6. See J. Joseph, 'Foucault and Reality', *Capital and Class* 82, 2003: 143-65, for a useful discussion of Foucault's attitude to power relations and the role of the state.

7. If the character of democratic bourgeois modernity can be determined as generally benign, then the range of discussion about any corrective measures needed to steer through various crises can exclude any revolutionary propositions. The range of debate can then be confined to the more limited disputes over the correct balance to strike on certain issues, such as the degree to which a national deficit should be reduced through public spending cuts. The notion that all such cuts are unnecessary is therefore never raised.

8. Material goods and benefits are seized en masse or manufactured in bulk by the profiteer, then parcelled out in small units to be sold back to people who do not assume that they have as much (or as little) right to ownership as the capitalist who gains a social advantage from the exchange.

9. For a recent examination of the change in the definition of the 'public' from a single entity to a more complex conception, see Mahoney et al., 2010.

10. This distinction, between a majority of individuals who own capital for personal or familial use, which gives them 'little or no control over other people', and those groups that possess assets employed as 'financial instruments', is made in Nitzan and Bichler, 2009: 37.

11. The core of the 'state apparatus' is defined by Jessop as 'a distinct ensemble of institutions and organisations' the function of which is to 'define and enforce collectively-binding decisions on a given population in the name of their 'common interest' or 'general will'' (2008: 9).

12. Interest in the promotion of 'joined-up government' was a significant feature of the British 'New Labour' project: see Fairclough, 2000: 51.

13. Cooley defines hierarchy as 'a condition of relational power' in which a 'dominant polity' has the right to make decisions, while the 'subordinate member' does not (Cooley, 2005: 5). A useful example of the executive assuming

power in an emergency is the removal of strategic decision-making from the Ministry of Agriculture, Fisheries and Food during the 2001 foot-and-mouth crisis, when the prime minister operated through the 'COBR' system (Cabinet Office Briefing Room, pronounced 'cobra'). See Hindmoor, 2009.

14. See Fisher et al., 2010.

15. A newspaper columnist observed the corollary to this principle, in which groups once regarded as powerful are treated with contempt by bourgeois commentators once they seem to have lost their influence: the example given was the working class, which, at the point at which it was no longer regarded as 'a political peril', ceased to be accorded any public respect (Toynbee, *Guardian*, 10 July 2010).

THREE

1. See Cobain, *Guardian*, 18 June 2009: 16; Norton-Taylor, *Guardian*, 1 August 2009: 2.

2. The first three of these qualities are taken from Acher's designation for the three orders of reality: see Archer, 2000: 162.

FOUR

1. If the dominant political environment is conceived in a particular way, this will of course effect what 'counts' as an event.

2. A 'natural' event, such as an earthquake or volcanic eruption, is supposed to occur without human intervention, and to demonstrate attributes that mark it out as independent. As a result, it provides a useful example of a phenomenon that 'interrupts' the social and has to be (or is automatically) classified. The creation of a 'public' event (one organised by human collectives) requires the concentration of resource and effort (together with the use of practical, material and symbolic power) that only human groups are capable of producing.

3. In some cases, events thought unusual or extraordinary are used to exemplify new distinctions or subdivisions, providing a home for the appearance of any subsequent cases thought broadly comparable.

4. See, for example, the controversy over the classification of drugs.

5. Metropolitan Police Service, n.d.; accessed 18 March 2010.

6. For an official account of MI5's history, see Andrew, 2010.

7. The present tendency in Britain to repeat, throughout a conversation, the specious reassurance that the speaker intends 'to be honest with you' is an example of this form of mimetic currency.

8. See the Civil Contingencies Act 2004, at www.opsi.gov.uk/acts/acts2004/ukpga_20040036_en_7.

9. See R. Carne, 'How Britain's "deep state" is covering up the mistakes that led to Iraq war', *Observer*, 25 July 2010: 5.

FIVE

1. Such types of 'demonstration' (see the discussion on Debord) are staged in the knowledge that they will achieve mass media circulation. Individuals present at such events often report a qualitatively different subjective experience. See,

for example, John Tulloch's account of the way his image was used in press reports after the 7 July London bombing, in R. Coward, 'They have given me somebody else's voice – Blair's voice', *Guardian* G2, 10 November 2005.

2. See Chapter 2, and as a further guide Bevir and Rhodes, 2003.

3. This emerges from the perception that individuals are sometimes faced with 'mutually exclusive' categories, and explains why some individuals declare themselves 'ashamed' of their country of origin; in order to maintain a political distinction, they are forced to deny their 'natural' place within a national category.

4. See also Norton-Taylor and Cowan, *Guardian*, 11 May 2006.

5. That which produces a condition through the act of utterance.

6. An example is the use by the British Labour government of coded terms like 'reform'; see Fairclough, 2000.

7. The movement from 'shock and awe' to 'target of opportunity', which appeared in news reports of the initial attack on Iraq, is an example; see Price, 2010.

8. An instance of this was Blair's speech to the September 2005 Labour Conference (27 September 2005), in which television coverage turned on the question of his longevity as party leader, rather than dealing with the themes he wished to animate.

9. See Abercrombie et al., 1980.

10. It is worth noting that the Household Cavalry, from which the troops were mustered, has traditionally provided a military force able to check civil unrest in the capital.

11. The Greek authorities created the Olympic Games Security Division (OGSD) for the purposes of policing the Games.

12. In rhetorical terms, this may be associated with 'negative identification' (Atkinson, 1984).

13. In 'We should not be hosting these Olympics', *Independent*, 3 August 2004.

SIX

1. This statement was taken from a news report, 'Morgan Freeman's 9/11 Take Panned', which appeared in the *New York Daily News* of 3 June 2002 (p. 4). It was written by Hayes et al. and cited subsequently in Trimarco and Depret's 'Wounded Nation, Wounded Time' (2005).

2. The time zone in London was five hours ahead of New York, so for British viewers it was just after three in the afternoon. The bulletin carried the caption 'LIVE', together with 'Breaking News', which alternated with the title 'Explosions in America'.

3. Although concerned primarily with the Twin Towers, the BBC report also showed the efforts of firefighters to control the blaze at the Pentagon.

4. Meyer, British ambassador to the USA from 1997 to 2003, recalled his initial response to the news of the first crash: he imagined that 'some small private plane … had wandered off course' (Meyer, 2006: 187). See also the accounts written by Handschuh and Epstein, among others, in Bull and Erman's *At Ground Zero* (2002), which carries twenty-five descriptions of September 11th, all written by trainee reporters who covered the event.

5. At this point, a police officer interrupted the interview as he tried to move people away from the scene of the explosion.

6. Later episodes are not, of course, always used to determine the meaning of earlier ones; any number of incidents, taken from any point within an extended period, might be employed to represent the overall quality of a particular event. The point is that the classification (and retrospective re-evaluation) of individual episodes – followed by the creation of a provisional storyline – is common to journalists and eyewitnesses alike.

7. An initial and anonymous claim made on behalf of the Democratic Front for the Liberation of Palestine was denied by the representatives of the organisation itself. See the remarks of Orla Guerin, BBC News 24's Israel correspondent, who described the 'strenuous, energetic and repeated denials' made by the DFLP's officials, who, she said, had been 'pleading' with their contacts to ensure that they were not held accountable: 11 September 2001. See also the comments about the DFLP made by Gaby Rado on Channel Four on the same day, reprinted in Price, 2010: 90.

8. Meyer makes reference to the inadequacy of Bush's first intervention, recalling the president's 'rather stumbling performance on television' (2006: 191). For an analysis of Bush's movements on the day of the attack, see Wood and Thompson's online article 'An Interesting Day: President Bush's Movements and Actions on 9/11' (n.d.).

9. See the very useful discussion of Bush's televised address on the evening of 11 September, in Montgomery's 'Talking War' (2005: 247–8).

10. Mahoney et al. provide an overview of the ways in which the public is convened and assembled in their edited collection *Rethinking the Public* (2010).

11. See Chapter 16 of Moore and Slater's *Bush's Brain* (2004) for an account of the rationale behind the decision to attack Iraq.

12. In Debrix's opinion, for example, it bewildered public, politicians and the media alike, and produced a 'virtual silence and absence of commentary … on the part of media networks', at least 'for a few moments' during the initial live transmission (Debrix, 2008: 3). It is this point which so nearly brings into focus a vital determinant of public communication during '9/11': the deficiency of political, rather than media, structures, and the relegation of the 'public' to the position of spectator. The media are, in fact, never really silent. Journalists, in particular, are used to filling in 'dead air' with speculative chatter, while the appearance of captions and rolling headlines fulfils the requirements of continuous commentary.

13. The second collision featured in early reports, while a recording of the first impact – captured by a crew making a documentary about the Fire Department of New York – did not feature in the first phase of coverage. Three film-makers, James Hanlon, Jules Naudet and Gedeon Naudet, had intended to make a feature about a probationary officer who was serving in the Fire Department. By chance, their footage included the impact on the North Tower of the first aircraft. See Reynolds, 2002.

14. In an early discussion of press coverage of '9/11', one author argued that 'despite the uniqueness of September 11, newspaper reports fit easily into the established frames and templates of journalism' (Berrington, 2002: 51).

15. Even among those who observed television coverage in 'real' time, a significant

number will have had their perceptions coloured by later repetitions of the same footage.

16. Of course, no two-dimensional relay is ever quite 'instantaneous', and the position occupied by the camera restricts the observer to a view taken from a particular angle.

17. This, in turn, may help to identify 'patterns of cause and effect, which may ... enable prediction of what is to come' (Hutchings, 2008: 6). The relationship between this process of stimulus and consequence, and its mapping onto imagined futures, is one of the themes of this book.

18. In his book on *Basic Content Analysis* (2nd edn), Weber gives the following list of semantic qualities: word, word sense, sentence, paragraph, theme, whole text (1990: 23)

19. The 9/11 Commission Report lists 2,479 'non-terrorist' deaths at the WTC, 184 at the Pentagon, and 40 in Pennsylvania (*9/11 Commission Report*, 2004, n. 188). Ferguson, in his book *Colossus*, gives the figure of 2,940 killed in the World Trade Center attacks, 189 in the strike against the Pentagon, and 44 dead in the Pennsylvania plane crash (2005: 325 n67).

20. 'Incident' is drawn from the Latin *incidere*, meaning 'to fall upon', suggesting a dangerous, or at the very least unexpected, and thus unwelcome event.

21. Noam Chomsky argued that this was 'the first time since the war of 1812 that the national territory has been under attack' (Chomsky, 2001: 11). He dismissed references to the 'Pearl Harbor analogy' because he believed that this was in effect part of a dependent colony (12). The attack was also notable for the initial absence of admissions of responsibility. There were, however, some early suggestions that Osama bin Laden was responsible: Gaby Rado, on Channel Four News, 11 September 2001, argued that the 'first suspicion has got to be' the 'bin Laden led group of terrorist organisations' (in Price, 2010: 90).

22. This is a matter of social and functional demarcation. Just as pedestrians are supposed to use the pavements, and motorists are meant to drive on the roads, so social life is directed through the means of demarcation, of division of function. When pedestrians and motorists move into the same spatial domain, as for instance when someone attempts to cross the road, a series of protocols comes into play. Similarly, when two different group activities intersect, a modus operandi must be in place. This is not to say that it is impossible to swap roles. For example, the executive can be reduced to the factotum: class relations are maintained, which is what the system requires; once established, 'social mobility' can take place to a greater or lesser degree, provided hierarchical roles are maintained. It does not matter who fills the roles concerned. A set of appropriate behaviours will inevitably be generated by the situation.

23. See the analysis of Hymes in Price, 1996.

24. The relationship between models of subjective and objective categorisation is discussed to good effect in Oakes et al., 2004: 108–13. For an example of the controversies that arise over how to characterise or label an event, see the analysis of changes in the depiction of military strategy which occurred during the opening phases of the Iraq War of 2003, in Price, 2010: 77.

25. The use of the term 'ideological' refers here to the production of attitudes rather than the creation of invariant belief; this approach is based on the

conviction that the ideological process is concerned with the attainment of goals, which does not necessarily require the imposition of distinct 'positions' on the subordinate.

SEVEN

1. Sir Ian Blair, who was at the time the chief constable of the Metropolitan Police, declared at the press conference of 22 July 2006 that '*Met police officers* have shot a man inside Stockwell Underground Station at approximately 10 a.m. this morning.' The *Guardian* reported that 'a man was chased by *officers* and shot around five times in the head at point-blank range' (Cobain et al., *Guardian* 23 July 2005; my emphasis). Some commentators had attributed the action to military personnel.

2. See, for example, Dodd, *Guardian*, 23 July 2005.

3. *Daily Express*, 'IT WAS JUST A TRAGIC MISTAKE' of 18 August 2005; see also 'Tragic victim who loved London', *Daily Mail*, 25 July 2005: 2–3.

4. See 'Innocent died in hail of bullets', *Sunday Express*, 24 July 2005: 2.

5. The Metropolitan Police issued a document emphasising that Kratos is based on 'a range of tactics', including 'an unarmed uniformed police officer stopping someone' (Metropolitan Police, n.d.; accessed 28 August 2008).

6. See Metropolitan Police Authority minutes, 8 August 2005. Other tactics associated with a 'shoot to kill' policy include 'a second separate strategy for dealing with a suspected suicide bomber targeting a major public event … [when] a commander has the authority to order a sniper to fire without warning from a hidden position' (Casciani, 2007).

7. See www.ipcc.gov.uk for details of the two IPPC reports into the Stockwell shooting.

8. '"Shoot to kill" is a vernacular term which the police themselves prefer not to use', Metropolitan Police Authority minutes, 8 August 2005.

9. In the *Sun* of 23 July this appeared as 'any death is deeply regrettable. But as I understand it the man was challenged and refused to obey instructions' (Parker et al., *Sun*, 23 July 2005: 4). The passage on the UK Police Service website read: 'The information I have available is that this shooting is directly linked to the ongoing and expanding anti-terrorist operation. Any death is deeply regrettable. I understand the man was challenged and refused to obey.'

10. The death could at this stage have been reported in a variety of ways – including murder, manslaughter and illegal killing. Verdicts of illegal killing were passed in two cases of police shootings, in 1997 and 2005, though these were overturned at, respectively, retrial and judicial review (see Inquest, at http://inquest.gn.apc. org/data_unlawful_killing.html).

11. Instead, attention was devoted to the dramatic character of the incident, supported by the extensive use of eyewitness evidence, accounts which themselves produced misleading impressions of de Menezes's movements and behaviour.

12. These are contained within Metropolitan Police Authority minutes, 8 August 2005.

13. See 'Menezes police "gave no warning"', BBC News online, 30 October 2008; accessed 30 October 2008.

14. See 'Menezes identification "definite:"', BBC News online, 28 October 2008; accessed 28 October 2008.

15. The speaker in this particular instance possessed not only privileged information, but also the authority to disseminate it.

16. *Setting* is a concept used by the linguist Hymes to describe the context in which a speech event takes place. It refers not only to the physical arena provided for formal utterance, but also to the psychological conditions encountered by participants (Price, 1998: 96).

17. The representatives of formal authority are also seen, following Wheeler (in Keeble, 2005), as 'actors'. They are treated, in everyday practice, as the first focus of enquiry for the press, their opinions actively sought through 'calls' or 'ring-arounds', unlike less exalted bodies, which are not usually asked to 'generate their own proactive copy' (Wheeler, cited in Keeble, 2005: 57).

18. In the days that followed the Stockwell shooting, the public were to learn a little more about the extent of the coercive powers which the police, armed forces and intelligence services had begun to develop.

19. See IPPC at http://statguidance.ipcc.gov.uk/index.php?id=4.

20. The following excerpt may demonstrate the reluctance of some in authority to keep the MPA fully informed: 'After that meeting in March 2002 a critical incident exercise weekend was conducted, called Operation Tavistock, at which Sir John Quinton represented the Authority. Unfortunately I can find no records of Sir John subsequently briefing the Authority in any formal way on the outcome of that weekend but it is clear that the MPS felt that through his attendance the Authority was being kept in touch with this policy as it was being developed' (Metropolitan Police Authority minutes, 8 August 2008).

21. 'Man shot at Stockwell tube station: We can confirm that at just after 10 am this morning, Friday 22 July, armed officers from the Metropolitan Police entered Stockwell tube station in south London. A man was challenged by officers and was subsequently shot … the man was pronounced dead at the scene. Stockwell tube station is closed and cordons of 200 metres are in place. As is routine, officers from the Met's Directorate of Professional Standards have been informed' (Bulletin 0000000232 cms.met.police.uk/news/major_operational_announcements). This appeared in the *Daily Mail* on 22 July as 'We can confirm that just after 10am armed officers entered Stockwell Tube station. A man was challenged by officers and subsequently shot. London Ambulance Service attended the scene. He was pronounced dead at the scene.'

22. Press management of the transition between themes might be expected to include some recognition that the original police statement was a falsehood; the actual process of adjustment, however, tended to concentrate on the novelty of the new situation, rather than the misrepresentations already offered.

23. 'Political interventions depend upon 'timeliness'. In other words, the actual function of rhetoric is to provide *alibis* to cover decisions made in advance of their public revelation.

24. The ubiquitous appearance of 'terrorism' as a catch-all description of a condition requiring a systemic response is described by Makdisi, who considers that the label constitutes a 'politico-juridical foundation for a universal campaign' (Makdisi, 2002: 267). The 'war on terror', therefore, represents 'the proposal for

a new system of governance and control whose declared enemies are indefinite and spectral' (267).

25. This marks an interesting revision of Althusser's conception of the police officer calling the citizen to account (1971), and the individual's immediate recognition of their place within the symbolic order. In the Stockwell case, the officers made no 'call to order', but executed an individual who turned out to be the citizen of another state.

26. So, for example, the Prevention of Terrorism Act of 1989 was introduced in Britain as temporary legislation requiring annual renewal and was used to proscribe organisations such as the IRA and INLA, armed nationalist groups that used, among other methods, bombings and assassinations to disrupt British occupation of the Six Counties.

27. The Italian state, for example, had by 1981 incarcerated some 3,500 individuals without trial, in some cases under a law ('insurrection against the powers of the state') that had remained on the statute books since the fascist era (Red Notes, 1981: 42).

28. For example, the whole narrative concerning 'weapons of mass destruction' may be seen as a rationale designed to unite competing agencies in the pursuit of an 'imperial' aim which could not be fully delineated in public. As Wolfowitz explained, 'the truth is that for reasons that have a lot to do with the U.S. government bureaucracy we settled on the one issue that everyone could agree on which was weapons of mass destruction as the core reason' (interview with Sam Tannenhaus, *Vanity Fair*, 9 May 2003).

29. The use of the ambush or 'hard arrest' in Northern Ireland, dating from the deployment of the SAS in 1976, provides one example (Urban, 1992). On the mainland, other instances can be found in the fairly regular calls to update public order tactics to deal with 'enhanced' threats. So, for example, the *Sunday Times* of 8 April 1990 carried an article on the Poll Tax Riot of the previous weekend, in which the group of reporters that formed the 'Insight' team speculated on the possible use of 'marksmen' to shoot armed assailants hiding in crowds. As with all such plans, the establishment of a convincing *scenario* is an important initial step. This particular narrative involved imagining a situation in which terrorists or criminals were ready to discharge weapons, using crowds of demonstrators as cover. The headline read 'Police plan a "shoot to kill: policy in riots' (Insight, *Sunday Times*, 8 April 1990).

30. See 'Menezes identification "definite"', BBC News online, 28 October 2008.

31. This is not to say that either society lacks democratic institutions which oppose these developments, but rather that most elements of civil society seem relatively powerless under the terms of conflict set by each nation's security apparatus, at least at the specific place and time in which fatal coercive force is applied.

32. Ian Blair attempted to turn this phrase into 'shoot-to-kill-to-protect' (see Twomey and Dixon, *Daily Express*, 25 July 2005: 1–4).

33. The shooting was attributed to a case of mistaken identity, in which the appearance and location of one suspect was supposedly confused with that of de Menezes. The *Panorama* report of 8 March 2006 revealed that one of the surveillance team was part of a specialist unit, the origins of which lay in Army operations in Northern Ireland. This was most probably 14 Intelligence Company (see Urban, 1992).

34. It is worth noting that police forces often publish requests for assistance featuring ordinary demonstrators whose supposed misdemeanours are unspecified and who, unlike at least three of the London suspects, were not photographed 'after the fact'. One example, which appeared on the website of the 'Post G8 Investigation Team, Lothian and Borders Police', gives no information about the offence that might have been committed. On 26 April 2006, the *Guardian* carried three pictures of demonstrators wanted by Scotland Yard, on the basis of their participation in protests outside the Danish embassy on 3 February 2006. The photographs were supposedly issued to the press because police had not been able to trace them by other means.

35. An undercover soldier, who was part of the team monitoring de Menezes's residence, revealed that he believed the suspect to be an 'IC1 male', meaning he thought he was a white European (*Panorama*, 'Stockwell: countdown to killing', 8 March 2006).

36. The caption at the top of page 5 inside the paper read 'CCTV images of the four suspects'.

37. Nonetheless, the 'wanted' genre can produce alternative and oppositional views; take for example the *Daily Mirror's* front-page treatment of George W. Bush during the build-up to the Iraq War.

38. As Schudson notes, there are contradictions even within the same article (in Benson and Neveu, 2005: 215).

39. In which the imagined members of a collective are presented with a common perspective and the urgency of recognising a 'duty' they should be willing to fulfil.

40. These points were framed as questions in an email enquiry to a *Guardian* journalist on 9 December 2005, which received no response. The *Guardian's* Editorial Code was published in January 2002.

41. The *Express* headline, in keeping with its overall attitude, read 'SHOOT ALL BOMBERS'. This declaration, which actually appeared without quotation marks, originated in remarks made by the mayor of London and the Conservative 'Homeland Security' spokesman.

42. For sources on press and media behaviour in emergencies, wars and crises, see Raboy and Dagenais, 1992; Zelizer and Allan, 2002; Noll, 2003; Allan, 2005; McNair, 2006. For specific incidences of police or military interventions in public order or security situations, see Gilbert, 1974; NCCL, 1980; Cramer and Harris, 1982; Gray, 2006.

43. See Allan, 2005: 67–81.

44. Tolson regards 'liveness', even where simulated, as 'indispensable' to television (2006: 12).

45. States of emergency can also be manufactured through the attempted control of spatial circumstances, and as a consequence the wider semiotic/discursive environment.

46. The caption to a photograph of Muktar Saed Ibrahim, which noted that he 'Turned to extremism during jail term' (*Daily Mail*, 27 July 2005), does not then prompt a study of social and political conditions in Britain's jails.

47. This, however, is not intended to support the conception of 'common sense' perpetuated in many academic critiques of news and agenda-setting. Fairclough attacks what he sees as 'common sense' assumptions, calling them 'the

conventions according to which people interact linguistically, and of which people are generally not consciously aware' (Fairclough, 1989: 2).

48. Propositional content is the essential meaning of a statement or utterance, and can therefore be expressed in a number of different guises.

49. In a column of 25 July, Phillips explained that new rules meant that armed police were directed to shoot suspected suicide bombers 'in the brain', adding that 'this is because even if a suicide bomber is shot in the chest, he could still detonate himself by a twitch of the finger' (Phillips, *Daily Mail*, 25 July 2005).

50. *Guardian* report by Ian Cobain, Rosie Cowan and Richard Norton-Taylor, 23 July 2005.

51. In both cases, the discourse of criminality was deployed when the 'terrorist' device proved difficult to sustain.

52. Neither of these events provides unique examples of the 'legitimate' use of armed coercion or force, in which civilians have been killed in political, criminal or public-order situations. Obvious examples of fatalities caused during political protests include the deaths of Kevin Gately at an anti-fascist demonstration in 1974 (see Gilbert, 1974) and Blair Peach at a similar mobilisa-tion in 1979 (see NCCL, 1980); neither, however, involved the discharge by police of firearms. Instances of fatal shootings carried out by police marksmen include the killing of Harry Stanley in 1999, Derek Bennett in 2001 and Keith Larkins in 2003.

53. One such incident, also based on 'mistaken identity', occurred on 8 July 2008, when armed police arrested a 21-year-old male commuter, ordering him to lie on the platform of Bournemouth station as they aimed their weapons (see 'A chilling echo of de Menezes', *Metro*, 8 July 2008). Another well-known parallel was the shooting by police of Abul Koyair during the Forest Gate incident in 2006 (Goodchild and Elliott, *Independent*, 11 June 2006).

54. For a fuller explanation of the realist position, see Archer, 2000; Price, 2007.

55. Preference for a thematic approach derives from dissatisfaction with the vague modes of enquiry marshalled beneath the category of 'discourse'.

56. A political point of view or perspective, which uses themes in order to achieve communication aims.

57. In the final moments of the embassy siege, witnesses recounted how members of the SAS assault group shot dead a number of hostage-takers who had, by this time, thrown down their own weapons (Cramer and Harris, 1982).

58. The preference for descriptions of the shooting as a 'tragedy' is analysed above.

59. Between '1990 and March 2003' four officers had been killed and 135 injured by the 'criminal use of firearms' (Waldren, 2007: 222).

60. Analysing the brief details provided on the thirty deaths, the number of individuals who were said to be armed with or in possession of real weapons was twelve; of these, two carried swords only, two carried air rifles, one carried a sword and a gun, and the remaining seven had guns of some description, of which four were discharged. Three individuals carried replicas. In eleven cases it is not clear from the information if the victims were armed are not. In four cases, the dead were entirely unarmed.

61. On 22 July, an armed officer chased the driver of the Stockwell Tube train into

the tunnel. See BBC News online, 1 October 2007; accessed 29 August 2008.
See also BBC News online, 3 November, 2008; accessed 3 November 2008.

62. See Cassidy, 2008: 93.

EIGHT

1. The *security state* refers to those structures and practices that, organised in the name of 'national security', operate in defence of the established social order. The security state emerges from the principles of rule associated with the 'prerogative' state (Neocleous, 2008: 37), and is formally distinct from the sites of 'democratic' governance associated with the 'normative' state and the rule of law (37). It remains, however, the effective site of coercive, patriarchal regulation within neoliberal democracies, and is composed of members of the political executive, senior police and intelligence officers, civil servants and state functionaries.

2. In a discussion of the political differences between the USA and the UK, one reporter cited another journalist, who noted that in America the divisions between the main parties was more extreme than in Britain, where 'the approach to the deficit was more grown-up', where politicians '*despite the usual artificial anger*' were 'broadly in agreement' (Hoggart, 16 October 2010: 24; my emphasis).

3. See Plunkett, *Guardian*, 25 August 2010: 12.

4. The BP advertisement appears in the November 2005 issue of *Prospect*.

5. For a discussion of such disingenuous tactics in the context of gendered address, see Ross, 2010a.

6. The Shell advertisement appears in an issue of the *New Statesman*, 28 June 2010.

7. This means not that subaltern or alternative positions do not appear within the form of the address, but that, where they are progressive or rebellious in some respect, they are placed in a context where they are enlisted in the service of capital (see McGuigan, 2009).

8. See the description of expropriation offered in Marx, *Capital, Volume One* (1954), p. 671ff.

9. See, for example, Lister, *Independent,* 10 October 2001.

10. The US Joint Chiefs of Staff *Joint Vision 20/20*, published in Washington DC in 2000, uses the uncertainty of the future to argue for the concentration of military power.

11. Ogilvy's 'Topoff' training for the US Department of Homeland Security in 2005 was described by its organisers as 'the most realistic test yet', offering 'agencies and jurisdictions a way to exercise a coordinated national and international response to a large-scale, multipoint terrorist attack' (www.iwar.org.uk/news-archive/2005/03-17-07.htm; accessed 19 June 2009).

CONCLUSION

1. Repressive governance includes the reform of welfare regulations (see Brooks, *Guardian*, 12 June 2009: 32) and the economic discipline enacted through employment laws.

2. Police and military planners must assume that an operative will have adopted a form of *psychological* antipathy to the 'subversive' enemy, since this cannot be delivered as a formal part of the 'curriculum'. See the comments made by police officers and TSG members describing the protestors at the G20 demonstrations in London, April 2009, as 'the great unwashed' (Davenport, 2009).
3. The training regimes set up by Western states are not devoted solely to internal repression, and have been exported to client regimes overseas (see Kuzmarov, 2009).

References

Abercrombie, N. (1980) *Class, Structure and Knowledge*, Oxford: Basil Blackwell.

Abercrombie, N., Hill, S., and Turner, B.S. (eds) (1980) *The Dominant Ideology Thesis*, London: Unwin Hyman.

ACPO (Association of Chief Police Officers) (2006) *Counter Terrorism Protective Security Advice for Shopping Centres*, London: National Counter Terrorism Security Office (NaCTSO).

ACPO (Association of Chief Police Officers) (2005/2007) *About Us*, www.acpo. police.uk/about.html (accessed 16 July 2010).

ACPO (Association of Chief Police Officers) (2009) *Counter Terrorism Protective Security Advice for Higher and Further Education*, London: ACPO.

Adam, B. (2004) *Time*, Cambridge and Malden, MA: Polity Press.

Adam, B., Beck, U., and van Loon, J. (2000) *The Risk Society and Beyond: Critical Issues for Social Theory*, London, Thousand Oaks and New Delhi: Sage.

Agamben, G. (2005) *State of Exception*, Chicago and London: Chicago University Press.

Agence France Press (2004) *Report on Athens Olympics*, 10 May.

Allan, S. (ed.) (2005) *Journalism: Critical Issues*, Buckingham: Open University Press.

al-Rehaief, M. (2003) *Because Each Life is Precious*, New York: HarperCollins.

Althusser, L. (1971) *Lenin and Philosophy and Other Essays*, New York and London: Monthly Review Press.

Altschull, J.H. (1995) *Agents of Power*, New York: Longman.

Ammon, R.J. (2001) *Global Television and the Shaping of World Politics*, Jefferson, NC: McFarland.

Andrew, C. (2010) *The Defence of the Realm: The Authorised History of MI5*, London and New York: Penguin.

Andrew, C., Aldrich, R.J., and Wark, W.K. (eds) (2009) *Secret Intelligence: A Reader*, Abingdon and New York: Routledge.

Archer, M. (2000) *Being Human: The Problem of Agency*, Cambridge: Cambridge University Press.

Athens Olympic Committee (2004) www.athens2004.com/athens2004. (accessed 10 December 2004: site now defunct).

Athens Olympic Committee (2004) Statement of Greek Premier, www.livingroom. org.au/olympics/archives/greek_premier, 31 July 2004 (accessed 10 December, 2004: site now defunct).

Atkins and Partners (2006) 'Software for Emergency Planning and Management', 13 June 2006, www.armedforces-int.com/article/emergency-planning-and-management.html (accessed 23 February 2010).

Atkinson, M. (1984) *Our Masters' Voices*, London: Methuen.

Austin, J.L. (1975) *How to Do Things with Words*, Oxford: Clarendon Press.

AWE (Atomic Weapons Establishment) (2007) *Proud to be AWE*, Bristol: AWE Media Group, www.awe.co.uk/safety/Onsite_safety_emergency_planning (accessed 23 February 2010).

Ayers, A. (2009) 'Imperial Liberties: Democratisation and Governance in the "New" Imperial Order', *Political Studies* (Sheffield: Political Studies Association) 57(1): 1–27.

Bach, K., and Harness, M. (1979) *Linguistic Communication and Speech Acts*, Cambridge, MA and London: MIT Press.

Badiou, A. (2007a) 'The Event in Deleuze', *Parrhesia* 2: 37–44, www.parrhesiajournal. org (accessed 12 October 2010).

Badiou, A. (2007b) *Being and Event*, London and New York: Continuum.

Badiou, A.. (2010) *The Communist Hypothesis*, London and New York: Verso.

Baker, E.A., and Hayward, A.L. (eds) (1956) *Cassell's New English Dictionary*, London, Toronto, Sydney, Melbourne, Auckland: Cassell.

Barbrook, R. (2007) *Imaginary Futures: From Thinking Machines to the Global Village*, London and Ann Arbor, MI: Pluto Press.

Barrett, D. (2009a) 'Police stop and search two-year olds', *Sunday Telegraph*, 16 August: 12.

Barrett, D. (2009b) 'Spy in the sky: flying camera tracks protesters', *Sunday Telegraph*, 16 August: 12.

Barrow, G. (2001) BBC News 24 Report, 11 September 2001 (transcript).

Bassnett, S. (2002) *Translation Studies*, New York and London: Routledge.

Bates, S. (2009) 'War Book reveals how Britain planned to cope with nuclear attack', www.guardian.co.uk/uk/2009/jun/23/Britain-nuclear-war-plan, 23 June (accessed 24 June 2009).

Baudrillard, J. (1996) *The Perfect Crime*, London: Verso.

Baudrillard, J. (2003) *The Spirit of Terrorism*, London and New York: Verso.

BBC News online (2003) 'Heathrow threat real says Blunkett', 14 February, http://news.bbc.co.uk/1/hi/uk_politics/2758753.stm (accessed 15 February 2003).

BBC News online (2003) 'Ministers highlight UK terror threat', 14 February 2003, at http://news.bbc.co.uk/1/hi/uk/2751361.stm (accessed 20 December 2010).

BBC News online (2003) 'Public relations disaster', 14 March, http://news.bbc. co.uk/1/hi/uk_politics/2758753.stm (accessed 15 February 2003).

BBC News online (2007) 'Police "failure" in Menezes death', 1 October, http://news. bbc.co.uk/1/hi/uk/7021401.stm (accessed 29 August 2008).

BBC News online (2008) 'Menezes identification "definite"', http://news.bbc.

co.uk/go/pr/fr/-/1/hi/uk/76695088.stm, 28 October 2008 (accessed 28 October 2008).

BBC News online (2008) 'Menezes police "out of control"', http://news.bbc.co.uk/go/pr/fr/-/1/hi/uk/7669657.stm, 30 October, 2008 (accessed 30 October 2008).

BBC News online (2008) 'Menezes police "gave no warning"', http://news.bbc.co.uk/1/hi/uk/7706033.stm, 3 November 2008 (accessed 3 November 2008).

BBC News 24 (2001) Bulletin on September 11th attacks, 11 September.

BBC TV News (2007) Bulletin on the Stockwell Shooting, 18 July.

Beck, U. (1992) *Risk Society*, London, Thousand Oaks and New Delhi: Sage.

Beck, U. (1997) *The Reinvention of Politics*, Cambridge and Malden, MA: Polity Press.

Beck, U. (2000) 'Risk Society Revisited: Theory, Politics and Research Programmes', in Adam, B., Beck, U., and van Loon, J. (eds), *The Risk Society and Beyond: Critical Issues for Social Theory*, London, Thousand Oaks and New Delhi: Sage, pp. 211–29.

Bell, A. (1991) *The Language of News Media*, Oxford: Blackwell.

Benham, R. (2007) 'The Birth of the Clinic', in South End Press Collective, *What Lies Beneath: Katrina, Race, and the State of the Nation*, Cambridge, MA: South End Press.

Benson, R. and Neveu, E. (eds) (2005) *Bourdieu and the Journalistic Field*, Cambridge: Polity Press.

Bergalli, R., and Sumner, C (1997) *Social Control and Political Order*, London, Thousand Oaks and New Delhi: Sage.

Berrington, E. (2002) 'Representations of Terror in the Legitimation of War', in Scraton, P. (ed.), *Beyond September 11th: An Anthology of Dissent*, London and Sterling, VA: Pluto Press.

Bevir, M., and Rhodes, R.A.W. (2003) *Interpreting British Governance*, London and New York: Routledge.

Bewes, T., and Gilbert, J. (2000) *Cultural Capitalism*, London: Lawrence & Wishart.

Bichler, S., and Nitzan, J. (2010) 'Systemic Fear, Modern Finance and the Future of Capitalism', in *Creative Commons*, July 2010, http://bnarchives.net/ (accessed 2 August 2010).

Billig, M. (1991) *Ideology and Opinions*, London, Thousand Oaks and New Delhi: Sage.

Bird, S., Rajeev, S., and Hennigan, T. (2005) 'The hard-working son who moved to London in search of a better life', *The Times*, 25 July: 3.

Blair, I. (2005) Press conference on the Stockwell shooting, 22 July 2005, www.police.uk/content (accessed 25 July 2005).

Blair, I. (2009) *Policing Controversy*, London: Profile Books.

Blair, T. (2005) Speech to Labour Party Conference, 27 September, at http://news.bbc.co.uk/1/hi/uk_politics/4287370.stm (accessed 20 December 2010).

Blair, T. (2007) Speech on 'Our Nation's Future', 12 January, at http://ukingermany.fco.gov.uk/en/news/?view=Speech&id=4616100 (accessed 20 December 2010).

Blondheim, M., and Liebes, T. (2003) 'From Disaster Marathon to Media Event', in Noll, A.M. (ed.), *Crisis Communications*, Lanham, MD: Rowman & Littlefield.

Blum, W. (1995) *Killing Hope: US Military and CIA Interventions since World War II* Monroe, ME: Common Courage Press.

Boggan, S. (2010) 'It took just one hour for internet experts to find out almost every private detail of my girlfriend's life', *Daily Mail*, 11 September 2010: 34–5.

Boltanski, L., and Chiapello, E. (2007) *The New Spirit of Capitalism*, London and New York: Verso.

Bonner, D. (2007) *Executive Measures, Terrorism and National Security*, Aldershot and Burlington, VT: Ashgate.

Booth, K. (2007) *Theory of World Security*, Cambridge: Cambridge University Press.

Borger, J. (2007) 'Turkish PM drops out of presidential race to placate army', *Guardian*, 25 April.

Bottero, W. (2004) 'Class Identities and the Identity of Class', in *Sociology* 38(5): 985–1003.

Boulton, A. (2010) Interview with William Hague, 17 October, at www.fco.gov.uk/en/news/latest-news/?view=Speech&id=23041594 (accessed 20 December 2010).

Bousquet, A. (2009) *The Scientific Way of Warfare:Order and Chaos on the Battlefields of Modernity*, London: Hurst.

Boyer, R. (1996) 'State and Market: A New Engagement for the Twenty-First Century?', in Boyer, R. and Drache, D. (eds), *States Against Markets*, London and New York: Routledge.

Boyer, R., and Drache, D. (eds) (1996) *States Against Markets*, London and New York: Routledge.

BP (2005) 'It's time to turn up the heat on global climate change', advertisement in *Prospect* magazine, November.

Brady, B. (2009) 'Police want water cannons to beat back city rioters', *Independent on Sunday* 5 July: 32.

Branigan, E. (1993) *Narrative Comprehension and Film*, London and New York: Routledge.

Brenner, N., Jessop, B., Jones, M., and MacLeod, G. (2003) *State/Space: A Reader*, Oxford: Blackwell

Brenner, N., and Theodore. N. (eds) (2002) *Spaces of Neoliberalism: Urban Restructuring in Western Europe and North America*, Oxford: Blackwell.

Brighton (2002) 'Management Speak: a master discourse?', *Critical Quarterly* 44(3), Autumn.

Brooks, L. (2009) 'In the workfare state, poverty is always an individual failing', *Guardian*, 11 June, at www.guardian.co.uk/global/2009/jun/11/welfare-reform-bill-workfare (accessed 4 January 2011).

Brown, C.M. (2008) *The National Security Council*, Project on National Security Reform, Washington DC.

Brown, G., and Yule, G. (1983) *Discourse Analysis*, Cambridge: Cambridge University Press.

Brown, J., Judd, T., and Stringer, R. (2005) 'A man chased by police ran onto a train. Five shots later he was dead', *Independent*, 23 July: 4–5.

Bruck, P.A. (1992) 'Discursive Movements and Social Movements', in Wasko, J., and Mosco, V., *Democratic Communications in the Information Age*, Norwood, NJ: Garamond/Ablex Publishing, pp. 138–58.

Bruner, J.S. (1957) 'On Perceptual Readiness', *Psychological Review* 64: 123–22.

Bull, C., and Erman, S. (2002) *At Ground Zero*, New York: Thunder's Mouth.

Bull, M. (2006) 'States of Failure', *New Left Review* 40, July–August: 5–25.

Bush, G.W. (2002) Speech of 9 May, at www.whitehouse.gov/news/releases.

Bush, G.W., and Blair, T. (2003) White House Press Conference, 31 January.

Buxton, D. (1980) *From the Avengers to Miami Vice: Form and Ideology in Television Series*, Manchester: Manchester University Press.

Cabinet Office (2004) *Emergency Preparedness*, www.cabinetoffice.gov.uk/media/131981/ep_chap_07.pdf (accessed 5 November 2010).

Cabinet Office (2005) *UK Resilience: Exercise Atlantic Blue*, at www.cabinetoffice.gov.uk/ukresilience/preparedness/exercise/atlantic/blue (accessed 23 February 2010).

Cabinet Office (2008) *National Risk Register*, London: COI Communications.

Cabinet Office (2009) *Civil Protection Lexicon*, www.cabinetoffice.gov.uk/media/230446/lexicon.pdf (accessed 5 November 2010).

Cabinet Office (2009) *Security for the Next Generation: The National Security Strategy of the United Kingdom, update 2009*, London: HMSO.

Cabinet Office (n.d.) *Why Exercise your Disaster Response*, www.cabinetoffice.gov.uk/ukresilience/preparedness/exercise (accessed 23 February 2010).

Cadwalladr, C. (2010) 'No regrets: Wikileaks chief damns his Afghan critics', *Sunday Times*, 1 August: 8–9.

Callon, M., Millo, Y., and Muniesa, F. (2007) *Market Devices*, Malden, MA., Oxford and Victoria: Blackwell.

Calvert, C. (2004) *Voyeur Nation*, Boulder, CO: Westview Press.

Calvert, J., and Leppard, D. (2005) 'Police shot wrong man', *Sunday Times*, 24 July: 1.

Cameron, A., and Palan, R. (2004) *The Imagined Economies of Globalization*, London, Thousand Oaks and New Delhi: Sage

Campaign (2010) 'BT stunned silence', 20 August: 3.

Campaign (2010) 'Does Peperami ad make a case for crowdsourcing?', 20 August: 12–13.

Campbell, D. (2005) 'The moment of decision: when do you pull the trigger?', *Guardian*, 26 July: 4.

Carr-Smith, J. (2010) Interview, ITV news bulletin, 30 July.

Casciani, Dominic (2007) 'Shoot to-kill-policy under debate', BBC News online, http://news.bbc.co.uk/1/hi/uk/7085244.stm (accessed 29 August 2008).

Cashore, B. (2009) 'Legitimacy and the Privatization of Environmental Governance: How Non-state Market-driven (NSDM) GovernanceSystems Gain Rule-making Authority, *Governance* 15(4): 503–29.

Cassidy, R.M. (2008) *Counterinsurgency and the Global War on Terror*, Stanford, CA: Stanford University Press.

Castle, S. (2004) 'Greece attacked for failing to enforce EU anti-terror laws', *Independent*, 8 June.

Cavelty, M.D., and Mauer, V. (2009) 'Strategic Warning and Reflexive Intelligence', *Security Dialogue* 40(2): 123–44, April.

Cawson, A. (1986) *Corporatism and Political Theory*, Oxford: Basil Blackwell.

Cerny, P.G. (1990) *The Changing Architecture of Politics: Structure, Agency and he Future of the State*, London, Newbury Park, New Delhi: Sage.

Chomsky, N. (2001) *9/11*, Seven Stories Press: New York.

City Security and Resilience Networks (2010) *Business Recovery and Emergency*

Planning, at www.csarn.org/BREP.html (accessed 20 December 2010).
Civil Contingencies Act (2004) at www.opsi.gov.uk/acts/acts2004/ukpga_20040036_en_7. (accessed 7 July 2010).
Civil Defence (1964) *Handbook No. 3: Exercises and Studies*, London: HMSO.
Clarke, J., and Newman, J. (2004) 'Governing in the modern world?', in Steinburg, D.L., and Johnson, R. (eds) *Blairism and the war of Persuasion*, Cambridge: Lawrence & Wishart.
Clarke, J., Newman, J., Smith, N., Vidler, E., and Westmarland, L. (2007) *Creating Citizen-Consumers*, London, Thousand Oaks and New Delhi: Sage.
Coaffee, J. (2009) *Terrorism, Risk and the Global City*, Farnham and Burlington, VT: Ashgate.
Cobain, I., (2009) 'How UK's torture policy was traced back up political ladder', *Guardian*, 18 June: 16.
Cobain, I., Cowan, R., and Norton-Taylor, R. (2005) 'They held the pistol to him and unloaded five shots', *Guardian*, 23 July: 1-2.
Cockerell, M., Hennessy, P., and Walker, D (1985) *Sources Close to the Prime Minister*, London: Macmillan.
Concise Oxford English Dictionary (1964) ed. Fowler, H.W., and Fowler, F.G., Oxford: Oxford University Press.
Connecticut, State of (2005) *Consequence Management Guide for Deliberately Caused Incidents Involving Chemical Agents*, January 2005, 2005_update_conseq_mngt_guide_feb_14th.pdf (accessed 23 February 2010).
Conservative Party (2010) *Invitation to Join the Government of Britain: Conservative Party Manifesto 2010*, London: Conservative Party.
Cooley, A. (2005) *Logics of Hierarchy: The Organisation of Empires, States, and Military Occupations*, New York: Cornell University Press.
Coombs, W.T. (2004) *Ongoing Crisis Communication*, London, New Delhi, Thousand Oaks: Sage.
Corea, G. (2006) 'US confirms Heathrow hijack plot', 22 June, at http://news.bbc.co.uk/1/hi/uk/5104672.stm (accessed 20 December 2010).
Cottey, A. (2007) *Security in the New Europe*, Basingstoke and New York: Palgrave Macmillan.
Couldry, N. (2000) *The Place of Media Power*, London and New York: Routledge.
Couldry, N. (2010) *Why Voice Matters: Culture and Politics after Neoliberalism*, Los Angeles, London, New Delhi, Singapore, Washington DC: Sage.
Couldry, N., Hepp, A., and Krotz, F. (eds) (2010) *Media Events in a Global Age*, London and New York: Routledge.
Couldry, N., and McCarthy, A. (eds) (2004) *Mediaspace: Place, Scale and Culture in a Media Age*, London and New York: Routledge.
Council of Europe (2007) *The Fight against Terrorism: Council of Europe Standards*, Strasbourg: Council of Europe Publishing.
Cox, A. (1988) 'Neo-corporatism versus the Corporate State', in Cox, A., and O'Sullivan, N. (eds), *The Corporate State: Corporatism and the State Tradition in Western Europe*, Aldershot: Edward Elgar.
Cox, A., and O'Sullivan, N. (eds) (1988) *The Corporate State: Corporatism and the State Tradition in Western Europe*, Aldershot: Edward Elgar.
Cramer, C., and Harris, S. (1982) *Hostage*, London: John Clare Books.

Crawford, N.C. (1994) 'A Security Regime among Democracies: Cooperation among Iroquois Nations', *International Organization* 48: 345–85.

Croft, S. (2010) 'New Security Challenges in an Interdependent World', in Hay, C. (ed.) (2010) *New Directions in Political Science*, Basingstoke and New York: Palgrave McMillan, pp. 189–210,.

Crouch, C. (2009) 'Privatised Keynesianism: An Unacknowledged Policy Regime', *British Journal of Politics and International Relations* 11(3), August: 382–99.

Curtis, A. (2005) 'The Power of Nightmares', 14 January, BBC, bbc.co.uk/1/hi/programmes /3755686.stm (accessed 24 October 2010).

Curtis, M. (1998) *The Great Deception: Anglo-American Power and World Order*, London: Pluto Press.

Curtis, M. (2010) *Secret Affairs: Britain's Collusion with Radical Islam*, London: Serpent's Tail.

Dagenais, B. (1992) 'Media in Crises: Observers, Actors or Scapegoats?', in Raboy, M., and Dagenais, B. (eds), *Media, Crisis and Democracy*, London, Newbury Park, New Delhi: Sage.

Daily Express (2005) 'Bombers are all sponging asylum seekers', front page headline, 27 July.

Daily Express (2005) 'SHOOT ALL BOMBERS', front page headline, 23 July 2005.

Daily Express (2005) 'Innocent died in hail of bullets', front page headline, 24 July 2005.

Daily Mail (2005) Editorial Comment: 'Another victim of the terrorists', 25 July.

Davenport, J. (2009) 'Jeers as Met chiefs defend tactics of G20 police', *Evening Standard*, 30 April, at www.thisislondon.co.uk/standard/article-23683475-jeers-as-met-chiefs-defend-tactics-of-g20-police.do.

Davies, C. (2010) 'We don't want to be seen as "self-pity city", but it is worse than the worst-case scenario', *Guardian*, 22 October.

Davies, P. (2010) Report on Icelandic volcano, Independent Television News, 15 April.

Davison, S (ed.) (2003) 'A Market State?', *Soundings* 24, Autumn 2003, London: Lawrence & Wishart.

Dayan, D., and Katz, E. (1992) *Media Events: The Live Broadcasting of History*, Cambridge, MA and London: Harvard University Press.

Dean, J. (2009) *Democracy and Other Neoliberal Fantasies*, Durham, NC and London: Duke University Press.

Dearing, J.W., and Rogers, E.M. (1996) *Agenda-Setting*, London, Thousand Oaks and New Delhi: Sage.

Debord, G. (1998) *Comments on the Society of the Spectacle*, London, New York: Verso.

Debrix, F. (2008) *Tabloid Terror: War, Culture, and Geopolitics*, London and New York: Routledge.

DeLanda, M. (2002) *Intensive Science and Virtual Philosophy*, London and New York: Continuum.

DeLanda, M. (2006) *A New Philosophy of Society*, London and New York: Continuum.

Der Derian, J. (2009) *Virtuous War*, London and New York: Routledge.

Devlin McAliskey, B. (2010) 'Bloody Sunday: Put Britain in the dock', 16 June, at www.guardian.co.uk/commentisfree/2010/jun/15/bloody-sunday-british-government-soldiers (accessed 20 December 2010).

Devon County Council (2009) *Don't Be Scared, Be Well Prepared!*, DCC Local Resilience Forum.

Dodd, V. (2005) 'Seconds to decide if suspect is suicide threat', *Guardian*, 23 July.

Dodd, V. (2009) 'Met used anti-terror laws to stop and search 58 under-10's', *Guardian*, 19 August: 13.

Dodd, V., Jones, S., Norton-Taylor, R., and Hooper, J. (2010) 'Six held by terror police hours before pope's historic address', *Guardian*, 18 September: 1-2.

Dörfer, I. (1997) *The Nordic nNations in the New Western Security Regime*, Washington DC and Baltimore, MD: Woodrow Wilson Center Press.

Doward, J. (2010a) 'Nuclear arsenals under scrutiny for safety lapses, fires and floods', *Observer*, 22 August: 6.

Doward, J. (2010b) 'Firefighters "lost control" of blaze at Aldermaston nuclear weapons base', *Observer*, 26 September, at www.guardian.co.uk/world/2010/sep/26/aldermaston-nuclear-blaze-firefighters (accessed 30 September 2010).

Duffield, M. (2001) *Global Governance and the New Wars*, London: Zed Books.

Du Gay, P. (2007) *Organising Identity*, Thousand Oaks, London and New Delhi: Sage.

Dunleavy, P. (1995) 'Reinterpreting the Westland Affair: Theories of the State and Core Executive Decision Making', in Rhodes, R.A.W., and Dunleavy, P. (eds), *Prime Minister, Cabinet and Core Executive*, London and New York: Macmillan.

Dutta, K. (2010) 'Cashing in on modern-day man's identity crisis', in *Campaign*, 20 August: 13.

Dyson, M.E. (2006) *Come Hell or High Water: Hurricane Katrina and the Colour of Disaster*, New York: Basic Civitas Books.

Emergency Response Planning Group (n.d.) www.emergencyresponseplanning.co.uk/6.html (accessed 20 April 2010).

Engelmann, P. (2009) *Badiou and Žižek: Philosophy in the Present*, Cambridge and Malden, MA: Polity Press.

English, R., and Townshend, C. (eds) (1999) *The State*, London and New York: Routledge.

Entman, R. (1993) 'Framing: Toward Clarification of a Fractured Paradigm', *Journal of Communication* 43(4): 51–8.

Ericson, R.V., Baranek, P.M., and Chan, J.B.L. (1991) *Representing Order*, Milton Keynes: Open University Press.

European Commission (2001) *European Governance: A White Paper*, 25 July, Brussels.

European Committee for the Prevention of Torture and Inhuman or Degrading Treatment or Punishment (2006), *Report to the Government of Greece*, Strasbourg, 20 December.

Evans, M., Coghlan, T., and Philip, C. (2008) 'Top al-Qaeda terrorist "was missile target in Bush campaign for favourable legacy"', *The Times*, 25 November: 37.

Evans, R., and Lewis, P. (2009) 'Police forces challenged over files held on law-abiding protesters', *Guardian*, 26 October: 1

Fairclough, N. (1989) *Language and Power*, London and New York: Longman.

Fairclough, N. (2000) *New Labour, New Language?*, London and New York: Routledge.

Ferguson, N. (2004) *Colossus*, London and New York: Penguin.

Fierlbeck, K. (2008) *Globalizing Democracy: Power, Legitimacy and the Power of Democratic Ideas*, Manchester: Manchester University Press.

Fisher, J., van Heerde, J., and Tucker, A., (2010) 'Does One Trust Judgement Fit All? Linking Theory and Empirics', *British Journal of Politics and International Relations* 12(2), May 2010: 161–88.

Fisk, R. (2010) 'Address to the fifth Al Jazeera annual forum', 23 May, http://english.aljazeera.net/focus/2010/05/201052574726865274.html (accessed 23 October 2010).

Fitzgibbon, D.W. (2004) *Pre-emptive Criminalisation: Risk Control and Alternative Futures*, London: National Association of Probation Officers.

Flaherty, J. (2007) 'Corporate Reconstruction and Grassroots Resistance', in South End Press Collective, *What Lies Beneath: Katrina, Race, and the State of the Nation*, Cambridge, MA: South End Press.

Foreign Staff (2007) 'Sunni dissidents in Iraq to be given arms by US', *The Times*, 12 June.

Fowles, J. (1996) *Advertising and Popular Culture*, London, Thousand Oaks and New Delhi: Sage.

Frankel, B. (1983) *Beyond the State?*, London: Macmillan.

Franklin, B., Hamer, M., Hanna, M., Kinsey, M., and Richardson, J. (eds) (2005) *Key Concepts in Journalism Studies*, London, Thousand Oaks and New Delhi: Sage.

Fraser, M. (2006) 'Event', *Theory, Culture and Society* 23: 129–32, http://tcs.sagepub.com/cgi/content/refs/23/2-3/129.

Fresco, A. (2010) 'Police pledge crackdown', *The Times*, 11 December: 1.

Furedi, F. (2002) *Culture of Fear*, London and New York: Continuum.

Furedi, F. (2007) *Invitation to Terror*, London and New York: Continuum.

Gamble, A. (2009) *The Spectre at the Feast: Capitalist Crisis and the Politics of Recession*, Basingstoke and New York: Palgrave Macmillan.

Ganser, D. (2005) *NATO's Secret Armies*, London and New York: Frank Cass.

Gardner, F. (2003) 'Q&A: terrorist threat', in BBC News online, http://news.bbc.co.uk/1/hi/uk/3199122.stm (accessed 17 November 2010).

Gardner, H. (2005) *American Global Strategy and the 'War on Terrorism'*, Aldershot and Burlington, VT: Ashgate.

Gerbner, G. (1992) 'Violence and Terror in and by the Media', in Raboy, M., and Dagenais, B. (eds), *Media, Crisis and Democracy*, London, Newbury Park, New Delhi: Sage.

Gibb, J. (2005) *Who's watching you?*, London: Collins & Brown.

Gilbert, T. (1974) *Only One Died*, London: Kay Beauchamp.

Gill, G. (2003) *The Nature and Development of the Modern State*, Basingstoke and New York: Palgrave Macmillan.

Gill, P. (2009) 'Securing the Globe', in Andrew, C., Aldrich, R.J., and Wark, W.K. (eds), *Secret Intelligence: A Reader*, Abingdon and New York: Routledge.

Global Outlook (2004) '26 Top Anomalies of 9/11', *Global Outlook* 8, Spring: 31–4.

Goffman, E. (1981) *Forms of Talk*, Oxford: Basil Blackwell.

Goldenburg, S. (2010) 'White House "overly optimistic" on oil spill', *Guardian*, 6 August: 19.

Goodchild, S., and Elliott, F. (2006) 'Tip-off by police informer led to Forest Gate raid', *Independent*, 11 June: 23.

Gordenker, L., and Weiss, T.G. (1993) 'The Collective Security Idea and Changing World Politics', in Weiss, T.G. (ed), *Collective Security in a Changing World*, Boulder, CO and London: Lynn Rienner.

Governmentattic.org (2009) *US Department of the Army Department of Defense Civil Disturbance Plan*, 'GARDEN PLOT', 15 February 1991, posted 9 September 2009 (accessed 30 July 2010).

Graef, R. (2010) 'These officers must NOT stay anonymous', *Daily Mail*, 23 September: 14.

Graham, P., Keenan, T., and Dowd, A.M. (2004) 'A Call to Arms at the End of History: Discourse-historical Analysis of George W. Bush's Declaration of War on Terror', *Discourse and Society* 15(2–3): 199–221.

Gray, C.H. (2001) *Cyborg Citizen*, New York and London: Routledge.

Gray, R. (2006). *Armed Response*, Virgin Books: London.

Green Party of England and Wales (2010) *Fair is Worth Fighting For*, Election Manifesto, London: Green Party.

Greenberg, K.J., and Dratel, J.L. (eds) (2008) *The Torture Papers: The Road to Abu Ghraib*, Cambridge: Cambridge University Press.

Grice, A. (2001) 'Bush's Speech to Congress', *Independent*, 22 September.

Grice, P. (1989) *Studies in the Ways of Words*, Cambridge, MA and London: Harvard University Press.

Grieco, J.M., and Ikenberry, G.J. (2003) *State Power and World Markets: The International Political Economy*, New York and London: W.W. Norton.

Grusin, R. (2010) *Premediation*, Basingstoke and New York: Palgrave Macmillan.

Guardian (2005) 'Faces of the suspects', front page headline, 23 July.

Guardian Agencies and Staff (2003) 'Soldiers drafted in to increase Heathrow security', 11 February, at www.guardian.co.uk/uk/2003/feb/11/september11.terrorism (accessed 20 December 2010).

Gupta, S. (2002) *The Replication of Violence*, London: Pluto Press.

Habermas, J. (1991) *Communication and the Evolution of Society*, Cambridge: Polity Press.

Hale, B. (2008) 'Five Muslims in "Terror Material" Case are Freed', *Daily Mail*, 14 February.

Hall, M. (2006) 'Bush and Blair's Toe-curling Chat', *Daily Express*, 18 July.

Hall, S. (2003) 'New Labour's Double-shuffle', in Davison, S. (ed.), 'A Market State?', *Soundings* 24: 10-24.

Halliday, M.A.K., and Hasan, R. (1976) *Cohesion in English Language*, London: Longman.

Handschuh, D. (2002) 'A Lens on Life and Death', in Bull, C., and Erman, S. (eds), *At Ground Zero*, New York: Thunder's Mouth Press.

Hansen, H.K., and Salskov-Iversen, D. (2002) 'Managerialised Patterns of Political Authority', *Critical Quarterly* 44(3), Autumn.

Harcup, T. (2004) *Journalism: Principles and Practice*, London, Thousand Oaks and New Delhi: Sage.

Harris, P. (2005) 'One suspect, five shots in the head', *Daily Mail*, 23 July: 4-5.

Harvey, D. (2005) *A Brief History of Neoliberalism*, Oxford: Oxford University Press.

Harvey, D. (2010) *The Enigma of Capital*, London: Profile Books.

Hasan, M. (2010) 'Some history on the lack of history, 22 July, at www.new-statesman.com/blogs/mehdi-hasan/2010/07/history-war-blair-britain (accessed 25 October 2010).

Hay, C. (ed.) (2010) *New Directions in Political Science*, Basingstoke and New York: Palgrave Macmillan, pp. 189–210.

Hayman, A., and Gilmore, M. (2009) *The Terrorist Hunters*, London, Toronto, Sydney, Auckland, Johannesburg: HellerBantam Press.

Head, M., and Mann, S. (2009) *Domestic Deployment of the Armed Forces*, Aldershot and Burlington, VT: Ashgate.

Heinrich, C.J,, Hill, C.J., and Lynn, E.L. (2004) 'Governance as an Organising Theme for Empirical Research', in Ingraham, P.W. and Lynn, L.E. (eds), *The Art of Governance: Analyzing Management and Administration*, Washington DC: Georgetown University Press.

Hennessy, P. (ed.) (2007) *The New Protective State*, London and New York: Continuum.

Hennessy, P. (2010) *Secret State: Preparing for the Worst, 1945–2010*, London and New York: Penguin.

Hennessy, P., and Berg, S. (2009) 'Rehearsing the end of the world', in http://news.bbc.co.uk/today/hi/today/newsid_8110000/810678., 23 June (accessed 31 July 2009).

Hepp, A., and Couldry, N. (2010) 'Introduction: Media Events in Globalised Media Cultures', in Couldry, N., Hepp, A., and Krotz, F (eds), *Media Events in a Global Age*, London and New York: Routledge.

Her Majesty's Government, UK (2003) *Iraq's Weapons of Mass Destruction:The Assessment of the British Government*, London: HMSO.

Hewitt, S. (2008) *The British War on Terror*, London and New York: Continuum.

Higginbotham, J., Pianesi, F., and Varsi, A.C. (2000) *Speaking of Events*, New York and Oxford: Oxford University Press.

Higginson, J. (2004) 'Anti-WMD unit is sent to Olympics', *Metro* 30 November.

Hildebrand, S., Crowe, S., and Fithian, L. (2007) 'Common Ground Relief', in South End Press Collective, *What Lies Beneath: Katrina, Race, and the State of the Nation*, Cambridge, MA: South End Press.

Hindmoor, A. (2009) 'Explaining Networks through Mechanisms: Vaccination, Priming, and the 2001 Foot and Mouth Disease Crisis', *Political Studies* 57(1): 75–94.

Hirsch, A. (2009) 'Police Accused of Misusing Terror Laws Against Peaceful Protests', *Guardian*, 23 March.

Hobsbawm, E. (2007) *Globalisation, Democracy and Terrorism*, London: Abacus.

Hoggart, S. (2010) 'Simon Hoggart's week: The flocking "bigot" who did for Brown', *Guardian*, 16 October: 24.

Holloway, D. (2008) *9/11 and the War on Terror*, Edinburgh: Edinburgh University Press.

Home Office (1964) *Exercises and Studies*, Civil Defence Handbook 3, London: HMSO.

Hood, C., James, O., Peters, B.G., and Scott, C. (2004) *Controlling Modern Government: Variety, Commonality and Change*, Cheltenham and Northampton, MA: Edward Elgar.

Horton, D., and Wohl, R. (1956) 'Mass Communication as Para-social Interaction', *Psychiatry* 19(3): 215–29.

Hoskins, A., and O'Loughlin, B. (2007) *Television and Terror*, Basingstoke and New York: Palgrave Macmillan.

Hoskins, A., and O'Loughlin, B. (2010) *War and Media*, Cambridge and Malden, MA: Polity Press.

Houen, A. (2002) *Terrorism and Modern Literature*, Oxford: Oxford University Press.

Howie, L. (2009) *Terrorism, the Worker and the City: Simulations and Security in a Time of Terror*, Farnham and Burlington, VT: Ashgate/Gower.

Hughes, S. (2007) *War on Terror Inc.*, London and New York: Verso.

Hulsse, R., and Spencer, A. (2008) 'The Metaphor of Terror: Terrorism Studies and the Constructivist Turn', *Security Dialogue* 39(6): 571–92.

Hunt, K., and Rygiel, K. (eds) (2007) *(En)Gendering the War on Terror*, Aldershot and Burlington, VT: Ashgate.

Hutchings, K. (2008) *Time and World Politics*, Manchester and New York: Manchester University Press.

Independent (2005) 'THE FOUR MOST WANTED', front page headline, 23 July.

Independent Police Complaints Authority (2005) at http://statguidance.ipcc.gov.uk/index.php?id=4 (accesed 23 August 2008).

Independent Television News (2003) 'Breakfast with Frost', 16 November.

Independent Television News (2005) Bulletin on the Stockwell Shooting, 16 August.

Independent Television News (2005) Bulletin on the Stockwell Shooting, 18 August.

Independent Television News (2007) Bulletin on the Stockwell Shooting, 2 August.

Independent Television News (2010) Bulletin on Volcanic Cloud, 15 April 2010.

Ingraham, P.W., and Lynn, L.E. (2004) *The Art of Governance: Analyzing Management and Administration*, Washington DC: Georgetown University Press.

Ingrams, R. (2009) 'Come the revolution, who will be there to protect us?', *Independent*, 21 March: 45.

ICGN (International Corporate Governance Network) (2009) *Corporate Governance Principles*, London: ICGN.

IPPR (2000) *Secure Foundations: Key Issues in Crime Prevention, Crime Reduction and Community Safety*, www.ippr.org.uk/publicationsandreports/publication.asp?id=24 (accessed 16 November 2010).

Irvine, J.T. (1989) 'When Talk Isn't Cheap: Language and Political Economy', *American Ethnologist* 16: 248–66.

Isin, E.F. (2000) *Democracy, Citizenship and the Global City*, London, New York: Routledge.

Ivie, R.L. (2005) *Democracy and America's War on Terror*, Tuscaloosa: University of Alabama Press.

Jappe, A. (1999) *Guy Debord*, Berkeley and Los Angeles: University of California Press.

Jeffery, K., and Hennessy, P. (1983) *States of Emergency*, London: Routledge & Kegan Paul.

Jenkins, P. (2003) *Advanced Surveillance: The Complete Manual of Surveillance Training*, Harrogate: Intel Publications.

Jervis, R. (1982) 'Security regimes', *International Organization* 36(2), Spring: 357–78.

Jessop, B. (2002) 'Liberalism, Neoliberalism, and Urban Governance: A State-theoretical Perspective', in Brenner, N., and Theodore. N. (eds), *Spaces of Neoliberalism: Urban Restructuring in Western Europe and North America*, Oxford: Blackwell, pp. 105–25.

Jessop, B. (2008) *State Power: A Strategic-Relational Approach*, Cambridge: Polity Press.

Jobson, R. (2008) *Harry's War: The True Story of the Soldier Prince*, London: John Blake Publishing.

Johnson, C., and Leslie, J. (2008) *Afghanistan: The Mirage of Peace*, London: Zed Books.

Johnson, R., and Walkerdine, V. (2004) 'Transformations under Pressure: Reforming Class and Gender Identities under New Labour', in Steinberg, D., and Johnson, R. (eds), *Blairism and the War of Persuasion*, London: Lawrence & Wishart.

Joint Chiefs of Staff (2000) *Joint 20/20 Vision*, Washington DC: US Government Printing Office.

Joseph, J. (2003) 'Foucault and Reality', *Capital and Class* 82: 143–65.

Judd, T (2010) 'The death of Karen Woo – by the man who survived', *Independent*, 16 August: 10–11.

Kalita, S.M. (2002) 'Seeking Solace in my Notebook', in Bull, C., and Erman, S. (eds), *At Ground Zero*, New York: Thunder's Mouth Press.

Karl, P.A. (1982) 'Media Diplomacy', *Proceedings of the Academy of Political Science*, 34(4): 143–52.

Kassimeris, G. (2004) 'We should not be hosting these Olympics', *Independent, 3* August.

Kavoori, A.P., and Fraley, T. (2006) *Media, Terrorism and Theory*, Oxford and Lanham, MD: Rowman & Littlefield.

Keane, J. (1992) 'The Crisis of the Sovereign State', in Raboy, M., and Dagenais, B. (eds), *Media, Crisis and Democracy*, London, Newbury Park, New Delhi: Sage.

Keeble, R. (2005) *The Newspapers Handbook*, 4th edn, London: Routledge.

Kiersey, N. (2009) 'Neoliberal Political Economy and the Subjectivity of Crisis: Why Governmentality is not Hollow', *Global Society* 23(4), October, London and New York: Routledge.

Kirchner, E., and Sperling, J. (2007) *EU Security Governance*, Manchester and New York: Manchester University Press.

Klaidman, D., and Thomas, E. (2000) 'A world on alert', *Newsweek*, 3 January 2000.

Klein, N. (2007) *The Shock Doctrine*, London and New York: Penguin.

Knight, G., and Dean, T. (1982) 'Myth and the Structure of the News', *Journal of Communication* 32(2): 144–61.

Knightley, P. (2004) 'How frightened are you?', *Independent on Sunday*, 8 August: 25.

Koumoutsakos, G. (2006) Press conference, Greek Foreign Ministry, 21 December 2006.

Kress, G., and van Leeuwen, T. (2001) *Multimodal Discourse: The Mores and Media of Contemporary Communication*, London and New York: Arnold.

Kuzmarov, J. (2009) 'Modernizing Repression: Police Training, Nation-Building and Political Violence in the American Century', *Diplomatic History* 33(2), April: 191–221.

Labour Party, UK (2010) *A Future Fair for All*, General Election Manifesto, 2010, labour.org.uk.

Lamport, L. (1978) 'Time, Clocks, and the Ordering of Events in a Distributed System', in *Communications of the Association of Computing Machinery* 21(7): 558–65.

Lane, J.-E. (2000) *New Public Management*, London and New York: Routledge.

Lansford, T., Pauly, R.J., and Covarrubias, J. (2006) *To Protect and Defend: US Homeland Security policy*, Aldershot and Burlington, VT: Ashgate.

Larrain, J. (1994) *Ideology and Cultural Identity*, Cambridge: Polity Press.

Lash, S., Szerszynski, B., and Wynne, B. (eds) (1996) *Risk, Environment and Modernity* London, Thousand Oaks and New Delhi: Sage.

Latour, B. (2005) *Reassembling the Social*, Oxford: Oxford University Press.

Laville, S. (2005) 'De Menezes shooting: UK's top anti-terror officer is singled out', www.guardian.co.uk/uk/2007/aug/01/topstories3.menezes (accessed 29 April 2009).

Lawson, T. (2006) 'Information, Communication and Learning Technologies: Equipping the Digital Citizen', in Breslin, T., and Dufour, B., *Developing Citizens*, London: Hodder Murray.

Lazuka, A. (2006) 'Communicative intention in George W. Bush's presidential speeches and statements from 11 September 2001 to 11 September 2003', *Discourse and Society* 17(3): 299–330.

Leake, C., Delgado, M., and Arbuthnott, G. (2010) 'Police have shot dead 33 people since 1995 – only two marksmen have ever been named', *Mail on Sunday*, 26 September: 24–5.

Leigh, D. (2010) 'Tories promised to run a "pro-American regime"', *Guardian*, 4 December 2010: 1.

Leishman, F., and Mason, P. (2003) *Policing and the Media*, Abingdon: Lawrence & Erlbaum.

Leiss, W., Kline, S., and Jhally, S. (1990) *Social Communication in Advertising*, London and New York: Routledge.

Lewis, P. (2009) 'Britain faces summer of rage – police', *Guardian*, 23 February: 1.

Lewis, P. (2009) 'CCTV in the sky: police plan to use military-style drones', *Guardian*, 23 January, at www.guardian.co.uk/uk/2010/jan/cctv-sky-police-plan-drones (accessed 20 December 2010).

Lewis, P. (2009) *Guardian*, 19 August.

Leys, C. (2001) *Market-Driven Politics*, London and New York: Verso.

Liberal Democratic Party (2010) Election Manifesto 2010, London: Liberal Democratic Party.

Lichtenberg, J. (2003) 'Precedent and Example in the International Arena', http://scholar.google.co.uk/scholar?q=related:Zmwj8tGKDHMJ:scholar.google.com/&hl=en&as_sdt=0,5&as_vis=1 (accessed 14 February 2011).

Lister, D. (2001) 'Army calls up film-makers to provide tactical advice', *Independent*, 10 October, www.independent.co.uk/news/world/America/army-calls-up (accessed 17 April 2009).

Lloyd's (2007) *Home-Grown Terrorism: What Does It Mean for Business?*, London: Lloyd's.

London First (2005) *Secure in the Knowledge: Building a Secure Business*, London: London First.

Lothian and Borders Police (2005) *Request for information on protestors*, Post G8 Investigation Team (accessed 1 August 2005).

MacKenzie, I. (2008) 'What is a Political Event?', *Theory and Event* 11(3), Baltimore, MD: Johns Hopkins University Press.

McCahill, M. (2002) *The Surveillance Web: The Rise of Visual Surveillance in an English City*, Cullompton: Willan.

McGrath, John E. (2004) *Loving Big Brother London*, New York: Routledge.

McGreal, C. (2010) 'William Hague says Britain will pursue "solid not slavish" relationship with US', 14 May, www.guardian.co.uk/politics/2010/may/14/hague-uk-us-clinton-Afghanistan (accessed 20 December 2010).

McGuigan, J. (2009) *Cool Capitalism*, London and New York: Pluto Press.

Machin, D. (2007) *Introduction to Multimodal Analysis*, London: Hodder Arnold.

McLaughlin, E. (2007) *The New Policing*, London, Thousand Oaks and New Delhi: Sage.

McNair, B. (2006) *Cultural Chaos: Journalism, News and Power in a Globalised World*, London and New York: Routledge.

Mahoney, N., Newman, J., and Barnett, C. (2010) *Rethinking the Public: Innovations in Research, Theory and Politics*, Bristol: Policy Press.

Makdisi, S. (2002) 'Spectres of "Terrorism"', *Interventions* 4(2): 265–78.

Mandelson, P. (2004) Opening speech, Progressive Governance Conference, Policy Network.

Mann, M. (2003) 'The Autonomous Power of the State: Its Origins, Mechanisms and Results', in Brenner, N., Jessop, B., Jones, M., and MacLeod, G. (eds), *State/Space: A Reader*, Oxford: Blackwell, pp. 53–64.

Manning, P. (2001) *News and News Sources* London, Thousand Oaks and New Delhi: Sage.

Manningham-Buller, E. (2003) The James Smart Lecture, 16 October, at www.mi5.gov.uk/output/director-generals-speech-at-the-james-smart-lecture-2003.html (accessed 20 December 2010).

Marketing (2010) 'Win the Hearts and Minds of Today's Digi-Savvy Youth', conference flyer, 15th Annual Youth Perspective Conference, London, 21 October.

Martin, A.P. (2002) *Harnessing the Power of Intelligence, Counter-Intelligence, and Surprise Events*, Cambridge, MA and Ottawa, ON: Professional Development Institute.

Martin, R. (2004) 'America as risk / securitizing the other', *Interventions* 6(3): 351–61.

Martin, R. (2007) *An Empire of Indifference*, Durham, NC and London: Duke University Press.

Marx, K. (1954) *Capital, Volume One*, London: Lawrence & Wishart.

Matheson, D., and Allan, S. (2009) *Digital War Reporting*, Cambridge and Malden, MA: Polity Press.

Mazzarella, W. (2004) 'Culture, Globalisation, Mediation', *Annual Review of Anthropology* 33: 345–67.

Metropolitan Police Authority (2002) Minutes, 8 August 2005, including minutes of 21 March 2002, at www.mpa.gov.uk/downloads/about/foi/log/kratos-attach.pdf (accessed 28 August 2008).

Metropolitan Police Service (2005) Bulletin 0000000232, 22 July, at cms.met.police. uk/news/major_operational_announcements (accessed 28 July 2005).

Metropolitan Police Service (n.d.) www.met.police.uk/communities_together/docs/ v_05-11-08_srb_anna_de_vries_1_.pdf (accessed 28 August 2008).

Metropolitan Police Service (n.d.) www.met.police.uk/so/counter_terrrorism_security_advisers (accessed 18 March 2010).

Meyer, C. (2006) *DC Confidential*, London: Phoenix.

Michael, J. (1982) *The Politics of Secrecy*, Harmondsworth: Penguin.

Microsoft News (2007) 'RAF pilots given "suicide scenario"', at www.news.uk.msn. com, 3 April (accessed 30 July 2009).

Miller, P., and Rose, N. (2008) *Governing the Present*, Cambridge: Polity Press.

Millo, Y. (2007) 'Making Things Deliverable: The Origins of Index-based Derivatives', in Callon, M., Millo, Y., and Muniesa, F., *Market Devices*, Oxford, Malden, MA, Victoria: Blackwell.

Milmo, C. (2009) 'Shoot to kill, Britain's answer to massacre at Munich Olympics', *Independent*, 9 May: 17.

Mirror (2005) 'IS THIS HOW WE MUST NOW LIVE?', front page headline, 22 July.

Misa, T.J., Brey, P., and Feenberg, A. (2003) *Modernity and Technology*, Cambridge, MA: MIT Press.

Molyviatis, P (2004) 'Statement on Greek Election to UN Security Council', 15 October, New York.

Montgomery, M. (2005) 'Talking War', in Allan, S. (ed.), *Journalism: Critical Issues*, Buckingham: Open University Press.

Moore, J., and Slater, W. (2003) *Bush's Brain: How Karl Rove Made George W. Bush Presidential*, Hoboken: John Wiley.

Moran, M. (2002) 'Understanding the Regulatory State', review article in *British Journal of Political Science*, April.

Morris, N. (2007) ' 'Problem' children to be monitored for signs of criminality', *Independent*, 28 March: 20.

Nair, Parvati (2006). 'Voicing Risk: Migration, Transgression and Relocation in Spanish/Moroccan Rai', *Interventions* 8(1): 67–82.

NaCTSO (National Counter Terrorism Security Office) (2009a) *Pursue Protect Prevent Prepare: The United Kingdom's Strategy for Countering International Terrorism*, London: HMSO.

NaCTSO (National Counter Terrorism Security Office) (2009b) *Project ARGUS Video for Higher Education*, Department for Innovation, Business and Skills, www. continuityforum.org/content/news/130842/project-argus-inc-video (accessed 5 November 2010).

NaCTSO (National Counter Terrorism Security Office) (2009c) *Project ARGUS Video – Crowded Places*, 11 February, www.mefeedia.com/watch/25167706 (accessed 5 November 2010).

NaCTSO (National Counter Terrorism Security Office) (n.d.) *The Threat*, www. nactso.gov.uk/threat.php (accessed 16 July 2010).

National Council for Civil Liberties (1980) *Southall 23 April 1979*, Nottingham: NCCL.

National Extremism Tactical Coordination Unit (2008) 'A Funding Method Of Domestic Extremism', 16 July, at www.policeoracle.com/news/A-Funding-Method-Of-Domestic-Extremism_16982.html (accessed 30 Septmber 2009).

Negri, A. (2003) *Time for Revolution*, London and New York: Continuum.

Neocleous, M. (2000) *The Fabrication of Social Order: A Critical Theory of Police Power*, London and Sterling, VA: Pluto Press.

Neocleous, M. (2008) *Critique of Security*, Montreal and Kingston, Ithaca, NY: McGill–Queen's University Press.

Newby, H., Bujra, J., Littlewood, P., Rees, G., and Rees, T.L. (1985) *Restructuring Capital: Recession and Reorganisation in Industrial Society*, London: Macmillan.

Newsweek (2001) 'How Scared Should You Be?', front cover, 8 October.

Nickel, P.M. (2009) 'Text, Portrayal, and Power: A Critique of the Transformation of the State Thesis', *Journal of Power* 2(3): 383–401, December.

9/11 Commission Report (2004) www.9-11commission.gov/report/911Report.pdf 9 (accessed 22 July 2004).

Nitzan, J., and Bichler, S. (2009) *Capital as Power: A Study of Order and Creorder* Abingdon and New York: Routledge.

Nofsinger, R.E. (1991) *Everyday Conversation*, London, Thousand Oaks and New Delhi: Sage.

Noll, A.M. (ed.) (2003) *Crisis Communications*, Lanham, MD: Rowman & Littlefield.

Norton-Taylor, R. (2009) 'MI5 officer gave false evidence in Guantanamo detainee case', *Guardian*, 21 April.

Norton-Taylor, R. (2009) 'Miliband's lawyers try to block CIA report on torture claims', *Guardian*, 2 May.

Norton-Taylor, R. (2009) 'The secret servants', *Guardian Weekend*, 11 July: 14–19.

Norton-Taylor, R. (2009) 'Ministers must assume war footing to defeat Taliban – army chief', *Guardian*, 31 July: 15.

Norton-Taylor, R. (2009) 'Suspect tortured while MI5 visited Morocco', *Guardian*, 1 August: 2.

Norton-Taylor, R. (2009) 'Leaked documents reveal No 10 cover-up over Iraq invasion', *Guardian*, 23 November: 5.

Norton-Taylor, R. (2010) 'Chilcot hears ministers were told of British Muslims radicalisation risk', www.guardian.co.uk/uk/2010/jan/20/chilcot-inquiry-british-muslims-terrorism-risk, 20 January (accessed 22 January 2010).

Norton-Taylor, R., and Cowan, R. (2010) 'July 7 reports fail to silence inquiry calls: official accounts of London attacks leave key questions unanswered', *Guardian* online, 11 May, www.guardian.co.uk/uk/2006/may/11/july7.immigrationpolicy (accessed 16 November 2010).

Oakes, P.J., Haslam, S.A., and Turner, J.C. (1994) *Stereotyping and Social Reality*, Oxford: Blackwell.

Offe, C. (1984) *Contradictions of the Welfare State*, Cambridge, MA: MIT Press.

Ogilvy (2005) 'Topoff' exercise for Department of Homeland Security, www.iwar.org.uk/news-archive/2005/03-17-07.html (accessed 19 June 2009).

O'Hara, D.T. (2008) 'Badiou's Truth and the Office of the Critic: Naming the Militant Multiples of the Void', *Boundary 2*, 35(1): 169–75.

Oliver, J., Oakeshott, I., and Smith, D. (2009) 'Whitehall lines up "doomsday" cutbacks', *Sunday Times*, 5 July.

Omand, D. (2007) 'Reflections on Secret Intelligence', in Hennessy, P. (ed.), *The New Protective State*, London and New York: Continuum.

Omand, D. (2009) 'The National Security Strategy:Implications for the UK

Intelligence Community', paper for the Institute of Public Policy Research, London: IPPR.

Operation Midway (2008) www.highways.gov.uk/business/22426.aspx www.mcga. gov.uk/c4mca/mcga07-home/emergencyresponse/mcga-searchandrescue/mcga-hmcgsar-sarsystem/dops-medway-excersise.html (accessed 1 March 2010).

Osborne, P. (1995) *The Politics of Time*, London and New York: Verso.

OED (*Oxford English Dictionary*) Online (2010) at http://dictionary.oed.com.

Ozkirimli, U. (2000) *Theories of Nationalism*, Basingstoke and New York: Palgrave Macmillan.

Pakulski, J., and Waters, M. (1996) *The Death of Class*, London, Thousand Oaks and New Delhi: Sage.

Pallister, D. (2009) 'British link with drone aiding the Israeli war effort', *Guardian*, 9 January: 20.

Panorama (2006) 'Stockwell: Countdown to Killing', 8 March, 2100 GMT, BBC One.

Parker, N., Sullivan, M., Kennedy, S., Rae, C., and Wheeler, V. (2005) 'I saw them unload five shots into him… bang, bang, bang, bang, bang', *Sun*, 23 July: 4.

Parkin, F. (1972) *Class Inequality and Political Order*, St Albans: Paladin/Granada Publishing.

Parr, A. (2005) *The Deleuze Dictionary*, Edinburgh: Edinburgh University Press.

Parsons, T. (2001) 'Out of a clear blue sky', *Daily Mirror*, 20 September, www.mir-ror.co.uk/news/allnews/page.cfm?objectid=11314790&method=full (accessed 13 February 2002).

Parsons, T. (2005) 'A tragedy – but police still deserve our support', *Daily Mirror*, 25 July.

Partington, A. (2003) 'Rhetoric, bluster and on-line gaffes', in Aitchison, J., and Lewis, D.M. (eds), *New Media Language*, London and New York: Routledge.

Perkins, A. (2006) *A Very British Strike*, London: Macmillan.

Perri 6, Leat, D., Seltzer, K., and Stoker, G. (2002) *Towards Holistic Governance: The New Reform Agenda*, Basingstokeand New York: Palgrave Macmillan.

Phillips, M. (2005) 'A terrible tragedy – but this is no time for weakness', *Daily Mail*, 25 July: 12.

Phoenix Resilience Training (2009) 'Who are Phoenix?', phoenixresiliencetraining. com/about/about.htm (accessed 16 November 2010).

Pianesi, F., and Varsi, A.C. (2000) 'Events and Event Talk: An Introduction', in Higginbotham, J., Pianesi, F., and Varsi, A.C., *Speaking of Events*, New York and Oxford: Oxford University Press.

Pick, O., and Critchley, J. (1974) *Collective Security*, London: Macmillan.

Pidgeon, N., Kasperson, R.E., and Slovic, P. (2003) *The Social Amplification of Risk*, Cambridge: Cambridge University Press.

Pierson, C. (1996) *The Modern State*, London and New York: Routledge.

Pindoria, P. (2010) 'Project ARGUS – Protecting Against Terrorist Attacks', 10 June, www.cityoflondon.police.uk/CityPolice/Departments/CT/Protecting-Against-Terrorist-Attacks (accessed 16 July 2010).

Plunkett, J. (2010) 'Ban on misleading BT surfing ad', *Guardian*, 25 August: 12

Porter, R. (2006) *Ideology: Contemporary Social, Political and Cultural Theory*, Cardiff: University of Wales Press.

Poulantzas, N. (1978a) *State Power Socialism*, London: Verso.

Poulantzas, N. (1978b) *Classes in Contemporary Capitalism*, London: Verso.

Price, S. (1998) *Media Studies*, London: Longman.

Price, S. (2007) *Discourse Power Address: The Politics of Public Communication*, Aldershot and Burlington, VT: Ashgate.

Price, S. (2010) *Brute Reality:Power, Discourse and the Mediation of War*, London and New York: Pluto Press.

Prime Minister's Office (2010) 'Establishment of a National Security Council', at www.number10.gov.uk/news/latest/news/2010/05/establishment-of-a-national-security-council-49953 (accessed 30 September 2010).

Punch, M. (2011) *Shoot to Kill*, Bristol: Policy Press.

Pythian, M. (2009) 'The British Experience with Intelligence Accountability', in Andrew, C., Aldrich, R.J., and Wark, W.K. (eds), *Secret Intelligence: A Reader* London and New York: Routledge.

Raboy, M., and Dagenais, B. (eds) *Media, Crisis and Democracy*, London, Newbury Park, New Delhi: Sage.

Radnedge, A. (2008) 'A chilling echo of de Menezes', *Metro*, 8 July: 1.

Red Notes (1981) *After Marx, Jail*, London: Red Notes.

Reiter, D. (1995) 'Exploding the Powder Keg Myth: Pre-emptive Wars Almost Never Happen', *International Security* 20(2): 5–34.

Rejali, D. (2007) *Torture and Democracy*, Princeton, NJ and Woodstock: Princeton University Press.

Reynolds, P. (2002) 'WTC film-makers still positive', 4 September, at http://news.bbc.co.uk/1/hi/world/americas/2236210.stm (accessed 10 June 2010).

Rhodes, R.A.W. (1995) 'Prime Ministerial Power to Core Executive', in Rhodes, R.A.W., and Dunleavy, P. (eds), *Prime Minister, Cabinet and Core Executive*, London and New York: Macmillan.

Rhodes, R.A.W., and Dunleavy, P. (eds) (1995) *Prime Minister, Cabinet and Core Executive*, London and New York: Macmillan.

Ribowsky, S. (2010) Evidence of Medical Examiner, cited in *9/11 Crime Scene Investigators*, Channel Five, 9 September.

Richards, B. (2007) *Emotional Governance: Politics, Media and Terror*, Basingstoke and New York: Palgrave Macmillan.

Ricœur, P. (1976) *Interpretation Theory: Discourse and the Surplus of Meaning*, Fort Worth: Texas Christian University Press.

Ripley, A. (2004) 'How the U.S. got Homeland Security Wrong', *Time: Special Report*, 29 March 2004.

Roberts, B. (2005) 'Brazilian's visa 2 years out of date', *Daily Mirror*, 29 July: 10.

Roberts, B. (2008) *Human Insecurity: Global Structures of Violence*, London and New York: Zed Books.

Robinson, M. (2008) 'Hybrid States: Globalisation and the Politics of State Capacity', *Political Studies* 56: 566–83.

Ross, C. (2010) 'How Britain's 'deep state' is covering up the mistakes that led to Iraq war', *Observer*, 25 July: 5.

Ross, K. (2010) *Gendered Media: Women, Men and Identity Politics*, Lanham, MD and Plymouth: Rowman & Littlefield.

Sagan, S. (1993) *The Limits of Safety: Organizations, Accidents and Nuclear Weapons*, Princeton, NJ: Princeton University Press.

Sager, F. (2009) 'Governance and Coercion', *Political Studies* 57(3): 537–58, Sheffield: Political Studies Association.

Sands, P. (2005) *Lawless World*, London and New York: Penguin.

Sapsford, C. (2002) 'One City, Many Worlds', in Bull, C., and Erman, S. (eds), *At Ground Zero*, New York: Thunder's Mouth Press, pp. 331–48.

Savage, M. (2008) 'The techie Challenge to save the lives of soldiers', *Independent*, 20 August: 11.

Schmitter, P.C. (1974) 'Still the Century of Corporatism?', *Review of Politics* 36: 85–131.

Schudson, M. (2005) 'Autonomy from what?', in Benson, R., and Neveu, E. (eds), *Bourdieu and the Journalistic Field*, Cambridge: Polity Press.

Scott, S. (2009) *Making Sense of Everyday Life*, Cambridge and Malden, MS: Polity Press.

Seager, A., and Bowers, S. (2006) 'BP attacked over CO_2 emissions', *Guardian*, 21 April, www.guardian.co.uk/environment/2006/apr/21/oilandpetrol.climate-change (accessed 14 February 2011).

Self, P. (1993) *Government by the Market? The Politics of Public Choice*, Basingstoke and London: Macmillan.

Sengupta, K. (2008) 'Unmanned spy planes to police Britain', *Independent*, 6 August: 4.

Sengupta, K. (2008) 'Afghan war ties to security at home', *Independent*, 3 August: 13.

Seymour-Ure, C. (2000) 'Prime ministers' and presidents' news operations: what effects on the job', in Tumber, H. (ed.), *Media Power, Professionals and Policies*, London: Routledge.

Searle, J.R. (1969) *Speech Acts: An Essay in the Philosophy of Language*, Cambridge: Cambridge University Press.

Sexton, J. (2007) 'The obscurity of black suffering', in South End Press Collective, *What Lies Beneath: Katrina, Race, and the State of the Nation*, Cambridge, MA: South End Press.

Sharman, N. (1999) 'Remaining awake through a great revolution: the rhetorical strategies of Martin Luther King Jr.', *Social Semiotics* 9(1): 85–105.

Shaw, M. (2005) *The Western Way of War*, Cambridge: Polity Press.

Shell (2010) 'Let's pass energy on to the next generation'. Let's Go, advertisement, *New Statesman*, 28 June.

Sheptycki, J. (2009) 'High Policing in the Security Control Society', in Andrew, C., Aldrich, R.J., and Wark, W.K. (eds), *Secret Intelligence: A Reader*, London and New York: Routledge.

Sheriff, J.K. (1994) *Charles Peirce's Guess at the Riddle*, Bloomington and Indianapolis: Indiana University Press.

Simons, H.W., (2006) 'What's in a News Frame?', paper for ATINER conference, 22–24 May, Athens.

Smith, H. (2004) 'Greece admits defeat over armed guards at the Olympics', *Guardian*, 4 June.

Solnit, R. (2008) 'Four years on, Katrina remains cursed by rumour, lies and racism', *Guardian*, 26 August: 28.

South End Press Collective, *What Lies Beneath: Katrina, Race, and the State of the Nation*, Cambridge, MA: South End Press.

Steinberg, D., and Johnson, R. (eds) (2004) *Blairism and the War of Persuasion*, London: Lawrence & Wishart.

Stewart, H., and Elliott, L. (2009) 'G20 warned unrest will sweep globe', *Observer Business and Media*, 22 March: 1.

Stothart, C. (2008) 'Fires, floods, pandemics: planning for the worst', *Times Higher Education Supplement*, 17 April: 16.

Straw, J. (2003) Address to the International Institute for Strategic Studies, London, 11 February.

Stubbs, M. (1983) *Discourse Analysis*, Oxford: Blackwell.

Sullivan, P.J., and Wirtz, J. (2008) 'Terrorism Early Warning and Counterterrorism Intelligence', *International Journal of Intelligence and Counter Intelligence* 21(1), Spring.

Sunday Times Insight Team (1990) 'Police plan a "shoot to kill" policy in riots', *Sunday Times*, 8 April: 1.

Sunstein, C. (2007) *Worst-Case Scenarios* Cambridge, MA and London: Harvard University Press.

Swinford, S., and Smith, M. (2010) 'Freedom fighter or information terrorist?', *Sunday Times*, Focus, 1 August: 13.

Tandridge District Council (2010) *Emergency Planning*, www.tandridge.gov.uk/Your-Coucil/Contactus/emergency/html, (accessed 23 February 2010).

Tannenhaus, S. (2003) Interview with Paul Wolfowitz, *Vanity Fair*, 9 May.

Taylor, J. (2009) 'Complaints of heavy-handed tactics as squats are raided', *Independent*, 3 April.

Taylor, J. (2009) 'Were police spies behind mass arrest of activists?', *Independent*, 14 April: 3.

Tayside Strategic Co-ordinating Group (2010) (http://civilcontingencies.dundeecity.gov.uk/dundee-city-council/civi (accessed 23 February 2010).

Teignbridge District Council (2008) *Corporate Emergency Plan*, Newton Abbott: Teignbridge District Council.

Therborn, G. (1978) *What Does the Ruling Class Do When it Rules?*, London: Verso.

Therborn, G. (1980) *The Ideology of Power and the Power of Ideology*, London: Verso.

Thomas, C. (2002) 'Global Governance and Human Security', in Wilkinson, R., and Hughes, S.(eds), *Global Governance*, London: Routledge.

Thomas, H. (1970) *The Suez Affair*, Harmondsworth: Penguin.

Thompson, H. (2010) 'The Character of the State', in Hay, C. (ed.), *New Directions in Political Science*, Basingstoke and New York: Palgrave McMillan, pp. 130–47.

Tolson, A. (2006) *Media Talk*, Edinburgh: Edinburgh University Press.

Townshend, C. (1999) 'State and Public Security', in English, R., and Townshend, C. (eds), *The State*, London and New York: Routledge.

Townshend, C. (2002) *Terrorism: A Very Short Introduction*, Oxford: Oxford University Press.

Toynbee, P. (2010) 'Tony Blair tried to bury it, but class politics looks set to return', Guardian online, 10 July, www.guardian.co.uk/commentisfree/2010/jul/10/john-prescott-class-politics-old-labour (accessed 16 November 2010).

Trimarco, J., and Depret, M.H. (2005) 'Wounded Nation, Wounded Time', in Heller, D. (ed.), *The Selling of 9/11*, New York and Basingstoke: Palgrave Macmillan.

Tuchman, G. (1972) 'Objectivity as Strategic Ritual', *American Journal of Sociology* 77(4): 660–79.

Turse, N. (2008) *The Complex: How the Military Invades Our Everyday Lives*, New York: Metropolitan Books.

Twomey, J., and Dixon, C. (2005) 'Police: we will shoot to kill again', *Daily Express*, 25 July: 1–4.

Twomey, J., and Pilditch, D. (2005) 'IT WAS JUST A TRAGIC MISTAKE', *Daily Express*, 18 August: 1.

Twomey, J., Pilditch, D., and Rao, N. (2010) 'Muslim plot to kill the Pope', *Daily Express*, 18 September: 1–4.

UK Government (2007) *The Governance of Britain*, London: HMSO.

United States Department of State (2007) 'Top Officials (TOPOFF) www.state. gov/s/ct/about/c16661.html (accessed 23 February 2010).

University of North Texas (2010) at www.pacs.unt.edu/public-administration/ University of North Texas, 19 February (accessed 23 February 2010).

Urban, M. (1992) *Big Boys' Rules*, London: Faber & Faber.

Urban Warrior (n.d.) at www.defense.gov/specials/urbanwarrior/.

US State Department (2010) *Afghanistan and Pakistan Regional Stabilization Strategy*, US Government, Department of State.

Usborne, D. (2010) 'Five years after Katrina, the US faces up to New Orleans's day of infamy', *Independent*, 15 July: 4–5.

Uttlesford District Council (n.d.) *A Guide to Business Continuity Planning* Emergency Planning Department, Uttlesford District Council (accessed 23 February 2010).

van Dijk, T.A. (1998) *Ideology*, London, Thousand Oaks and New Delhi: Sage.

Varon, J. (2004) *Bringing the War Home: The Weather Underground, the Red Army Faction, and Revolutionary Violence in the Sixties and Seventies*, Berkeley, Los Angeles, London: University of California Press.

Virilio, P. (2007) *The Original Accident*, Cambridge and Malden, MA: Polity Press.

Venteurelli, E.J.C. (1993) 'The European Community and Communication', *European Journal of Communication* 18(4), December.

Verkaik, R. (2010) '101,000 stop and searches. No terror arrests', *Independent*, 29 October: 16.

Verkaik, R., and Bennetto, J. (2005) 'Shot dead by police 30, Officers convicted o', *Independent*, 21 October: 1–2.

Voulgarakis, G. (2004) Press statement, Athens Olympic Committee, at www. athens2004.com/athens2004. (accessed 10 December 2004: site now defunct).

Waldren, M.J. (2007) *Armed Police: The Police Use of Firearms Since 1945*, Stroud: Sutton.

Watson, G. (2010) 'In praise of Parliament', *Times Higher Education Supplement*, 16 September.

Watt, E.D. (1982) *Authority*, London: Croom Helm.

Webb, J. (2004) BBC Radio Four Today programme on US Presidential Election, 4 November.

Weber, M. (1978a) *Economy and Society*, Vol. 1, New York: Bedminster.

Weber, R.P. (1990) *Basic Content Analysis*, London, Thousand Oaks and New Delhi: Sage.

Weiss, T.G. (ed.) (1993) *Collective Security in a Changing World*, Boulder, CO and London: Lynne Rienner.

White, M., Hill, S., Mills, C., and Smeaton, D. (2004) *Managing to Change? British Workplaces and the Future of Work*, Basingstoke and New York: Palgrave Macmillan.

Wilkinson, R., and Hughes, S. (eds) (2002) *Global Governance*, London: Routledge.

Willey, J., and Flanagan, P., (2005) 'Policeman pumped 5 bullets into head and body of terrorist', *Daily Express*, 23 July: 4.

Williams, J. (2008) 'News blackout', BBC News blog at www.bbc.co.uk/blogs/theeditors/2008/02/news_blackout.html, 29 February.

Wilson, J. (2008) *Launch Pad UK: Britain and the Cuban Missile Crisis*, Barnsley: Pen and Sword Books.

Wintour, P. (2010) 'Straw: I drew up secret plan to keep Britain out of Iraq war', *Guardian*, 21 January: 1-2.

Wintour, P., and Watt, N (2010) 'Charles and Camilla caught up in violence after student fees vote', *Guardian*, 10 December: 1.

Wood, A., and Thompson, P. (n.d.) 'An interesting day: President Bush's movements and actions on 9/11', at www.historycommons.org/essay.jsp?article=essayaninterestingday (accessed 10 June 2010).

Wood, E.M. (1986) *The Retreat from Class*, London and New York: Verso.

Wood, E.M. (2003) *Empire of Capital*, London and New York: Verso.

Woodward, B. (2002) *Bush at War*, New York: Simon & Schuster.

Young, I.M. (2003) 'Feminist Reactions to the Contemporary Security Regime', *Hypatia*, Special Issue: *Feminist Philosophy and the Problem of Evil*, 18(1), February: 223–31.

Zakaria, F. (2010) 'What America has lost', *Newsweek*, 13 September: 8.

Zelizer, B. (2002) 'Photography, Journalism and Trauma', in Zelizer, B., and Allan, S. (eds), *Journalism after September 11th*, London and New York: Routledge.

Zelizer, B., and Allan, S. (eds) (2002) *Journalism after September 11th*, London and New York: Routledge.

Žižek, S. (ed.) (1994) *Mapping Ideology*, London and New York: Verso.

Index